A Process Spirituality

A Process Spirituality

Christian and Transreligious Resources for Transformation

Sheri D. Kling

LEXINGTON BOOKS
Lanham • Boulder • New York • London

Published by Lexington Books
An imprint of The Rowman & Littlefield Publishing Group, Inc.
4501 Forbes Boulevard, Suite 200, Lanham, Maryland 20706
www.rowman.com

6 Tinworth Street, London SE11 5AL, United Kingdom

British Library Cataloguing in Publication Information Available

Library of Congress Cataloging-in-Publication Data

Names: Kling, Sheri D., 1960- author.
Title: A process spirituality : Christian and transreligious resources for transformation / Sheri D. Kling.
Description: Lanham : Lexington Books, 2020. | Includes bibliographical references and index. | Summary:"A Process Spirituality argues for a hopeful and relational vision of the God-world relationship characterized by mutuality, value, change, and transformation, whichincorporates a constructive reimagining of the work of Whitehead and Jung"— Provided by publisher.
Identifiers: LCCN 2020011605 (print) | LCCN 2020011606 (ebook) | ISBN 9781793630421 (cloth) | ISBN 9781793630438 (epub)
Subjects: LCSH: Process theology. | Spirituality—Christianity. | Whitehead, Alfred North, 1861-1947. | Jung, C. G. (Carl Gustav), 1875-1961.
Classification: LCC BT83.6 .K55 2020 (print) | LCC BT83.6 (ebook) | DDC 230/.046—dc23
LC record available at https://lccn.loc.gov/2020011605
LC ebook record available at https://lccn.loc.gov/2020011606

Contents

List of Tables vii

Preface ix

Acknowledgments xxiii

PART ONE: FRAGMENTATION **1**

1 A House Divided 3

2 Integrating Resources 25

PART TWO: INTEGRATION: THEORETICAL, EMPIRICAL, PRACTICAL **53**

3 Theoretical: An Integrated, Relational Cosmos 55

4 Empirical: An Integrated, Relational Psyche 87

5 Practical: The Integrative Power of Dreams 115

6 Synthesis 155

PART THREE: TRANSFORMATION **173**

7 Construction 175

8 Transformation 211

References 235

Index 247

About the Author 257

List of Tables

Table 5.1 Brain Regions Involved in Dreaming 127
Table 5.2 Hoss's Findings 132

Preface

EXPERIENCE

"[A]ll theology begins in experience."[1] So claim Carol P. Christ and Judith Plaskow in their 2016 collaboration, *Goddess and God in the World: Conversations in Embodied Theology*. In other words, the particular perspective of every theologian is rooted in her or his *lived* and *embodied* experience, and therefore any theological ideas that issue forth are unavoidably springing from the personal and communal wellsprings that her or his body *experienced*. J. Pittman McGehee, a Jungian analyst and Episcopal priest, similarly claims that "All theology is autobiography."[2] Without argument, I know that what is communicated in this project flows directly and indirectly from the decades that led up to this moment in time and the spatial locations and historical contexts within which I am writing now and have lived throughout my entire life.

Within these pages are echoes of Roselle, New Jersey and West Lafayette, Indiana; of rural northeast Georgia and the booming suburbs of Atlanta; of Hyde Park in Chicago, and Claremont, California. Illuminating its margins are images of an invaluable web of friendships, family joys and sorrows, intra-school racial tensions, troubadour performances throughout the southeastern United States, as well as a temporary sojourn through eight acres of pasture and a 100-year-old farmhouse complete with picturesque barn and spring peeper calls at twilight. It is all here. Yet it is impossible to deny that the painful experiences—like the irritating sand that presses the oyster into pearl manufacture—are probably what have most motivated my theological study and spiritual practice.

Irritating grains of sand begin to pile up almost immediately when you grow up with a father who suffers deeply from mental illness within a family system that is not capable of acknowledging or ameliorating his unrest. Abandonment, abuse, and rage flow unimpeded downstream from one generation to another and create eddies of black water along the threatening edges of awareness. All of that lays a broad foundation. But it was my father's suicide when I was ten years old that shoved me headlong into an abyss that fractured my personality into far-flung parts of alienation, depression, anxiety, existential loneliness, and frequent despair. That same descent initiated me into mysteries for which I was unprepared emotionally. Years followed during which life centered around denying my own painful bodily reality and retreating into a cerebral and spiritual world where I doggedly maintained that if I could only figure it all out, I could find some sanctuary, some purchase in the material world.

Somewhere along the way, a psychotherapist asked me about my dreams, and I began to see patterns in the images that emerged. I was introduced to Jungian authors who interpreted myths and fairy tales as representing archetypal journeys through psychological terrain, and found that whenever I felt "stuck" in my own journey, a story that seemed to explain everything would suddenly land in my lap. I began to see my life less as a series of random acts of suffering and more as an individual thread in a much larger—and much richer—tapestry; and because the stories never ended in the dark abyss, I began to entertain hope for my own rebirth. Meanwhile, uncanny and deeply meaningful coincidences happened on a regular basis, linking my inner world to the human and natural world that confronted me. Through such events—what C.G. Jung calls *synchronicities*—I began to believe that the whole world is God's mouthpiece, that it seemed to see and know me, and that if the world *could* see and know me, then maybe I was not so alone after all.

During this time, I was blessed by a church community that loved and held me, with pastors at the helm who engaged me in theological discussions (or, I should say, who responded enthusiastically to my never-ending prompts). As a naturally curious adult with a commitment to life-long learning, I delved into other religious traditions, read medieval mystics, examined studies at the margins of the new physics, consciousness, and healing, and discovered Marcus Borg, John Shelby Spong, and biblical historical criticism before I even knew the term. Tensions in my theological world began to arise, and frustrations over the Church's failure to share academic scholarship combined with the increasingly conservative face of public Christianity left me questioning whether I could even continue to call myself "Christian."

Around the year 2000, I was introduced to a life-giving spiritual language in Joyce Rockwood Hudson's book *Natural Spirituality: Recovering the Wisdom Tradition in Christianity*.[3] Hudson weaves Jungian thought and Christianity into a seamless whole that became the means through which I could remain a Christian. At the same time, she introduced me to a community of dream workers who meet every year at the Natural Spirituality Regional Gatherings held in north Georgia and the Haden Institute's Summer Dream and Spirituality Conference held in the mountains of western North Carolina. In these places—as well as in the Mythic Journeys conferences I helped to organize in 2004 and 2006 in Atlanta—I found my spiritual tribe.

There are more dreams, synchronicities, and what might be called religious or even mystical experiences in my life than I can reasonably share here, but a few deserve description in the following paragraphs. One such experience occurred while I was traveling alone in the southwestern United States in 1995 during a brief visit to the Canyon de Chelly National Monument in Arizona. I had just completed a half-day "shake and bake" tour of the Canyon—so nicknamed because the open-air truck bounced along the sun-soaked Canyon floor—and decided to visit the overlooks along the canyon rim above. I drove my rented Plymouth to the first overlook and parked it in the empty parking lot. I walked out to the edge of the rim and sat on a rock where I marveled at the beauty hundreds of feet below me—so high up was I that the people walking around below looked like ants and the truck I had just left was the size of a hazelnut. As I watched the hawks flying above, I suddenly entered into a new frame of consciousness wherein I felt to the marrow of my bones that I was infinitesimally tiny in the whole scheme of things yet intimately connected to everything. I *felt* that connection in a way unlike any other insight I had ever had. Just as quickly, I was snapped back into regular awareness. I can say with complete certainty that I have been trying to integrate that experience ever since that moment.

A small synchronicity that has cheered me every time I recall it happened on the grounds of a small college near Asheville, North Carolina, where I was attending a music camp in 2003. I had lost my last full-time "day job" in software marketing earlier that year and had spent the summer in an intense period of discernment. In those months, I spent as much time in silence and in nature as I could, and also fell deeply in love with a man who had just made it clear that my feelings for him were not mutually reciprocated. I sat on a hillside, wrote in my journal, and wept until I could weep no more, pleading heavenward that I "needed a nature moment." Suddenly, an entire flock of goldfinches exploded the tree just in front of me into a raucous celebration of yellow. It may not have been the color purple, but it would surely have pissed God off if I had not smiled.

One more—or rather, a series of dreams. Several months before I moved from north Georgia to Chicago to begin my theological studies, I had a dream whose central image was of a huge snake that had been hacked into large pieces—still alive and writhing—and shipped to me in a foam cooler. In the dream, I was horrified, and kept trying to dispose of the thing, even planning to push it down into the large trash compactor at my "old complex" (the condominium community where I had lived for many years; a friend who is a Jungian analyst named that one of the best representations of repression that he had ever heard). For me, the dream was saying that this "transformation stuff" (imaged by the snake who can represent new life) was not what I had "ordered" and not what I wanted. That dream led me to complete my first exegetical paper on the story in the Garden of Eden and the symbolic motif of the tree, the woman, and the snake. It seemed for several months that snake images kept popping up in my studies, and finally, about six months later, I had another dream. This was a simple auditory dream that intoned one sentence: *You will not be resurrected until you allow yourself to be bitten by the snake.* I could not make much headway on how to understand that, so I set the dream aside.

Four years later, during my second year of doctoral course work at Claremont School of Theology, I found myself deep in the worst spiritual abyss I had encountered to that point. I was wracked with depression, anxiety, health issues, self-doubts, and relationship woes that were so intense that I lost all footing in the worldview that I had held for many years. I had long been wrestling with what I knew was a dying God image—that of the demanding and love-denying Father—and questioned whether anything I had ever said or believed about God or dream work or spiritual practice made any sense or was in any way efficacious. I knew I had to reject this punitive God, and yet I had no idea what would remain if I did. I did not know if there would be any form of faith left in me. At that same time, being enrolled in a class on becoming a public scholar, I was asked to articulate a vision and mission for my future work. I told my classmates that I was in the process of breaking up with God—or at least with the abusive-father-bad-boyfriend-God-image that I had come to hold. Bellowing that I was "good enough!" at the heavens felt freeing—and emptying. There was no faith left in me and I entered the silence yet again. It was almost an afterthought when I suddenly realized one day that in the previous two nights, I had had two dreams; in each dream, I had been bitten by a snake.

You will not be resurrected until you allow yourself to be bitten by the snake.

That simple awareness of my dream activity caused an inrushing of a new kind of faith. A faith in which I no longer needed a specific God image, where it was enough to know deep in my core that there was something bigger than me that loved me, and that whatever That was, It or He or She was working in my life and connecting me to its Heart of Reality.[4]

METHODOLOGIES

As is standard fare in both process theology and practical theology, this project is based on questioning the doctrinal assumptions that stress God's transcendence over God's immanence in the world. Such an approach fits this project because the lived experiences of Christian dream workers are not supported by doctrinal assumptions that preference God's transcendence. Yet whereas a doctrinal methodology would typically critique and dismiss such lived experience, I assume—as does liberation and feminist theology—that such experience must lead to a reasoned critique of the doctrine. Rosemary Radford Ruether, a preeminent feminist theologian, acknowledges that feminist theology has typically used the experiences of women as a hermeneutical lens. Moreover, she argues forcefully that this consideration of experience as a viable source should not be limited to feminist theology because

> what have been called the objective sources of theology, Scripture and tradition, are themselves codified collective human experience. Human experience is the starting point and the ending point of the hermeneutical circle. Codified tradition both reaches back to its roots in experience and is constantly renewed or discarded through the test of experience. "Experience" includes experience of the divine, experience of oneself, and experience of the community and the world, in an interacting dialectic.[5]

With all apologies to McGehee and Thomas, it would be unacceptable for this project to merely "reduce theology to autobiography";[6] therefore, I am relieved that Christ and Plaskow name the methodological approach I have been intuitively applying for most of my theological life as the *embodied theological method*.[7] This method is described as "a new way of constructing theologies" that acknowledges such insights as:

- "Theology is rooted in experience";
- All religious texts, traditions, and mystical experiences "felt to have revelatory status" are all "received by finite individuals who interpret [such text, traditions and experiences] through their own language and cultural constructs"; and
- Theologies "can and must be judged by rational and ethical criteria" using measures of consistency, coherence, comprehensiveness, and clarity.[8]

It is the sum total of my own psycho-spiritual-physical experiences that led me to wind my way to the Claremont School of Theology so as to complete a Ph.D. in Religion with a focus on Process Studies, researching the work of Alfred North Whitehead and various process theologians, alongside that of Carl Gustav Jung. As well, the discoveries made in my own spiritual study and experiences have incited what I believe to be novel theological insights. If it is true, as process theology argues, that God's possibilities or initial aims introduce novelty into the world, and that integration and self-transcendence move us toward Beauty, Harmony, and Value, then it is certainly one task of process theologians to construct new psycho-religious forms that can serve those purposes in a process-friendly spirituality.

Within the broader framework of the *embodied theological method* already described, I have freely used other methodologies depending on the purposes of each chapter. Chapter 1 is primarily *analytical* of the problem as I see it, taking an inductive analytical approach where I use actual experience to develop broader theories. Chapter 2 is primarily *descriptive* of the resources I am bringing to bear on the problem. Chapters 3, 4, and 5 use a *hermeneutical* approach in which I explore the meaning of each of my resources when viewed through the lenses of my core criteria of *value*, *relationality*, and *transformation*. Chapter 6 uses a *comparative* methodology in which I compare the ideas and functions that Whitehead and Jung each describe in proprietary terms to see what fruits emerge from their synthesis. I will not make one-to-one comparisons of the ontological nature of each thinker's concepts but will, instead, claim functional resonances between terms. This is an essential part of this project because both Whitehead and Jung coined their own terminology to describe aspects of reality that are practically impossible to quantify. As their terminology is inherently metaphorical, my approach (explained in chapter 2), therefore, finds it less helpful to pit, for example, Whitehead's *eternal objects* directly against Jung's *archetypes*, and more helpful to reach deeply into each term to understand how it *functions* and then to compare those functions to discuss ways in which they are *resonant*.

Chapters 7 and 8 are primarily *constructive* chapters where I develop new theories and practices. Here I construct new theories of dreaming and of the God-Self in the psyche, drawing from Whiteheadian and Jungian resources while combining those resources in novel ways to create a generative synthesis that is more robust and liberative than existing alternatives and that supports the creative transformation of individuals and communities toward wholeness and flourishing. Paraphrasing Stanley R. Hopper, I am writing here neither as a strict Whiteheadian nor as a strict Jungian; I am arguing neither as a philosopher nor an analyst; I am not even constructing this project as an ensiled theologian. Rather, I am "trying to explore a zone or an environment in which [these various] modes of thinking might find some common ground."[9]

Rather than seeing this project as either "Whiteheadian" or "Jungian" I see it as one that uses Whiteheadian and Jungian resources to reform psycho-spiritual practice. It is therefore key that this project is understood to be inherently *interdisciplinary*. As such, I do not use theology or tradition as the "final arbiter" of the data on experience, but will also draw from process philosophy, Jungian psychology, cognitive research into the dreaming brain, and qualitative research to support my claims. In this interdisciplinary approach,

I am being true to both my Whiteheadian and Jungian roots. Whitehead saw religion, philosophy, and science as fields that were all attempting to understand the actual world[10] and therefore could not be separated quite so cleanly as we might be tempted to think. In fact, it was only through "harmonization" of those disciplines that Whitehead believed philosophy could avoid the "taint of ineffectiveness."[11] Similarly, my approach is grounded in the stance that it is only through a creative and generative synthesis of the disciplines included in this project that a robust and liberative psycho-spiritual praxis may be constructed; we do not live our lives in disciplinary silos. An *anthropological* methodology posits spirituality as intrinsically human and that therefore does not spring from "Christian theological categories, or even from history, but rather from the capacity for spirituality in every individual."[12] Discussions of the human psyche and how God can be alive there from a psychological standpoint are therefore germane. Here I will include material from various branches of psychology that examine what is called *nondirected thinking* or *primordial experience* and mystical and religious experience and its effects.

I must also note that earlier versions of comparative material examining Whitehead, Jung, symbolism, and dreams were presented at a conference sponsored by the Whitehead Research Project on Whitehead's book *Symbolism* and appear in the book *Rethinking Whitehead's* Symbolism: *Thought, Language, Culture*, published by Edinburgh University Press in 2017. Ideas similar to some in this work but focused on using Whitehead's thought as a metaphysical framework for transpersonal psychology also appear in "Whitehead's Metaphysics as a Cosmological Framework for Transpersonal Psychology," published in Vol. 47, Issue 2 of *The Humanistic Psychologist* in 2019.

CORE COMMITMENTS

Having been a regular church-going Lutheran all my life in churches that were not particularly strident, I avoided the blatant misogyny that is often witnessed in some forms of Christianity. Moreover, having grown up with a college-educated mother who generally worked outside the home, I was able to envision possibilities for myself that other women might have been denied. So I was unprepared for the torrent of sorrow that engulfed me when I read Rosemary Radford Ruether's *Sexism and God-Talk*. Having been bullied by young girls and young women of color during most of my grade school and high school years, I was unprepared for the flood of compassion that moved through me when I watched the movies *Bamboozled* and *Do the Right Thing* by Spike Lee and read *Jesus and the Disinherited* by Howard Thurman. An immersion in religion and science with a focus on ecology while getting a master's degree exposed me to a multitude of books that spoke of ecological destruction and our human failure to protect the common home we share with all life on this earth, and so I became acutely aware of this suffering too. If it is true, as paraphrased of Leon Bloy, that *there are places in the heart that do not yet exist; pain must be in order that they be*, then my heart—along with the hearts of all of humankind—now carries a multitude of places that did not exist on the day I was born. Every single one of those places has contributed to this constructive psycho-spiritual/theological project and are reflected in its core commitments and in the overarching framework of assumptions upon which it rests.

In this project and in my work overall, I am committed to:

- valuing embodied, lived experience;
- hearing the pain of the world and responding to it;
- expressing ideas about divinity that make sense not only of my own "personal experiences, but also of the world"[13];
- acknowledging divinity in the world and a God who is both transcendent and immanent;
- valuing diversity and religious pluralism and recognizing the intrinsic—not just instrumental—value of all beings, all genders, all races; to that end, I have used inclusive and gender-neutral language in my own writing, and reflected the same in quotations where it did not become too clumsy to do so;
- integrating life-affirming knowledge discovered through the sciences;
- promoting what I call the *common flourishing* of all beings and ecosystems while focusing on spiritual tools for developing the "fullness of humanity for the flourishing of all"[14];
- working as a reformist within a Christian paradigm that is neither exclusive nor limited to resources within classical Christian theistic frameworks;
- constructing a viable spirituality that is robust, liberative, and transformative and that will produce more joy, more love, more compassion, and more wholeness for those who embrace it;
- promoting the primary mission of the Church as facilitating deep encounter with God, self, and world based on the assertion that we cannot expect Christians to live as Jesus lived without having the inner spiritual life that Jesus had; and
- constructing liberative resources that are *transreligious*.

OVERARCHING CONCEPTUAL FRAMEWORK

In some ways, this project is a continuation of work that began in 1983 at Claremont School of Theology with conversations between James Hillman, depth psychologists, and process thinkers. Spearheaded by Catherine Keller, then a doctoral student, those conversations became a volume edited by David Ray Griffin entitled *The Archetypal Process: Self and Divine in Whitehead, Jung, and Hillman*. At the time, Keller described the project as a search for Eros in cosmos and psyche common to all three figures' work.[15] The focus here is not an analysis of the similarities and differences between the two schools of thought for its own sake—though both are acknowledged. Rather, this project explores the *functional resonances* of the two that can be *generatively synthesized* to construct a *robust and liberative imaginal praxis* that can be enlisted to foster personal wholeness and communal transformation of consciousness.

In the same way that Hillman claims to have found a "third way of doing metaphysics" that he calls "metaphysical *praxis*,"[16] I have found what might be called *embodied psycho-spiritual praxis* to be an effective *perspectival center*[17] for this project. From this center, I argue that the embodied encounter with the collective unconscious—what has been called *primordial experience*[18]—experienced in such practices as dream work reveals the presence of God in all reality as well as our interwovenness and participation within that sacred reality. From this perspective, God offers novelty and transformation to humans through the God-image in the psyche, and it is this archetypal Self that acts as an activation point where the process or event of God meets the process or event of the human psyche; it is the thread in the net of interwovenness that connects human and divine and through which creative transformation moves. Therefore, in the dynamic within process theology between what Roland Faber describes as either the "empiricist" or the "rationalist" orientations,[19] I prioritize the empiricist inclination with its commitment to the world as characterized by infinite flux, and seek therefore to positively influence the field of process studies and theology by adding new empirical elements drawn from psychology and dream research. Like Marjorie Suchocki, I too understand my own humble revisionism as "serving the soteriological function of all theology."[20] My personal experience and study has admittedly formed me with a bias toward what I perceive to be valuable within Jungian psychology and the process-relational worldview—I will, therefore, attempt to bracket that bias by acknowledging criticisms and limitations within the two systems. As is true of Polly Young-Eisendrath's and James Hall's approach to Jung, within this project I seek to define and revise Jung's and Whitehead's ideas in order to find a new, meaningful perspective in the synthesis.[21]

This is an inherently and unapologetically interdisciplinary project that works to creatively and generatively synthesize key resources from the disciplines of theology, philosophy, psychology, and Christian spirituality without being an exhaustive analysis of any one discipline. My approach is not systematic and I am more concerned with being true to what may still be life-giving and transformative within the resources used than with conforming strictly to the traditions or texts within any one field. In a way, this work is an invitation to those interested in process-relational thought, Jungian thought, and spiritual transformation to open their disciplinary borders a bit and come together in an experiential and imaginal effort to do more good in the world.

Because of my commitment to interdisciplinarity, it cannot pragmatically be within the scope of this project to exhaustively describe or analyze all of the elements that inform it and so I will name below key assumptions that contribute to the overarching conceptual framework within which this project is constructed.

- The term "God" herein refers to what John B. Cobb, Jr. calls "a unitary actuality which is supremely worthy of worship and/or commitment"[22] and to what may be described as the primordial mystery at the base of all life. This is the reality that William James described as "working in things rather than above them,"[23] and what Norman Pittenger calls "the cosmic thrust toward good."[24] While my conception of God is certainly informed by Christian tradition, its contours and characteristics are not strictly limited to that tradition.
- This project assumes a liberal-progressive Christian theological foundation which insists that Christianity is not essentially patriarchal (although it is currently manifestly so) and rejects all patriarchal thinking that is dependent upon mind-body dualism and devaluation of the body, the feminine, and the natural world. It also assumes that contemporary liberal theologies—including process-relational, liberation, and eco-feminist theologies—bring necessary and valid critique to the tradition and provide invaluable resources.
- It assumes a relational, panentheistic, and radically incarnational theological framework that presupposes a participatory theory of agency as described by Philip Clayton and Simpson Zachary.[25] This theory incorporates the best of liberal theologies without losing what is described as mystical, incorporates a speculative mindset, and views God as "empowering, persuading, and saving love" while rejecting descriptions of God as "coercive determiner of history."[26]
- It assumes a kenotic doctrine of creation[27] and a kenotic Christology (referenced later as present in the process that Jung describes as individuation—a self-kenotic mindset in which the ego bows to the Christ as Archetypal Self to manifest divine action in the world).
- Finally, it assumes that neither the Christian canon nor God's self-revelation are closed or final.

The circumstances of my birth, the innate abilities and education with which I have been blessed, the histories of my family and social networks, and a myriad of other elements have co-constituted my being in such a way that I speak and write from a specific social and historical location. I am a white, heterosexual woman who grew up in what would probably be described as a lower middle-class household with early exposure to people of other faiths and other races. For most of my life, I have also had access to pathways and resources not available to everyone; these allowed me to pursue college and graduate education and to invest in psychological counseling when needed. I therefore do not claim to speak for all people or even all Christians.

MOTIVATION

While pursuing a career as a performing singer and songwriter, I traveled as a troubadour, sharing songs and stories written from personal experience. Time and time again, audience members' reactions confirmed the wisdom that what is deeply personal is often broadly universal. In this project, while I make assertive claims on what ails us in contemporary America and propose a Christian-influenced psycho-spiritual praxis constructed with Whiteheadian and Jungian resources, I do so admittedly through the limited lenses of my own experience and interpretations of the broader context within which I find myself. Therefore, I do not see the alternatives or solutions I propose as universally normative. Similarly, in *A Process Christology*, Griffin refuses to formulate any kind of universal doctrine of salvation that presupposes a "fundamental spiritual problem" that is ontologically true for all of humankind in all times and places. Such a task, frequently undertaken by Christian theologians, would be "impossible, due to the differences between cultures, eras, and individuals."[28] Such a move is not only problematic due to the differences that are ignored, but also because focusing only on an "originating sin" removes other significant factors from consideration. He writes,

> But what of the alienation of man's conscious life from the unconscious symbolizations that his civilization has fostered? What of the lack of wholeness fostered by the specialization of civilization, embodied supremely in the assembly line? What of modern man's difficulty in honestly believing there is a divine reality, and, hence, any ultimate meaning to life? These problems can, of course, be interpreted as flowing from some underlying perversity common to man, defined as self-centeredness or pride. But such interpretations seem more ingenious than illuminating.[29]

Like Griffin, I find it to be much more appropriate to show how my own theological position can be relevant to my context, allowing others to write for their own contexts.[30] While I am not proscriptive regarding solutions and practices, I do make claims about a metaphysical reality that must be universally available to all humans equally, and I do believe that the arguments made herein will resonate with many people. It is for them that I have hewn the pathway through *Fragmentation*, *Integration*, and *Transformation* that follows this preface.

I begin by identifying the problem of Fragmentation, move into comparing and synthesizing resources for Integration, and finally construct theory and practice for Transformation. This *elemental* structure of the project is not its deepest layer because, for me, the fruits of this project must *do real work* in the world. As a result, there is also—alongside this elemental layer—an *existential* layer at which the theoretical, empirical, and practical resources are only useful if they reveal our metaphysical reality to be one that is characterized by *value*, *relationality*, and *transformation*. In other words, our condition of fragmentation will not be healed until we can experience the cosmos as one for which we *matter*, to which *we belong*, and in which *we can experience positive change*. As we traverse the elemental journey, it is my hope that we also realize the existential journey because while dream work is merely one practice that reveals a metaphysical reality of value, relationality, and transformation, *knowing* this God-world reality *in our lived experience* is the real destination.

NOTES

1. Carol P. Christ and Judith Plaskow, *Goddess and God in the World: Conversations in Embodied Theology* (Minneapolis: Fortress Press, 2016), 290.
2. J. Pittman McGehee and Damon J. Thomas, *The Invisible Church: Finding Spirituality Where You Are* (Westport, CT: Praeger, 2008), 62.
3. A revised edition of the book has since been released under the title *Natural Spirituality: A Handbook for Jungian Inner Work in Spiritual Community*.
4. Ann Belford Ulanov and Alvin Dueck, *The Living God and Our Living Psyche: What Christians Can Learn from Carl Jung* (Grand Rapids, MI: Wm. B. Eerdmans Publishing Co., 2008), 69.
5. Rosemary R. Ruether, *Sexism and God Talk: Toward a Feminist Theology* (Boston: Beacon Press, 1993), 12.
6. Christ and Plaskow, *Goddess and God in the World*, xiv.
7. Christ and Plaskow, xiv.
8. Christ and Plaskow, 290–93.
9. Stanley R. Hopper, "Language as Metaphorical: A Reply to John Cobb," in *The Archetypal Process: Self and Divine in Whitehead, Jung, and Hillman*, ed. David Ray Griffin (Evanston, IL: Northwestern University Press, 1990), 129.
10. Thomas E. Hosinski, *Stubborn Fact and Creative Advance* (Lanham, MD: Rowman & Littlefield Publishers, 1993), 232.
11. Hosinski, *Stubborn Fact and Creative Advance*, 232.

12. David B. Perrin, *Studying Christian Spirituality* (New York: Routledge, 2007), 40.

13. Christ and Plaskow, *Goddess and God in the World*, xv.

14. Philip Clayton and Simpson Zachary, *Adventures in the Spirit: God, World, Divine Action* (Minneapolis: Fortress Press, 2008), 260.

15. Catherine E. Keller, "Psychocosmetics and the Underworld Connection," in *The Archetypal Process: Self and Divine in Whitehead, Jung, and Hillman*, ed. David Ray Griffin (Evanston, IL: Northwestern University Press, 1990), 133.

16. James Hillman, "Back to Beyond: On Cosmology," in *The Archetypal Process: Self and Divine in Whitehead, Jung, and Hillman*, ed. David Ray Griffin (Evanston, IL: Northwestern University Press, 1990), 218.

17. Roland Faber, *God as Poet of the World: Exploring Process Theologies* (Louisville, KY: Westminster John Knox Press, 2008), 14.

18. Ann Belford Ulanov and Barry Ulanov, *Religion and the Unconscious* (Philadelphia: Westminster John Knox Press, 1985), passim.

19. Faber, *God as Poet of the World*, 17.

20. Faber, 17, 37.

21. Polly Young-Eisendrath and James Hall, *Jung's Self Psychology: A Constructivist Perspective* (New York: The Guilford Press, 1991), 1.

22. John B. Cobb Jr., *God and the World* (Philadelphia: Westminster Press, 1969), 20.

23. Bernard M. Loomer, "The Size of God," in *The Size of God: The Theology of Bernard Loomer in Context*, ed. William D. Dean and Larry E. Axel (Macon, GA: Mercer University Press, 1987), 23.

24. W. Norman Pittenger, *The Lure of Divine Love: Human Experience and Christian Faith in a Process Perspective* (New York: Pilgrim Press, 1979), 62.

25. Clayton and Zachary, *Adventures in the Spirit*, 204.

26. Faber, *God as Poet of the World*, 3.

27. Clayton and Zachary, *Adventures in the Spirit*, 181.

28. David Ray Griffin, *A Process Christology* (Philadelphia: Westminister Press, 1973), 18.

29. Griffin, 18.

30. Griffin, 19.

Acknowledgments

First and foremost, I would like to thank the members of the faculty at the Claremont School of Theology who guided my studies there and advised me in my research. My deepest gratitude goes to Philip Clayton for being a generous, encouraging, and challenging coach. Ever since our first meeting at a Religion and Science Student Society event in 2010 at the Lutheran School of Theology at Chicago (where I was invited to be a student responder to his presentation) and the following weekend's conference at Goshen College where we first discussed my unusual research interests, I was eager to work with him. His expertise, guidance, and flexibility were indispensable. I also want to thank Roland Faber, Monica Coleman, and Bruce Epperly who led me through my studies in process philosophy and theology with both expertise and openness, and Andrew Dreitcer and Frank Rogers for their teachings around spirituality and formation. Having come to know Kelly Bulkeley and his work through the Psychology, Culture, and Religion Group in the American Academy of Religion and the International Association for the Study of Dreams, I was thrilled when he agreed to serve on my committee. Dr. Bulkeley's work at the intersection of psychology, religion, cognitive science, and dreaming has been key to this project.

I must acknowledge Anna Case-Winters in whose process theology class at McCormick Seminary in Chicago I was first inspired to connect Whitehead with Jung. Other process thinkers who were very influential in my work that must be recognized are John B. Cobb, Jr., David Ray Griffin, Marjorie Suchocki, Thomas Hosinski, and Jay McDaniel. It would also be remiss were I not to acknowledge the incredibly formative experiences I had with the full faculty and staff of the Lutheran School of Theology at Chicago and Claremont School of Theology. The entire ecosystems of each place and the wise and encouraging faculty and fellow students all contributed to my own "becoming." In addition, although they would not know me from Adam's housecat, I feel I must also acknowledge Christian de Quincey in whose book *Radical Nature: the Soul of Matter* I first met Alfred North Whitehead and Clarissa Pinkola Estes in whose book *Women Who Run with the Wolves* I first encountered Carl Gustav Jung.

I would like to acknowledge Sheree Aston and my former colleagues at Western University of Health Science along with other faculty and staff there who encouraged me in my studies. Other significantly formative communities that I would like to thank include the members and current and former staff of the Lutheran Church of the Resurrection in Marietta, Georgia, Nacoochee Presbyterian Church in Sautee, Georgia, and all those involved in the Natural Spirituality Regional Gatherings in North Georgia, the Haden Institute Summer Dream and Spirituality Conferences in North Carolina, and the Mythic Journeys conferences in Atlanta. I would especially like to thank Joyce Rockwood Hudson and Jerry Wright for their wise mentorship over many years.

I give thanks for my colleagues at the School of Theology of the University of the South in Sewanee, Tennessee, my current vocational home. I am grateful for the opportunity to contribute to our endeavors together. I am also grateful to Michael Gibson, senior acquisitions editor at Lexington Books for believing in this project and finding its appropriate place there and to Tim Blevins of 1517 Media for introducing us. Finally, I would like to thank my parents, Richard and Lucille Bayne, my brother, Jeff Kling, and all other family and friends who have walked with me and loved and encouraged me along this serpentine pathway of faith, frustration, and fulfillment.

Part One

FRAGMENTATION

Chapter 1

A House Divided

INTRODUCTION

We who currently live in the United States are deeply and painfully divided. Can we not feel this to be true in our very bones? How often do we experience a general sense of personal contentment? How often can we say we bask in the glow of family love and support? Can we equally express strength and vulnerability, uniqueness and connection, and deeply relate in intimate ways with our closest loved ones? How frequently do we enjoy the company of friends and neighbors and the joy of fellowship and good food shared at a communal table? Are we able to easily name three to four close friends or family members that we know will have our backs when times get tough? How regularly do we—along with the neighbors in our broader communities—feel the satisfaction of meaningful work done well? Can we survey the communities in our state and know that the people who live in them *all* have equal access to nutritious food, clean water and air, good education, and to the natural world that is essential for the flourishing of human life? Are we and our neighbors regularly able to access, appreciate and be inspired by the aesthetic beauty and value reflected in both human-created art and in our interactions with non-human beings? Can we voice our complaints and convictions, and know that we have the power to change what ails us individually and communally? Are affirmative answers to the questions above not the very definition of what it means to be human, whole, and to flourish individually and communally? I certainly cannot speak for everyone in the United States, but the characteristics inferred by these questions are not those that I witness regularly in our broader culture and I do not seem to be alone in that assessment.

In 1951, Paul Tillich described the human condition as one of "disruption, conflict, self-destruction, meaninglessness, and despair in all realms of life."[1] Somewhat more recently, Jürgen Moltmann linked this inner state of "alienation of the human being from [his or her] bodily existence" to the "external ecological crisis of modern industrial society."[2] In fact, in *God in Creation*, Moltmann describes the current environmental state as not just a crisis for the earth, but as "nothing less than a crisis in human beings themselves."[3] James W. Heisig points out that widespread environmental destruction as well as other social forces related to specialization, scientific materialism, and problematic approaches to both aesthetics and technology were all attributed by mathematician-philosopher Alfred North Whitehead to the modern human's non-relationally aware and ratio-centric ego—or "self-defeating particularity."[4]

Modernity's heroic ego, champion of numerous achievements of which humankind can be proud, has been a "mixed blessing," notes Jungian analyst and seminary professor Robert L. Moore (as has been argued for decades by Catherine Keller and other feminist scholars and theologians) because the down side of the consciousness and autonomy it engendered have been "alienation from the physical world, from the body, and from the unconscious." This ego is inflated, unrooted, and denies its limitations along with its "embeddedness in the physical and social world"[5] from which it was born and on which it depends. According to archetypal philosopher Richard Tarnas, the same evolutionary processes that have allowed a centered and autonomous human self to emerge have simultaneously moved our cultural, religious, philosophical, and scientific outlooks to an overall worldview that has emptied the external world of any "intrinsic meaning and purpose," removing from it "all those qualities with which the human being is uniquely identified."[6] The precious human autonomy achieved has been paid for by the painful experience of human alienation. Moreover, the epistemological separation of subject and object in the human mind, while liberating to some degree, has also been problematic.[7]

Progress itself may indeed be partially responsible for creating the very polarity with which we wrestle and within which we suffer, anxious and lonely. Robin Robertson notes that the amazing scientific and technological advancements we have made have also severed us from our "instinctual roots."[8] Long before the 2016 election season, Robertson claimed that tensions had reached a breaking point. He describes wrenching and ongoing societal swings between the "twin poles of spirit and instinct" that have bounced us between the poles of a sexual revolution on the one hand and the "born again" movement on the other, or between the left-wing focus on societal responsibility and systemic evil and the right-wing focus on personal responsibility and immorality.[9]

We have made astonishing progress as a culture. We can point to countless examples of inventions and advancements that have been made that have ended misery, improved public health, and left us speechless with their aesthetic beauty. Yet we are relentlessly at war with ourselves, with each other, and with the planet. There are numerous symptoms to which we can point; in this chapter, I will highlight the ways in which we are divided people living within a divisive culture and sketch out the wholeness that may help us flourish individually and communally.

A DIVIDED PEOPLE

We do not have to look very far for the evidential tracings of the kind of division and alienation that Tillich, Moltmann, Tarnas, and Robertson have described. As will be shown in this chapter, we are divided *societally*, as evidenced in our political polarization and the rise of hate groups. We are divided *interpersonally* as evidenced in increasing loneliness and isolation. Finally, we are divided *intrapersonally*, as is evidenced by the exploding usage of antidepressants and the correlation between early adverse childhood experience and morbidity, mortality, and disability that is somehow related to the divided psyches that result from trauma.

Ideological and Societal Fragmentation

By all accounts, the 2016 presidential election in the United States only deepened our already chasmic political polarization. In 2014, the Pew Research Center reported that "Republicans and Democrats are more divided along ideological lines—and partisan antipathy is deeper and more extensive—than at any point in the last two decades."[10] Following are some of the highlighted statistics:

- The overall share of Americans who express consistently conservative or consistently liberal opinions has doubled over the past two decades from 10 percent to 21 percent;
- Ninety-two percent of Republicans are to the right of the median Democrat, and ninety-four percent of Democrats are to the left of the median Republican;
- Partisan antipathy has grown to where 27 percent of Democrats view the Republican Party as a threat to national well-being and 36 percent of Republicans view the Democratic Party in the same way.[11]

Another indicator of expanding societal fissures is described by Mark Potok, senior fellow at the Southern Poverty Law Center, who reports that the number of hate groups in the United States rose 14 percent, as did the number of "conspiracy-minded" antigovernment "Patriot" groups. Recent years have brought us extremist violence in the form of terror plots, the slaughter of both African American churchgoers during a prayer meeting and Jewish worshippers celebrating Hanukkah, and the bombing or burning of numerous mosques. In fact, more people were killed by extremist groups in the United States in 2015 than in any year since 1995's Oklahoma City bombing.[12] Yet an alarming body count is just the tip of the iceberg. According to Potok, "Violence motivated by racial, ethnic or religious animus fractures society along its most fragile fault lines and sends shock waves through entire targeted communities. More hatred and fear, particularly of diversity, are often the response."[13] Fractured communities and the anxiety that results have been harnessed by unscrupulous political candidates who attempt to capitalize on America's fears. Whereas such extreme hate appeared in the past to be mostly on the fringes of American political life, in 2020 it is front and center.

Interpersonal Fragmentation

Not surprisingly, societal division and alienation is also manifest in our closest relationships. Reporting on a General Social Survey conducted by the National Science Foundation in 2014, Janice Shaw Crouse alerts us to the fact that Americans are lonelier than ever before. More than one quarter of the 1,500 interviewees "said that they have no one with whom they can talk about their personal troubles or triumphs."[14] Moreover, when family members are excluded, *more than half* affirmed that statement. What are the consequences of such loneliness and self-perceived social isolation? According to neuroscientist John Cacioppo, chronic loneliness can cause depression, affect prevalence toward chronic diseases like diabetes, and is even correlated to an increase in the likelihood of dementia.[15] Though loneliness can serve a protective purpose, it can also become a negative physiological trigger. Cacioppo writes,

> Our stress response contributed to survival across human history, but in contemporary society, chronic stress also contributes to morbidity and mortality . . . Partly, we're showing that the brain is organized in part to deal with and to promote salutary connections to other people. The fundamental question was "what is the social nature of our brain?" One of the things that surprised me was how important loneliness proved to be. It predicted morbidity. It predicted mortality. And that shocked me. When we experimentally manipulated loneliness, we found surprising changes in the "personalities" of people. There's a lot more power to the perception of being socially isolated than any of us had thought.[16]

Intrapersonal Fragmentation

Americans are suffering socially *and* psychosomatically. Citing a report from the National Center for Health Statistics, Peter Wehrwein notes an increase in antidepressant use in the United States among teens and adults (people aged twelve and older) of almost 400 percent between 1988 and 1994 and 2005 and 2008.[17] The report also states:

- Twenty-three percent of women in their forties and fifties take antidepressants, a higher percentage than any other group (by age or sex).
- Women are two and one half times more likely to be taking an antidepressant than men.
- Fourteen percent of non-Hispanic white people take antidepressants compared with just four percent of non-Hispanic blacks and three percent of Mexican Americans.
- Less than a third of Americans who are taking a single type of antidepressant (as opposed to two or more) have seen a mental health professional in the past year.[18]

The symptoms of our cultural disease go beyond the increasing usage of psycho-pharmaceuticals. In 1998, physician-researchers Vincent J. Felitti and Robert F. Anda released the findings of a collaborative study between Kaiser Permanente's Department of Preventive Medicine in San Diego (Felitti) and the U.S. Centers for Disease Control and Prevention (CDC, Anda). Known as the ACEs study, their research was conducted to examine the relationship between childhood traumatic stress and the leading causes of morbidity, mortality, and disability in the United States, including cardiovascular disease, chronic lung disease, chronic liver disease, depression and other forms of mental illness, obesity, smoking, and alcohol and drug abuse. A major epidemiological study of 17,000 participants, the ACEs research analyzed "the effect of traumatic experiences during the first eighteen years of life on adolescent and adult medical and psychiatric disease, sexual behavior, healthcare costs, and life expectancy."[19] The findings were stunning.

> It became evident that traumatic life experiences during childhood and adolescence were far more common than generally recognized, were complexly interrelated, and were associated decades later in a strong and proportionate manner with outcomes important to medical practice, public health, and the social fabric of the nation. In the context of everyday medical practice, we came to recognize that the earliest years of infancy and childhood are not lost but, like a child's footprints in wet cement, are often life-long.[20]

In two waves of research, ten categories of adverse childhood experience were ultimately identified that included physical/emotional/sexual abuse, having an alcoholic or drug abuser in the household, physical/emotional neglect, violence in the home, and divorce or an incarcerated parent.[21] Based on their responses, participants were given an ACE score that represented the numerical total of each category experienced. Of these 17,000 middle-class Americans with high-quality health insurance, it was determined that only one third had an ACE score of 0, 17 percent had an ACE score of four or more, and 11 percent had an ACE score of five or more. Moreover, women had a significantly higher likelihood of having experienced five or more ACE categories than men.[22]

How can such early experience affect our physical health and behavior? Jungian analyst Donald Kalsched's work is helpful here. He argues that although trauma can happen at any age, it is particularly difficult in early childhood "where, because of the immaturity of the psyche and/or brain, we are ill-equipped to metabolize our experience."[23] For young children, trauma is not just a bad memory—it threatens to shatter their very "psycho-somatic unity." While the kind of complete shattering that might destroy the developing personality is rare, what can happen instead, Kalsched asserts, is *dissociation.* Such dissociation protects the self from annihilation, but replaces the unitary self with a multiplicity of parts held together by an archetypal story. The parts "cease to know about each other so that the personality does not have to suffer the unspeakable horror of trauma *as a whole.*"[24] Various aspects of the experience—for example, sensation, affect, and image—are fragmented, compartmentalized and "encoded in segmented 'neural nets' in the brain." While such fragmentation protects against the unbearable experience of the whole, it also obliterates the necessary meaning of the whole. After such experience, notes Kalsched, "we no longer make sense to ourselves. We can't tell our own story as a coherent narrative."[25]

In other words, painful energies and affect are distributed and held in a dissociated way in the psyche and body, where the emotional pain and discomfort are not felt consciously but often dealt with unconsciously through self-medication and self-soothing behaviors. The effects of such dissociation are borne out by the ACEs study, wherein high ACEs scores were directly correlated with higher incidences of a wide range of risky behaviors and public health ills including alcoholism, alcohol abuse, smoking, and illicit drug use; depression and suicide attempts; chronic obstructive pulmonary disease, ischemic heart disease, and liver disease; financial stress and impaired worker performance; and higher risk for intimate partner violence and sexual violence overall.[26]

The lasting effects of developmental trauma seem to be more than psychological. Bessel van der Kolk, M.D., a Boston-based psychiatrist and recognized expert on PTSD, explains in his book *The Body Keeps the Score: Brain, Mind, and Body in the Healing of Trauma* how early adverse experience produces physiological changes, including "a recalibration of the brain's alarm system, an increase in stress hormone activity, and alterations in the system that filters relevant information from irrelevant. We now know that trauma compromises the brain area that communicates the physical, embodied feelings of being alive." Such changes result in hypervigilance to danger, repetition of relational problems, and many other negative perspectives.[27] One sixth of the ACEs study population had a score of four or more and, at those levels, their incidences of such risks were exponentially higher than for those with scores of even one or two. Extrapolated to the total population of the United States—currently over 330 million[28]—we can estimate that over 55 million Americans have an ACE score of four or more. It is no wonder that Robert W. Block, former president of the American Academy of Pediatrics claims that "Adverse childhood experiences are the single greatest unaddressed public health threat facing our nation today."[29] Felitti and Anda conclude:

> The influence of childhood experience, including often-unrecognized traumatic events, is as powerful as Freud and his colleagues originally described it to be. These influences are long-lasting, and neuroscientists are now describing the intermediary mechanisms that develop as a result of these stressors. Unfortunately, and in spite of these findings, the biopsychosocial model and the bio-medical model of psychiatry remain at odds rather than taking advantage of these new discoveries to reinforce each other.[30]

Pointed examples in this section highlight the fragmentation in American culture at the societal, interpersonal, and intrapersonal levels, all of which result in the societal ills reflected in political polarization, hate groups, loneliness, isolation, rising antidepressant usage, and costly and debilitating effects of adverse childhood experience. In the next section, I will show how the roots of such fragmentation lie in the very culture and worldview within which we are embedded.

A DIVISIVE CULTURE

Rarely, if ever, do we as individuals even consciously think about our worldview. A worldview is the water within which we swim and the unconscious backdrop to our language, our decisions, our assertions, and our beliefs about the world and other beings. It is the invisible frame upon which our cultural experience is draped, yet it also directly forms those very experiences.

Although this is far from an exegesis of the entirety of Western culture and its influences, there are entrenched elements upon which our culture is based, yet these assumptions are hardly even noticed, let alone examined. The elements with which we are primarily concerned herein are mind-body *dualism* and its handmaidens, *mechanism* and *dismissal of the nonrational.*

Dualism

When Block bemoans the fact that the bio-psycho-social and the bio-medical models are "at odds," he may not even be consciously aware that they are "at odds" because psyche and matter—or mind and body—have been at odds in the Western paradigm since the Enlightenment. In other words, as long as there is no scientifically accepted and meaningful description of how mind and body interact—as is generally the case in the Western mechanistic and dualistic views—we will continue to act in "self-defeating particularity" and contrary to the realities of our embodied and embedded lives. Until that split is healed and we can experience embodied human life as something other than one of alienation, isolation, and despair, we will see no respite from the disastrous consequences of such bifurcation in our relationships to our bodies, to each other, and to the very ecosystems on which our lives depend.

In this regard, medicine and the natural sciences have been slow to recognize what humanities scholars have argued for decades. Process theologians John B. Cobb, Jr. and David Ray Griffin have linked our modern sense of alienation or estrangement from embodied life with "the dualistic view that human beings are totally different in kind from the rest of the world."[31] Murray Stein, a training Jungian analyst at the International School for Analytical Psychology in Zurich, Switzerland, concurs with this description of the human condition when he writes that "with the passing of active tribalism, there has come the modern experience of anomie and lack of kinship with the universe."[32]

Dismissal of the Nonrational

If the non*physical* is not considered, the non*rational* is actively dismissed. Yet both Freud and Jung understood all humans to have a *nonrational* unconscious that is dynamic in nature, and they appreciated its powerful impact on human experience and perception through its irruptive breaks into conscious awareness. For both men, it is the unconscious that gives humans access to the ongoing flow of life and energy that fuels all beings. Freud referred to this flow in the psyche as *primary-process thinking* while Jung used the term *nondirected thinking*. For both Freud and Jung, such contact with primordial

human experience—the most basic strata of human experience and instinct—carried enormous power and emotional punch.[33]

Nondirected Thinking and Religion

The flow of Jung's nondirected thinking was not just about sex or death, as it was with Freud, but about life, creativity, generativity, expression, and the desire of this unconscious flow of life to be differentiated into actualized reality. Jung was certain that our deepest unconscious reality seeks integration and speaks through the language of symbols to draw people toward an individuated state of wholeness wherein the opposing forces of the psyche are integrated and unconscious shadow materials—and the vitalizing energy they hold—can be utilized and released for expressive purposes.

Unlike Freud, who thought religion was infantile and destructive, Jung believed religion to be inextricably and vitally bound up with humanness and a "necessary fact" in human experience. He understood the encounter with primordial experience to be akin to what religion understands to be the "original mystery" typically referred to as "God." He also asserted that none of his second-half-of-life patients had been healed without regaining a "religious outlook."[34] Jung elaborated on that statement in a letter wherein he explained that people "since times immemorial" had always held some kind of view of the wholeness of the world that then facilitated the wholeness of the individual person within that frame. Movement toward individual wholeness, he insisted, was an "instinctual activity," a *drive* of the mind that requires an *object* in order to be satisfied, in the same way that hunger requires food. Therefore, when people lose a religious frame of reference, they are no longer "rooted in their world" and the human need for meaning "remains unanswered because the rational, biological goals are unable to express the irrational wholeness of human life."[35]

Experiences of the numinous or transcendent have historically been facilitated through the structures of religion. Until relatively recently, direct experience of the transpersonal, that engagement with deep unconscious forces, was facilitated by creative and intuitive modes of being such as "religious belief and spiritual practice, ritual and dance, artwork and poetry, romance and relationship, music and dreams" and any other mode of activity that is "open to the nonrational side of experience."[36] In *Teaching Jung*, David Tacey notes that

> The increasingly rational nature of modern life has had a destructive impact on our traditional forms of transcendence. Typically, the modern person has little or no access to religion or spirituality, to ritual or poetry, and even romance and

relationship have become attenuated, commercialized, and clichéd. Many of our nonrational outlets and avenues have been blocked, devalued, or destroyed.[37]

It is the *lack of the experience of this kind of wholeness*—rootedness in our world and a sense of meaning that goes beyond our individual experience—that our societal fragmentation reveals. Yet that kind of encounter with a sacred reality is unfathomable for most modern people for two main reasons: (1) we are generally unaware of a way to understand a religious reality that is neither *supernatural* nor merely *subjective*; and (2) if such a religious reality exists, we are generally unaware of a way to access it in our ordinary, day-to-day lives. To understand where we may go from here, it is necessary to briefly examine religion's function regarding the depths of human experience as well as its role in connecting individuals to what is transpersonal and whole.

Primordial Experience and Transpersonal Reality

Ann and Barry Ulanov understand religion to be a "true container" for primordial experience that serves: (1) to protect the individual from being overwhelmed and swept away by their encounter with the numinous or primordial and thereby safeguard human sanity; and (2) to protect individual autonomy and freedom by giving the individual an extra-mundane authority and point of reference, so that one does not fall under the spell of "mass mindedness," or be in lock-step with the collective.[38] Yet Edward F. Edinger would also warn us that though collective religion may serve a protective role regarding the powerful depths of the unconscious, it may also rob us of the more personal and growth-producing aspects of the unconscious as well as our individual relationship to it.[39] "All religious practices," writes Edinger, "hold up to view the transpersonal categories of existence and attempt to relate them to the individual."[40]

Those *transpersonal* or *suprapersonal* categories are articulated via a culture's myths and sacred stories and are typically present in that society's collective rituals of life. The religious practices embodied in those collective rituals serve to protect us from both ego inflation and alienation,[41] because they provide meaning and orient the individual morally.[42] But contemporary Western culture is marked by the collapse of myth and symbol and their replacement with a scientific materialism that presents itself as "sober fact."[43] Yet Gerald H. Slusser argues that it is our mythic statements that allow life to flow because such statements both "frame" the way in which we view the world and relate us in a meaningful way to psychic wholeness. "Meaninglessness," he writes, "inhibits fullness of life and is therefore equivalent to illness."[44] Edinger, too, doubts that collective human life can survive for very long without a shared system of transpersonal categories, or myth and symbol.[45] He argues that when people do not have functioning suprapersonal categories to explain human life, they are more likely to fall into the dangerous condition of either extreme ego inflation or deflation.[46]

Projection and Inflation

In the absence of suprapersonal categories, there are no transpersonal targets for projection, yet the elimination of such targets for projection does not eliminate the need to project; projection just moves from being transpersonal to being personal. Without a transpersonal target toward which to point the powerful, unconscious energies of life, humans will either project them onto other human beings[47]—seeing their new love interest, for example, as a "god" or "goddess"—or on such matters as personal power, social reform movements, or any number of other "-isms." When this happens, personal, secular, and political actions "become charged with unconscious religious meaning"; such a move endangers societies because unconscious religious motivation all too easily turns to destructive fanaticism.[48] On the other hand, when collective life is stable and individuals share a living myth, people are capable of projecting their inner God-image (what C. G. Jung called the Self) onto the communal religion and that religion then contains the Self and inhibits widespread inflation or alienation.[49] When such a religious container for projections of the inner God-image is lacking, all those energies then have nowhere to go other than back to the individual, activating that individual's psyche in a way that can cause major problems.[50]

The problems Edinger identifies that result from the loss of religious projection include individuals: (1) losing their inner connection to the Self/divine, resulting in alienation and a sense of life's meaninglessness; (2) assuming the divine energies, resulting in a sense of inflation and hubris; (3) projecting religious energies onto secular or political movements, as noted above; or (4) individuals may be forced to confront the kind of questions that lead them to discover the god-image within themselves, at which point the loss of religious projection will have served a positive developmental purpose.[51] The very birth of depth psychology Edinger describes as a "symptom of our time" in that its emergence has been initiated by the loss of religious projection and the breakdown of a collective symbol system.[52]

Inflation of the individual is diametrically opposed to any kind of community or sense of unity within a society. The kind of relational "communion"—or what Victor Turner calls *communitas*[53]—has typically been wrought through collective ritual experience. As framed by Kelly Bulkeley, a scholar working at the intersection of psychology, religion, and cognitive science, Turner's work in cultural anthropology reveals the way rituals *change* people and the way they participate in social conventions. Rituals use symbols and "liminal" space to move individuals from one stage of life to another and, more importantly, create an experience—even if only temporary—of society "as an *un*structured, *un*differentiated community of equals bound together by an essential unity." Having experienced that essential unity and relatedness, members of a community are then able to fully and creatively participate in the hierarchical structures that inevitably arise among groups.[54] Yet where can contemporary Americans go to experience our "essential unity" today? The answer to that question of late does not seem to be "to church."

Religion and the Church

What is the state of traditional religion in the United States today? According to Pew Research's Religion and Public Life Project, "One-fifth of the U.S. public—and a third of adults under 30—are religiously unaffiliated today, the highest percentages ever in Pew Research Center polling." This group includes atheists, agnostics, and people who say they "have no particular religious affiliation (14%)." At the same time, forty-six million unaffiliated adults identify as religious or spiritual due to belief in God, a connection with nature, or a practice of prayer. More than a third can be classified as "spiritual" but not "religious."[55] Judging by the numbers, it does not appear that traditional approaches to religious symbols are working to function as a unifying, collective container for the transpersonal in contemporary American society.

Have theologians and church leaders responded to our spiritual crises in ways that are helpful? Not necessarily. Though the Christian New Testament emphasizes being led by the Spirit, not long after its formation, the Church began to stress this aspect of faith less and less, according to Griffin. Increasingly, being a "Christian" has been defined more by one's doctrinal beliefs rather than by the presence or work of God's Spirit in one's actual life.[56] Griffin attributes this in part to the fact that Christian theologians did not construct a "genuinely Christian account of God's mode of acting upon the world in general, and human experience in particular."[57] Cobb concurs that churches are failing to meet the religious needs of people because of "our general theological failure."[58] While Griffin thinks most of the "beliefs about the past have lost their hold,"[59] Jung attributes this condition to modern humans' aversion to inherited truths. For moderns, science and religion cannot be reconciled because "Christian tenets have lost their authority and psychological justification."[60] According to Jung, traditional religious symbols and even the word "God" can no longer mediate the transcendent because such symbols are no longer alive. As we have already seen in Edinger, we no longer understand a God image at our center and we do not generally have the worldview or tools to re-imagine God.[61] Though shocking at the time,

Cobb thinks the "death-of-God theologians" were stating something truthful because what most Christians meant when they spoke of God had become empty of "conviction and reality."[62] What has taken the place of faith, for many, is a psychology of experience; a symptom, for Jung, "of a profound convulsion of spiritual life."[63]

In his blog "Is Biblicist Christianity Bankrupt?," Michael Dowd stakes his claim that Christians must embrace scientific evidence and rejects the idea that ancient texts must be considered the only authoritative sources for human life.[64] Instead, he believes that when we honor the evidence provided by history and the sciences, we honor "the authority of scripture," and unless we do this, the Church will "continue its slide into irrelevance or extinction."[65] Yet, while embracing scientific evidence would certainly be a step forward, much in human experience cannot be so neatly categorized. Jung believed that our task now is to rediscover for ourselves the life of the Spirit in order to bring savor to life.[66]

The negative effects of a culture and worldview that is based in dualistic and mechanistic thinking and that rejects what is nonrational are rampant. Such a dismissive stance robs us of appreciation for, and access to, the deep primordial experience that is the source of life and vitality as well as the ability to derive creative responses to life that our nondirected thinking engenders. We have traded our targets for transpersonal projection for the burdensome weight on the individual person of that which used to be held by transpersonal categories and values, resulting in ego inflation and ideological devotion to any number of "isms." Many have turned their backs on what they perceive to be an irrelevant Church with walking-dead symbols that can no longer serve as a collective site of ritual experience and unity. As a result, we have no shared values upon which we can rest; such values could serve to smooth our relations with the "others" to whom we are regularly exposed and of whom we are naturally wary or even fearful until we get to know them. The dividedness we experience and the problems it engenders are not individually created; they are a paradigmatic problem.

A Paradigmatic Problem

In our current era, Tarnas describes three fundamental factors at play in the Western context. The first is a pervading "metaphysical disorientation and groundlessness" that is marked by the absence of any kind of overarching purposes, meaning, or metanarrative that could provide humans "a nourishing coherence and intelligibility." The second factor is the deep alienation and personal isolation that marks our industrial, information-soaked but imagination-thirsty society; the "spiritual estrangement of the modern psyche in a disenchanted universe," as well as the bifurcation between humans and the natural cosmos. Finally, Tarnas points to the critical need for deeper insight into the powerful unconscious forces and tendencies that shape us for good and for ill.[67]

If we draw back our lens to take in the widest frame, we see that all the forces described in the sections above have contributed to a state where the planet we depend on for our very life and breath is now on the verge of ecological collapse. Though evidence of climate change relentlessly mounts in 2020, the United States is politically frozen, impotent regarding any of the steps that might help. Species are becoming extinct in record numbers, toxic wastes have polluted both watersheds and low-income communities, transnational corporations pillage economically poor countries for their precious resources, populations grow exponentially beyond what the Earth can support, and still, Americans consume ever more, every year. Yet, rather than despairing at this moment of "climactic urgency," Tarnas strikes a hopeful note, suggesting that we are poised at "an extraordinary threshold" that could bring about "a genuinely fundamental transformation in the underlying assumptions and principles of the cultural world view."[68] What is in contention now is our basic understanding of reality, our role in the cosmos, and how we relate to life.[69]

Can we recover an appreciation of the importance of nondirected thinking and the access such thinking gives us to our primordial source of vitality, dynamism, and creativity in human life? Our culture has lost the necessary function that religion provides in being a container for primordial experience, and by providing targets for transpersonal projection and ritual. We have seen how the loss of ritual and transpersonal projection result in psychological ego inflation and diminished communal bonding. Finally, we have begun to see the devastating effects that a faulty paradigm can have on us as individuals, on our society, and on planetary health. We have reached a moment of crucial decision where our very survival hangs in the balance. In such a high-stakes moment, when the outcome is uncertain, the anxiety so great, and the potential birth pangs so convulsive, we need an alluring alternative, a vision of wholeness toward which we can be drawn.

The Wholeness We Need

Certainly, there are existing alternative systems of thought that offer a wealth of resources to undergird such a holistic worldview. Works ranging from theologian Sallie McFague's *Body of God* to numerous voicings of deep ecology principles to historian of religions Mary Evelyn Tucker's and ecological philosopher Brian Swimme's cinematic *Journey of the Universe* have reached into the scientific story of the creation of the cosmos as a unifying vision. A torrent of scientists have—along with Al Gore's *An Inconvenient Truth* and

Greta Thunburg's inspiring calls for action—sounded the alarm about the need for a unified response to the global ecological crisis. Other theologians have stressed *panentheism*[70] as a compelling framework within which to understand both vertical and horizontal relationships between God, humans and the natural world. Yet these disparate resources—that rarely seem to stray beyond the confines of academia's hallowed halls—do not seem to be adequate to the task of real and lasting change.

Through what means might real and lasting *transformation* occur? In making his case for the transformative power of dreams, Bulkeley points to the work of philosopher Michael E. Zimmerman as key to understanding the entrenched societal fragmentation and life-threatening behavior loops in which we find ourselves. In "Quantum Theory, Intrinsic Value, and Panentheism,"[71] Zimmerman argues that in order to engender deep respect for the natural environment we must "move from atomistic, dualistic ego consciousness toward relational, nondualistic consciousness." Our human penchant for the kind of independent self-determination that sees the world only as instrumentally valuable is highly problematic. Alternatively, Zimmerman affirms quantum physics as a "new metaphysics" that "overcomes Cartesian dualism" by essentially relating all levels of being (a vision of the world shared by panentheism and ecofeminism) but then despairs that such "inspiring expressions of nondualistic consciousness" are not enough to spur real change in attitudes.[72] Why? Because even such compelling paradigms are only operative at the cognitive or rational level and therefore do not transform dualistic rationality.[73] In other words, such cognitive insights do not offer us an *experience* of our "membership in the web of all being."[74] Zimmerman argues that neither panentheism nor quantum theory can bring about nondualistic experience on their own.[75]

We cannot *think* our way into a new way of being. Cognitive knowledge in and of itself cannot provide the experience of a relational and meaning- and value-filled world that asks us to contribute our own attainment of value back to it. I am convinced that we will solve neither the ecological crisis nor our estrangement from each other and its attendant social ills until we transform our relationship with embodied life itself and rediscover *within it* what is sacred. Like Bulkeley and Zimmerman, I, too, assert that theories of wholeness, whether psychological, physical, or metaphysical are not enough to overcome the crippling societal, interpersonal, and intrapersonal effects of fragmentation; only *an embodied transformational experience of wholeness* holds any hope for shifting human consciousness and behavior.

What is needed now, claims James W. Heisig, is a reformation of popular imagination by "weaving" into that imagination "insights about eternal value flowing through the temporal" because the popular imagination must be enlisted in the reformation of civilization.[76] Such work, I believe, is inherently *psycho-spiritual* in nature. Connecting the spiritual with the psychological is fundamentally a return to the roots of psychology. Kenneth Pargament notes that psychology's "founding figures" from William James to G. Stanley Hall "saw no reason to separate spirituality from psychological study and practice," but naturally included mystical phenomena and conversion experiences.[77] Only later, with psychology's positivistic alignment with the natural sciences did psychology begin to see spirituality in "oversimplified, stereotypical terms" that, in the cases of Freud and Skinner, focused "on the dark side of faith to the exclusion of its other qualities."[78] Drawing similarities between religious life and psychoanalysis, Michael Argyle notes that in both, "people are seeking salvation, trying to solve their problems and find out how to live a better life."[79] Though Naomi Goldenberg, a leading author in the field of religious studies and gender, has been a very vocal critic of Jung, she acknowledges as helpful his attitude toward religious systems because he "hypothesized that there is a religious process in every human being" and that people would be "more secure" if they could remain connected to their religion, be guided by it, and then see its "basic process within." Those who cannot do so satisfactorily are "both cursed and blessed." Cursed because their way is not made easier by established text or doctrine and blessed because their way may be creatively freer.[80]

What, then, is spirituality? According to David B. Perrin, spirituality integrates all aspects of life into a unified whole, allowing life to be marked by the "overall spirit of good will" inherent in authentic living. In such an authentic life, one is committed to healthy critique of oneself and one's relationships, and gains a deeper appreciation of self and other.[81] We can understand such authentic spirituality as something intrinsic to human nature; it includes a capacity for both transcendence and self-transcendence; and it is a "lived reality that is shaped into a way of life."[82] Yet this "lived reality" seems to be in short supply in the modern world. Heisig enlists Thomas Berry to show how the "classic Western spirituality" that is behind both the present religious and scientific-technological paradigms responsible for our fragmentation are "really at odds with how we experience the world,"[83] specifying these four conceptions as problematic:

- The identification of the divine as transcendent to the natural world, so that the natural world becomes less capable of communicating divine presence;
- The establishment of the human as transcendent to the natural world, so that the world is transformed into crass matter, raw material for human consumption;
- The millennial vision of a blessed future accessible to history through technological progress; and

- The stress on salvation dynamics to the neglect of creation dynamics, so that our eyes could be turned away from our abuse of the earth to focus on moral revivalism and dedication to pious causes.[84]

What is called for now, Heisig and Berry suggest, is a cosmology that values differentiation, subjectivity, relational *communion* at both the micro and macro levels, and numinous experience.[85] Though we may answer Zimmerman by merely facilitating an experience of nondualistic consciousness, such an isolated experience of oneness is not a viable solution if it means a loss of the appreciation of embodied multiplicity. The wholeness we seek must still be pushed beyond just psycho-spiritual experience to include the frame or worldview upon which such an experience rests. In addition, we require a theoretical and empirical framework through which we can rationally appreciate such an experience.

SUMMARY

In this chapter, I have demonstrated the fragmentary nature of human existence in the contemporary United States of America, and have shown this fragmentation to be societal, interpersonal, and intrapersonal. We have explored the devastating consequences of the largely unexamined worldview upon which Western culture is based and have called into question its dualistic and mechanistic mindset as well as its dismissal of what is nonrational. I have shown how the ineffectiveness of organized religion in general and the Christian Church in particular have led to the loss of transpersonal projection and collective ritual, resulting in rising individual inflation and communal disconnection. Finally, I have argued in this chapter that until contemporary people in the United States experience a real, transformative encounter with a transpersonal Reality that reflects our wholeness and value, our relatedness to everything, and the hope of transformative change, we will continue to be fragmented as individuals and as a society.

In order to move us toward the necessary changes, it is essential that we be able to access and describe such transformative experience through a theoretical and empirical framework that can be appreciated rationally as well as nonrationally. Therefore, I will argue in this work that a framework that generatively synthesizes the process thought of Alfred North Whitehead and the analytical psychology of Carl Gustav Jung—where consciousness, particularity, and multiplicity are prized alongside integrated wholeness—uniquely presents such embodied transformational experiences as a reunification that maintains diverse and particular value and feeling rather than as merely a regression to a pre-conscious monistic unity. Such a framework, I believe, provides the theoretical and empirical foundation through which such transformative encounters with transpersonal Reality can be facilitated.

NOTES

1. Paul Tillich, *Systematic Theology, Volume I* (Chicago: University of Chicago Press, 1973), 39.

2. Jürgen Moltmann, *God in Creation: A New Theology of Creation and the Spirit of God* (Minneapolis, MN: Fortress Press, 1993), 48.

3. Moltmann, *God in Creation*, xiii.

4. James W. Heisig, "The Mystique of the Nonrational and a New Spirituality," in *The Archetypal Process: Self and Divine in Whitehead, Jung, and Hillman*, ed. David Ray Griffin (Evanston, IL: Northwestern University Press, 1990), 175.

5. Robert L. Moore, "Psychocosmetics: A Jungian Response," in *The Archetypal Process: Self and Divine in Whitehead, Jung, and Hillman*, ed. David Ray Griffin (Evanston, IL: Northwestern University Press, 1990), 157.

6. Richard Tarnas, *Cosmos and Psyche: Intimations of a New World View* (New York: Viking Adult, 2006), 24–25.

7. Tarnas, *Cosmos and Psyche*, 25.

8. Robin Robertson, *Jungian Archetypes: Jung, Gödel, and the History of Archetypes*, Revised (New York: iUniverse, 2009), 248.

9. Robertson, *Jungian Archetypes*, 150.

10. "Political Polarization in the American Public," The Pew Research Center for the People and the Press (Washington, D.C.: Pew Research Center, June 12, 2014), http://www.people-press.org/2014/06/12/political-polarization-in-the-american-public/.

11. "Political Polarization in the American Public."

12. Mark Potok, "The Year in Hate and Extremism," Southern Poverty Law Center, February 11, 2016, https://www.splcenter.org/fighting-hate/intelligence-report/2016/year-hate-and-extremism.

13. Potok, "The Year in Hate and Extremism."

14. Janice Shaw Crouse, "The Loneliness of American Society," *The American Spectator* (blog), May 18, 2014, http://spectator.org/59230_loneliness-american-society/.

15. "The Profound Power of Loneliness: National Science Foundation," National Science Foundation, February 3, 2016, http://www.nsf.gov/discoveries/disc_summ.jsp?cntn_id=137534.

16. "The Profound Power of Loneliness."

17. Peter Wehrwein, "Astounding Increase in Antidepressant Use by Americans," Harvard Health Blog, October 20, 2011, http://www.health.harvard.edu/blog/astounding-increase-in-antidepressant-use-by-americans-201110203624.

18. Wehrwein, "Astounding Increase in Antidepressant Use by Americans."

19. Vincent J. Felitti and Robert F. Anda, "The Relationship of Adverse Childhood Experiences to Adult Medical Disease, Psychiatric Disorders and Sexual Behavior:

Implications for Healthcare," in *The Impact of Early Life Trauma on Health and Disease: The Hidden Epidemic*, ed. Ruth A. Lanius, Eric Vermetten, and Clare Pain (Cambridge, New York: Cambridge University Press, 2010), 78–79.

20. Felitti and Anda, "The Relationship of Adverse Childhood Experiences," 86.

21. Subsequent studies, such as the Philadelphia Urban ACE Study, have added other categories, such as peer-to-peer bullying and poverty. "Findings from the Philadelphia Urban ACE Survey" (Philadelphia: Institute for Safe Families, September 18, 2013).

22. Felitti and Anda, "The Relationship of Adverse Childhood Experiences," 79–80.

23. Donald Kalsched, *Trauma and the Soul: A Psycho-Spiritual Approach to Human Development and Its Interruption* (London, New York: Routledge, 2013), 10.

24. Kalsched, *Trauma and the Soul*, 11.

25. Kalsched, 23.

26. Felitti and Anda, "The Relationship of Adverse Childhood Experiences," 78.

27. Bessel van der Kolk, *The Body Keeps the Score: Brain, Mind, and Body in the Healing of Trauma*, Reprint edition (New York, NY: Penguin Books, 2015), 2–3.

28. "Population Clock," accessed January 3, 2020, https://www.census.gov/popclock/.

29. "Adverse Childhood Experience Study (ACES)," *Advokids: A Legal Resource for California Foster Children and Their Advocates* (blog), accessed September 16, 2016, http://www.advokids.org/adverse-childhood-experience-study-aces/.

30. Felitti and Anda, "The Relationship of Adverse Childhood Experiences," 86.

31. John B. Cobb Jr. and David Ray Griffin, *Process Theology* (Louisville, KY: Westminster John Knox Press, 1976), 18.

32. Murray Stein, "Jung's Green Christ," in *Jung's Challenge to Contemporary Religion*, ed. Murray Stein and Robert L. Moore (Wilmette, IL: Chiron Publications, 1987), 6.

33. Ulanov and Ulanov, *Religion and the Unconscious*, 26–27.

34. Kalsched, *Trauma and the Soul*, 169.

35. Kalsched, 169–70.

36. David Tacey, "The Challenge of Teaching Jung in the University," in *Teaching Jung*, ed. Kelly Bulkeley and Clodagh Weldon, AAR Teaching Religious Studies (New York: Oxford University Press, 2011), 15.

37. Tacey, "The Challenge of Teaching Jung in the University," 15.

38. Ulanov and Ulanov, *Religion and the Unconscious*, 25, 36–38.

39. Edward F. Edinger, *Ego and Archetype: Individuation and the Religious Function of the Psyche* (Boston; London: Shambhala, 1992), 64.

40. Edinger, *Ego and Archetype*, 64.

41. Edinger, 64.

42. Gerald H. Slusser, "Jung and Whitehead on Self and Divine: The Necessity for Symbol and Myth," in *Archetypal Process: Self and Divine in Whitehead, Jung, and Hillman*, ed. David Ray Griffin (Evanston, IL: Northwestern University Press, 1990), 87.

43. Slusser, "Jung and Whitehead on Self and Divine," 87.

44. Slusser, 87.
45. Edinger, *Ego and Archetype*, 64.
46. Edinger, 64.
47. Robert A. Segal, "Jung on Myth," in *Teaching Jung*, ed. Kelly Bulkeley and Clodagh Weldon, AAR Teaching Religious Studies (New York: Oxford University Press, 2011), 86.
48. Edinger, *Ego and Archetype*, 64–65.
49. Edinger, 65.
50. Edinger, 65.
51. Edinger, 67–68.
52. Edinger, 68–69.
53. Kelly Bulkeley, *Visions of the Night: Dreams, Religion and Psychology* (Albany, NY: State University of New York Press, 1999), 44.
54. Bulkeley, *Visions of the Night*, 44–45.
55. "'Nones' on the Rise," The Pew Forum on Religion & Public Life (Washington, D.C.: Pew Research Center, October 9, 2012), http://www.pewforum.org/2012/10/09/nones-on-the-rise/.
56. David Ray Griffin, "Holy Spirit: Compassion and Reverence for Being," in *Religious Experience and Process Theology*, ed. Bernard Cargas and Harry J. Lee (New York: Paulist Press, 1976), 109.
57. Griffin, "Holy Spirit," 109.
58. John B. Cobb Jr., "Spiritual Discernment in a Whiteheadian Perspective," in *Religious Experience and Process Theology: The Pastoral Implications of a Major Modern Movement*, ed. Harry J. Cargas and Bernard Lee (New York: Paulist Press, 1976), 350.
59. Griffin, "Holy Spirit," 110.
60. C. G. Jung, *Modern Man in Search of a Soul* (Orlando, FL: Harcourt Harvest, 1955), 232.
61. Stein, "Jung's Green Christ," 3.
62. Cobb Jr., "Spiritual Discernment in a Whiteheadian Perspective," 351.
63. Jung, *Modern Man in Search of a Soul*, 202.
64. Michael Dowd, "Is Biblicist Christianity Bankrupt?" *Evolutionary Christianity* (blog), n.d., http://evolutionarychristianity.com/blog/general/is-biblicist-christianity-bankrupt/.
65. Dowd, "Is Biblicist Christianity Bankrupt?"
66. Jung, *Modern Man in Search of a Soul*, 122–23.
67. Tarnas, *Cosmos and Psyche*, xiv.
68. Tarnas, xiii.
69. Tarnas, xiii.
70. Panentheism is the view that all is held within God while God is both immanent in and transcendent to the cosmos as opposed to pantheism which is the view that the cosmos is equivalent to God and God does not transcend it.
71. Michael E. Zimmerman, "Quantum Theory, Intrinsic Value, and Panentheism," in *Postmodern Environmental Ethics*, ed. Max Oelschlaeger (Albany, NY: State University of New York Press, 1995), 277–307.

72. Bulkeley, *Visions of the Night*, 39–40.

73. Bulkeley, 40.

74. Bulkeley, 40.

75. Zimmerman, "Quantum Theory, Intrinsic Value, and Panentheism," 296.

76. Heisig, "The Mystique of the Nonrational and a New Spirituality," 200.

77. Kenneth I. Pargament, *Spiritually Integrated Psychotherapy: Understanding and Addressing the Sacred* (New York: The Guilford Press, 2011), 7.

78. Pargament, *Spiritually Integrated Psychotherapy*, 8, 12.

79. Michael Argyle, *Psychology and Religion: An Introduction* (London, New York: Routledge, 2000), 10.

80. Naomi R. Goldenberg, "Jung After Feminism," in *Beyond Androcentrism: New Essays on Women and Religion*, ed. Rita M Gross, American Academy of Religion Aids for the Study of Religion (Missoula, MT: Scholars Press for the American Academy of Religion, 1977), 54.

81. Perrin, *Studying Christian Spirituality*, 18.

82. Perrin, 18–19.

83. Heisig, "The Mystique of the Nonrational and a New Spirituality," 172.

84. Heisig, 172.

85. Heisig, 173.

Chapter 2

Integrating Resources

INTRODUCTION

What is needed now to solve the problem of fragmentation is a generative synthesis of (1) a metaphysical/*theoretical* framework that coheres with (2) a psycho-physical/*empirical* framework, both of which are supported by (3) a spiritual *practice* that facilitates transformative lived experience that confirms both frameworks through direct experience. This is the kind of wholeness to which this project points. Here, authentic spirituality is enhanced and deepened by an appreciation of what is psychological to the human—the development of consciousness and insights into one's unconscious reactions to the slings and arrows of daily life. Even more specifically, it is deepened by a view of reality that is, as it was for Jung, subjectively real, ineffable, and mytho-poetic, and that presents us with collective, pre-personal, and daimonic contents.[1]

In this chapter, I will argue that the resources of Whitehead's process thought and Jung's analytical psychology are necessary and useful in the twenty-first century by first showing what is still compelling and relevant in their thinking, establishing their shared areas of interest, and then describing *resonances* between these two thinkers' systems of thought. I will also show where Whitehead and Jung contrast with one another, such as in their approaches to metaphysical speculation, in what is psychological versus what is ontological, and in *logos* versus *mythos* thinking. While it is not surprising that such creative and adventurous thinkers would be the targets of criticism, some of those critiques may be more valid than others; I will therefore look at Whitehead's critics who charge him with using off-putting language, and being elitist and overly optimistic as well as critics of Jung who question his archetypal theory, and charge him with Nazism and anti-Semitism, gender essentialism and misogyny, and with supporting the status quo. Finally, I will note the limitations that each of our theoretical, empirical, and practical resources have, what this project requires from them, and introduce the idea that each system may bring to the others the very strengths that we require *in toto*.

WHY THEM, WHY NOW?

Why resurrect early twentieth-century teachers for this project? Primarily because they are both still relevant—possibly even more so now than in their own time. Craig Chalquist describes it as "remarkable" that so little of Jung's work is out of date and points to his influence on such areas as systems theory, field theory, existential therapy, evolutionary psychology, eco-psychology, and more. While behaviorist theory in psychology has proven to be inadequate, Jung's relevance continues to grow, according to Chalquist.[2] Whitehead's relevance, too, has grown. Hosinski describes him as a philosopher who was speculatively bold yet incredibly humble regarding his achievements.[3] In recent years, Whitehead's thought has been instrumental in educational reform in China and where it has influenced that country's postmodern development. It is also impacting many other fields outside of philosophy and theology, such as ecological awareness, political thought, ethics, and aesthetics.[4]

Why interweave Whiteheadian and Jungian resources at this time? Such work is necessary now because neither system on its own can achieve widespread change. Bernard Lee notes that the overly technical language typically used to express philosophical and theological concepts means such ideas are less likely to be embraced by non-academic readers. In particular, Whitehead's language is heavily rational, resulting in limited general awareness. Reflecting on the greater success of the Jungian movement than the Whiteheadian,[5] Griffin acknowledges Whitehead's belief that people are "moved more by images than by concepts." While Whiteheadians have "rationalized" their intellectualized stance, he argues that they have actually been giving "hungry people stones, in the form of indigestible concepts."[6] Charles Hartshorne equally recognizes the need for a "philosophical religion" to go beyond concepts. In *She Who Changes*, feminist and process thinker Carol Christ notes Hartshorne's view that religions require symbols because through symbol "the insights of the mind become part of the feelings of the body and can be shared in community."[7]

Creation, fragmentation, and flux are a necessary part of any world of diverse multiplicity but this is a hard truth for the human heart. Yet it is also true that experiences of integration and transformation at the personal and communal levels seem somehow to carry the grace and power that make bearable and beautiful the fragmentary multiplicity of reality. That same grace and power can re-orient individuals and communities toward a hopeful awareness of our rightful belonging and participation in the interconnected community of life as well as our potential for the creative attainment of value and beauty: to live and to live well, to enjoy what I call *common flourishing*. I believe that such common flourishing is promoted in the work of Whitehead and Jung. Feminist and Jungian writer Susan Rowland notes the difficulty posed because of a postmodernism that rightfully questions the preeminence of human reason as the source of human identity; Jung's work, she argues, challenges Enlightenment reason without fragmenting consciousness.[8]

If Whiteheadian and Jungian frameworks are to be useful here, their schools of thought must positively address the limitations and deleterious effects of a dualistic worldview, the fragmentary nature of human experience, the ability of humans to encounter a life-giving source of dynamism in their everyday lives, the inherent value of all beings and of diversity, the validity of non-sensory experience, the relationship of mind to body (and how such emotional realities as adverse childhood experience can impact adult physical health), and allow access to resources for positive change within everyday human experience that are transformative, liberative, and salvific. In describing process thought as a "living option," Loomer reflects the demand I now place on both systems of thought: that "the heights and depths of existence," from religious experience to everyday resources for a meaningful life must be "experienced within the concrete realities of this world."[9]

In a nutshell, Whitehead and Jung are present at this table because they are both relevant, offer ways of thinking about the world and the psyche that promote the well-being of all, and can be compellingly combined to achieve the task that neither system can achieve in isolation. Even more importantly, they come to the table as viable theoretical and empirical resources that can: (1) show that individuals *matter* and that embodied experience has *value*; (2) show that individuals *belong* to a greater web of being that is *relational* and overcome dualistic bifurcations between mind and body, self and world, and self and God; (3) describe a God that is real, intimately related to the world, and accessible through embodied human experience; and, (4) show how painful and limiting past experience and decisions can be transcended and *transformed*, hope and faith restored, and new possibilities realized through encounter with a God who is a dynamic, life-giving reality at the base of human experience.

WHITEHEAD AND JUNG

This is not the first time that Whitehead and Jung have shared a dance. As noted earlier, a conference held at Claremont School of Theology in the

1980s gathered together John Cobb, David Griffin, Catherine Keller, James Hillman, and other Jungian and process scholars. The occasion resulted in a collection of essays entitled *The Archetypal Process: Self and Divine in Whitehead, Jung, and Hillman.*[10] Other than isolated writings by Steve Odin,[11] Chae Young Kim,[12] and Grant Maxwell,[13] there is little evidence of further scholarship along these lines.[14] So why revisit this topic? For one core reason: because a synthesis of process and Jungian resources along with a spiritual practice of dream work, can generate fruitful outcomes that are accessible, compelling, and effective for personal and communal healing and transformation of consciousness. According to Griffin, during the *Archetypal Process* conference there was a recognition that both movements have much in common, including a desire "to return soul and divinity to the world." Attending scholars suggested that a joining of the two movements might be successful in fighting "soul-denying" and "divinity-excluding" forces that both oppose.[15]

The potential for complementarity between the two movements is suggested in a rudimentary comparison. As I have elsewhere summarized, Whitehead's cosmos,

> is always in the process of becoming: reality is dynamic, creative, and event-based and one in which momentary events—or subjects—co-create themselves through their internal, active encounters with both an objective past and future possibilities for actualization. Each moment of what he called *concrescence* enjoys subjective immediacy *and* internal relations to the whole, is mentally and physically one, and seeks to attain its own value in the world before it becomes an objective datum for the future. The thrust of the creative advance is toward intensity of experience and a transpersonally-envisaged, ever-flowing integration of contrasts that achieves beauty and peace, the point of which, for individuals, is to particularize the whole to enjoy one's unique perspective.[16]

Jung's analytical psychology describes an embodied human psyche that is formed through its encounters with an objective and autonomous "other"—the collective unconscious—that plays a compensatory role in offering powerful transpersonal energies and images of transformation to allow the individual to integrate one's psychic oppositions and offer the value of one's own authentic contribution to the whole of life. Individuating is to be a "real" person in real relationship with others and with the God image in the psyche—the Self—that is the ever-flowing source of vitality. Within both schools of thought, the fullness of life of the individual contributes to the fullness of life of the whole.

RESONANCES

There are many ways in which Whitehead's and Jung's thought could be said to be *resonant*. The term *resonance* is intended here in the musical sense, wherein a vibrating string on a guitar may cause an adjacent string to vibrate sympathetically and in a frequency that might be described as "harmonious." Resonance here suggests a certain degree of *congruence*, rather than identity or equivalence. Resonance is *evocation*. It is meant to describe the potential—clearly unprovable since both men are deceased—for the thought of one man to resonantly engender a positive feeling in the other as to the subject under discussion. The resonances proposed in this section range from their intellectual sophistication, creativity, and visionary nature to their shared ability to communicate using a wide spectrum of scientific to poetic expression and their pragmatic grounding in experience. Both appreciated nonsensory perception and described a unified mind and body. Both rejected many aspects of modernism and were stalwart defenders of value, feeling, and aesthetic imagination. They were also both rooted in the Church yet were vocal critics of its current forms and doctrine. In short, they had much in common.

Jung and Whitehead were recognized as men of great intellect—even as "stellar thinkers"—and Slusser further describes them as "among the most seminal, complex, and sophisticated of any recent writers."[17] Heisig sees the primary gifts of Whitehead, Jung, and Hillman to be their "rational adventures" and their "creative vitality of thought."[18] J'nan Morse Sellery calls them "adventurers of ideas"[19] and "poets" who both had to allow creative ideas to emerge. While both relied on earlier, foundational narratives, they, like all poets and visionaries, according to Morse, deepened, broadened, and creatively re-invented those narratives.[20] Each could be scientifically precise, expressing difficult concepts with scholarly intellectualism; yet Robertson points to Jung's work as abounding "in poetic passages that better capture the majesty of their subject,"[21] words that apply equally to Whitehead.

Whitehead departs from what W. Norman Pittenger calls the "older mode of metaphysics" where one begins with "general principles assumed to be true rather than studying concrete phenomena." Instead, Whitehead begins on the ground of first-hand human awareness, then "takes off" like an aviator to observe from the highest and widest perspective possible, finally returning to direct experience.[22] Though it could be said that Whitehead used his ideas to "unflinchingly explore experience with the aid of those ideas,"[23] and Jung used his own and his patients' experiences to suggest possible models within which to understand those experiences, both were deeply bound to *experience*. Though both could be considered advanced thinkers, Whitehead considered the "infinite fullness of experience" to be "supreme over thought"[24] and Jung would have wholeheartedly agreed. One of Whitehead's most radical notions is that we can extrapolate about the nature of the entire cosmos from what we can learn from our most intimate and basic human experience; in fact, it is embodied human experience that provides our only evidential data for philosophical reflection.[25] Similarly, Jung believed that knowledge rests on the facts of nature[26] and that his own experience was a reliable basis for determining the overall human situation.[27] Moreover, Jung saw human life not as a "chance development in the universe" but as the outcome of a universe steeped in meaning.[28]

Empirical and pragmatic, Jung would not dismiss the paranormal experiences of others as superstition because if such experiences were psychic realities he wanted to know why, even if those experiences did not align with his preconceived assumptions.[29] Similarly, Whitehead affords nonsensory perception "primacy"[30] and, in fact, insists that to dismiss "instances of non-sensuous perception" would be to commit a "fatal error barring the advance of systematic metaphysics."[31] Both men shared an atypical comfort with paradoxical thinking: Jung believed both the scientific-technical and religious-nonrational aspects of life to be part of one dipolar reality[32]; Whitehead, too, holds science and religion in "creative relation," believing both to be part of the same world.[33] In general, process thought emphasizes the kind of wholeness that holds both the aesthetic *and* the scientific, the felt *and* the measurable, together.[34] Jung, writes Tacey, is an "amalgam of mythos and logos, story and science"; his thought belongs neither to "the arts faculty or in the life science faculty" but rather to a "university system that does not yet exist, one in which the whole of life is studied and taken seriously. Jung is the scientist and artist of life integration."[35] For both Whitehead and Jung, rational thinking is inextricably interwoven with feeling and aesthetic value.

Neither man saw biology as solely determinative of the individual or culture; both rejected the kind of physicalism that understands human consciousness to be merely an *epiphenomenon* of physical life.[36] Both Jung and Whitehead saw intelligence as having unconscious roots. Jung's system allows for the interaction of conscious and unconscious processes without reducing either to "brain functions or learning theories."[37] As Faber notes, Whitehead similarly refused a bifurcated world that reduces subjectivity and personality to physical processes alone; instead he insisted on retaining the "*unity* of experience."[38]

Before the emergence of postmodernity, Jung and Whitehead rejected core ideas of the modern worldview, such as the mechanistic doctrine of nature, sensate empiricism, and the denial of divine presence or influence in the world.[39] Korean scholar Chae Young Kim recognizes this area of commonality when he writes that despite their different academic backgrounds, they shared a disdain for mechanistic/materialistic philosophies and psychologies and realized that "contemporary philosophy and psychology had excluded the transcendental dimension of life."[40]

Neither accepted a "value-free" or "contextless" reality: Whitehead believed that "Value is inherent in actuality itself" because it is God's purpose to attain value in the temporal world.[41] For him, the epistemological process is teleological, "characterized by both interest and goal," and "fulfilled only in an (eschatological) process whereby the world itself becomes whole."[42] According to Rowland, although Jung tended toward "grand narratives" regarding his psychology, he never suggested that such narratives provided any kind of "neutral foundation for knowledge"; rather, much of his work she describes as personal myth because Jung's ego-based reason depended upon the objective other in his own psyche, the "superior unknowable unconscious. Jung never pretends to a reason shorn of 'personal' factors."[43] Rowland goes on to argue that Jung's work has a certain "affinity with postmodernism" in his theory of the unconscious because that unconscious is "unrepresentable, *unwritable*" and "inconceivable." Jung's collective unconscious, his "founding presence" becomes a "founding absence from the writing." For Jung, then, as in postmodernism, language is neither reliable nor transparent regarding meaning, truth, and knowledge.[44] Heisig describes Whitehead's approach as "congenial" to Jung's archetypal psychology because both men rejected any "unknowable" that was outside of human experience. Similarly, Whitehead saw all attempts to formulate metaphysical principles in precise terms as "asymptotic" and "metaphorical."[45]

Both Whitehead and Jung criticized traditional doctrines of God and formulated alternatives that they felt were positive and beneficial for humanity. Often, they seem to point to similar realities using differing terms. Their shared acceptance of nonsensory perception led them to reject seeing ideas and feelings in oppositional terms. Griffin notes that Whitehead considered a thought to be "a tremendous mode of excitement" that has "great importance," and even, in some cases, "holiness," and considers this to be "parallel to Jung's focus on 'numinous' ideas."[46]

Both systems posit a processive nature to the lives of both the individual soul and the world, with growth and positive change held as core values. Griffin suggests that both men held the psyche or soul in high regard as something with great power.[47] Though Jung certainly focused more on the individual psyche, Rowland considers his theory to be one of psyche *and* culture as well as "a therapeutic methodology."[48] While Jung's focus on individuation and Whitehead's focus on the web of internal relations may appear to be at odds, differences fade to the background when their underlying goals are in view. Although many process thinkers stress the relationality of process thought—the understanding that individuals are internally constituted by their relationships—it is the achievement of value that is the *reason for becoming* in the first place. Kraus writes that everything exists for itself, and for its significance to the whole. Those dialectical poles are inseparable. "Thus," she argues, "becoming is for the purpose of being (signification in the universe) and being is for the purpose of novel becoming (the emergent individual self)." The value attained by each new "growing together" or "concrescence" as it takes the past world into itself, must, in turn, be taken into account by the future.[49]

Interestingly, both Whitehead and Jung were sons of pastors, one Anglican and the other Reformed.[50] Both believed that the central aspect of religion lay not in its outer forms, but in the active involvement of one's heart. In other words, writes Kim, "Whitehead and Jung thought of the subject's internal experience as the essence of religion." For Whitehead, this internal experience was grounded in what he called "solitariness," and being apart from "collective enthusiasms." For Jung, inner experience stemmed from being possessed by, or having an encounter with, the *numinosum*, a phrase he drew from the work of Rudolf Otto.[51] In Whitehead's "solitariness," one experiences a transformation of consciousness, and for Jung as well, one must draw away from the collective in order to be transformed; Jung uses the term religion to denote a consciousness changed by direct experience of the *numinosum*.[52]

Kim notes that Jung and Whitehead vehemently argued for religion that is open to self-critique and transformation, or else it has a tendency to lose its original power, becoming "a dead formal tradition."[53] While Jung wrote that the importance of a *religious attitude* in one's psychic life could not be overrated, in his pursuit of religion's transformation he was unwilling to completely jettison the past because a religious outlook requires a sense of historical continuity.[54] Kim summarizes their strong core commonalities in this way: "the essence of religion is not in the memory of doctrines but the experience of solitariness and *numinosum* which is always refreshing and extending the human's consciousness."[55]

In summary, among many similarities, of primary importance is the fact that both Whitehead and Jung begin with actual, lived human experience rather than abstract, disembodied grand theory, yet both believed that we could extrapolate from the specific to the whole, from the personal to the transpersonal. Both challenged many modernist assumptions, such as reigning theories of perception and physicalism. Moreover, both men believed that religion and philosophy must be self-critical and open to change.

CONTRASTS

While their thought shares many resonances, of course there are significant differences between Whitehead's and Jung's approaches to their specific areas of concern. Though certainly not an exhaustive analysis of every difference or potential conflict between process thought and analytical psychology, in this section I will look at the differing ways they approach metaphysical speculation, what is psychological versus what is ontological, and their individual preferences toward *logos* versus *mythos* thinking.

From Griffin's perspective, Whitehead deals mainly with concepts while Jung deals primarily with images and while Whitehead was focused on cosmology first and the soul in a secondary way, Jung was most interested in the soul first and cosmology later. In contrast to his eloquent and lengthy discussion of the cosmos, regarding the self, Hopper acknowledges that Whitehead appears to say little. Yet, in digging deeper, he finds that in *Process and Reality*, Whitehead relates soul and mind to actual entity and actual occasion, leading him to believe that soul has been a central part of Whitehead's project all along.[56] In Whitehead's insistence that the essence of actuality is process, and process is inherent in God's nature, process is therefore inherent in personal identity. The soul, then, synthesizes its environment to create a new actualization, and, in doing so, introduces novelty. Moreover, when Whitehead places God at the initiation of every creative act, that initiation is the result of the "soul's indwelling Eros."[57]

Another apparent contrast is that regarding the ills of the world, Keller has accused Whitehead of "ontological serenity" and distinguishes Whitehead's tendency to "sublimate diagnosis too much into descriptions" from Jung's tendency to "turn diagnosis too easily into prescriptions." On the other hand, though Keller's work has moved away from Jung, she claims his insight into the "great dramas of unwholesomeness" to be "hardly paralleled in depth and imagination."[58] Probably the most significant areas of difference between Jung and Whitehead are evident in their approaches to metaphysical speculation, their psychological versus ontological perspectival centers, and the degree to which they preference *logos* or *mythos*, the rational or the nonrational.

Metaphysical Speculation

Whereas Whitehead specialized in speculative metaphysics, Jung generally avoided it, refusing to theorize beyond the limits of experience because he believed such metaphysical leaps to be "always in danger of becoming nonsense on one side, or the mere subjective projection of its author on the other."[59] For the most part, he restricted himself to descriptions of what he encountered in his clinical work and his personal deep dives into the unconscious. This may have been due as much to Jung's opinion that psychology had not been in existence long enough to have developed "a theoretical superstructure"[60] as it was to his personal proclivities. Rowland writes that

Jung seemed to resist the idea of theory altogether, "with its connotations of objectivity, rationality and scientific validity," believing that ideas create people more than the reverse.[61] On the other hand, Robertson describes Jung as a "superb model-maker" but one who did not confuse his models with reality.[62] Hillman reminds us that the abstractions of depth psychology typically do not generalize beyond the phenomenon witnessed.[63]

Jung's reluctance to embrace metaphysics applies equally to speculation about God or the numinous reality that one encounters within. He sees his stance as strictly phenomenological when he argues that God "is an experience, not a concept."[64] Jung concerned himself only with factual occurrences and experience but he considered the same idea held by numerous individuals—whether based in objective reality or not—to be a "psychic fact" or *consensus gentium.*[65] Because the unconscious—by Jung's definition—is an "*unthinkable*, not knowable, not securely mappable" power, it cannot possibly "be adequately theorized."[66] Finding more in common with Lao Tzu's insistence that "The Tao that can be told of is not the eternal Tao," Jung believed that the metaphysics entertained in Western religion had actually become an obstacle to religious experience.[67] He insisted on bringing metaphysics closer to experience because understanding can only be achieved psychologically.[68]

Psychological versus Ontological

Slusser notes that whereas Whitehead wanted to create a coherent and logical system of ideas, Jung thought such a system unreachable "because we have no Archimedean point outside the psyche from which to frame such a system."[69] Had Jung been aware of—and persuaded by—Whitehead's additional mode of perception in the form of causal efficacy, whereby experiencing subjects are able to perceive the objective past physically, internally, and unconsciously, he might not have concluded that all comprehension is psychic. To be fair, Jung did not assume that no objective world existed outside the mind, only that we cannot get outside the psyche. Heisig compares Jung's problem of the *psychological circle*—where "consciousness cannot become an object to itself"—to what he calls Whitehead's "ontological circle," or the claim that it is a "fiction" to imagine a world made up of subjects without internal relations to objects.[70] We can safely assume, on the other hand, that Whitehead and Jung would agree that holding *any* metaphysical or scientific truth "for all time"[71] would be a "fallacy of misplaced concreteness."[72]

Logos versus Mythos

Another point of distinction is the degree to which each valued rational consciousness or preferenced *logos* to unconscious *mythos*. Clearly,

Whitehead placed a higher value on rationality while Jung held the conscious and unconscious aspects of human life to be equally valid and necessary. For Jung, *mythos* was not something that civilization could ever—nor *should* ever—eliminate. In contrast, Whitehead believed that the advance of civilization *required* that humans reject the "uncontrollable" and superstitious symbols of their "savage past" and felt that humans are both attracted to and repulsed by symbols because "hard-headed men want facts and not symbols."[73] Although Keller is no stranger to Whitehead's poetic and mystical side, she blames his philosophical preferences for "mathematic pattern" over "music," his "lack of mythos," and his "Victorian sanguinity" for leaving "psyche starved for images."[74] On the other hand, Whitehead also understood symbolism—at least, of language—to be "essential for the higher grades of life."[75] Slusser makes the case that Whitehead's work is replete with symbols that convey unconscious processes; even his term *actual occasion* is symbolic.[76] In his most mystical moments, Whitehead may have agreed with Jung that our "regrettably demythologized and desouled world" demanded both logos "accountability to the rationally critical functions" *and* "an appreciation of the mythos perspective."[77]

In summary, there are differences between Whitehead's and Jung's perspectives on metaphysical and psychological reality. Whitehead deals primarily with concepts, while Jung focuses on images. Jung generally avoided metaphysical speculation while Whitehead is metaphysical speculator *par excellence*. Whitehead draws an "ontological circle" while Jung draws a "psychological circle" and Whitehead typically preferences rationality while Jung equally values rationality and nonrationality. Despite these differences—and *maybe even because of them*—we can interweave the most life-enhancing aspects of their thought into a liberative tapestry that is founded upon lived experience.

CRITIQUES AND RESPONSES

As beautiful and as life enhancing as the threads in our tapestry are, we must not avert our eyes from the valid critiques that have been pointed at both Whitehead and Jung. At the same time, we must remember that both men—as well as their successors—were clay-footed humans with certain limitations to their thinking. As a result, both have drawn criticism. In this section, critiques will be briefly acknowledged, and responses will be sufficiently noted. A key assumption—especially in a project that relies on the embodied theological method—is that experience is the lens through which their theorizing must be finally judged. Both clearly acknowledged the need for reformation of any thought that is not supported by empirical experience. Therefore, as we approach this task from a feminist-influenced embodied theological method that preferences experience, we are free to utilize the resources in each school of thought that are liberative and life-giving while being equally free to question any perspective that does not stand up to empirical evidence or is not liberative and life-enhancing. As Whitehead, in his humility, surmised: dogmatic certainty and finality of statement in philosophical matters is an "exhibition of folly,"[78] and we might say the same regarding psycho-spiritual matters.

Whitehead and Whiteheadians

Language

It is true that Whitehead's writing style—described by Griffin as "literal" and "prosaic"[79]—can be quite off-putting. As Carol Christ notes in *She Who Changes*,

> In order to read Whitehead's most profound ideas about the nature of God, one must wade through his opaque and difficult *Process and Reality*, a work filled with neologisms (made-up words and words used in other than their normal sense) that is daunting even to professional philosophers. Whitehead believed that philosophy should be modeled on mathematics, which means that his goal was to use language with a kind of numerical precision, not to communicate with anyone unfamiliar with his technical vocabulary.[80]

Legend has it that while hundreds of interested listeners attended the first lecture in the series that was eventually published as *Process and Reality*, by the last lecture, attendance was in the single digits. It is not just that his work is academic and dense, but that his technical jargon and detailed exploration of minute concepts can make one want to commence head banging. Yet, even amid his highly technical writing in *Process and Reality*, he can wax poetically and mystically eloquent. Anil Kumar Sarkar describes these as Whitehead's "extreme tendencies," and notes his two "dominant moods" as "extreme philosophic and scientific analysis" and "extreme emotional expression."[81] Whiteheadian thought is often criticized for being overly conceptual. Though Loomer sees Whitehead as "balanced," he decries the loss of balance in subsequent Whiteheadians who tend to emphasize "the logical side of things."[82] Griffin, meanwhile, acknowledges that Whitehead can occasionally write in a "lyrical" fashion, but bemoans the fact that most Whiteheadians can tend toward the "dull, prosaic style appropriate to the disenchanted world of the mechanists."[83]

Elitist and Overly Optimistic

Such feminist theologians as Lucinda Huffaker have pointedly critiqued process thought not only as being "overly abstract" and "rational," but also as "elitist," and not easily accessible to marginalized communities. She criticizes Whitehead for being too optimistic regarding evolutionary advancement and not critical enough of political dynamics and power structures.[84] Some aspects of process thought, she argues, maintain "patriarchal imbalances" by "overvaluing conscious experience and prioritizing novelty and dynamic process to the disparagement of continuity and rest."[85] Yet Huffaker seems to disregard Whitehead's prioritization of unconscious perception and internal relations, and his frequent acknowledgment that God seeks both order *and* novelty. In fact, Pittenger reminds us that in Whitehead's system, "everything contributes to make a unity of some sort" that is interested in "cosmos, not chaos, with order not anarchy." He notes that a perspective often lost in contemporary society is how our constant mode of information overload and the requisite requirement for skill specialization limits the knowledge any individual can hold and contributes to the fragmentation of human existence. Such a condition results in a loss of a sense of wholeness and humans can begin to see themselves as unrelated parts. Instead, process thought works from the foundational assumption "that there is cosmos and not chaos" writes Pittenger, "it is also concerned to *show* that this is the case."[86]

Those who criticize Whitehead for an overly "optimistic" view of "evolutionary advancement" often wish him to be more critical of societal power structures and less willing to view indigenous religions as "primitive." As Monica Coleman contends,

> Both *Religion in the Making* and *Adventures of Ideas* reflect a social Darwinism that describes the evolution of religions and societies as moving from lower to higher. The civilizations and religions that he describes as tribal and social tend to be ones that we could call "indigenous" today. The civilizations and religions that are described as rational and civilized are associated with Europe (Christianity) and Asia (Buddhism). In Whitehead's scheme, African traditional religions are "lower," "social" religions that are merely a stage in the evolutionary process toward a "rational religion." [supersessionism] Using Whitehead for any postmodern discussion of evil and wholeness requires a rejection of these aspects of his discussion.[87]

In some ways, Whitehead seems to expect that evolving societal forms will naturally increase in complexity and become more "harmonious" and more "interesting." In company with other feminist theologians, Coleman, William R. Jones, and Thandeka argue that Whitehead does not distinguish between the suffering that is "endemic to the entire human race" and the more targeted "suffering which is meted out by one ethnic group to another."[88] Moreover, whereas Whitehead's God can sometimes appear to be quite "rational" with "the manners of an English gentleman," Coleman reminds us that "a postmodern theology cannot guarantee a happy ending,"[89] a statement with which Whitehead would ultimately agree.

It is true that Whiteheadian thought can be overly conceptual and too ratiocentric. Bringing the imaginal perspective inherent in Jungian thought to the table could balance the heavy inclination in process thought toward concepts and rationality and its intent to appeal to reason. Whitehead's generous perspective on progress has already been addressed by Keller and other process theologians who urge us to reclaim the chaotic *tehom*, but it can be brought into balance even more through a synthesis with Jungian thought and its deep respect for the "shadow side of reality."[90]

Jung and Jungians

Naomi Goldenberg, a feminist scholar of the psychology of religion, relates that her study of the feminist movement initially led her to become interested in Jung's work.[91] Whereas "traditional religions reinforced the subjugation of women," and before many alternatives of religious expression for women began to emerge, she saw Jung as "the thinker to whom I turned for methods of understanding religious growth outside of traditional institutions."[92] In 1977, Goldenberg offered a "feminist revision of Jung" to enable the constructive use of his work so a feminist might be able to "accept and reinterpret what feels right about it for herself."[93] Some of the problems she addressed then were her perceived "veneration" of Jung, the man; his sometimes contradictory statements; and the sexism of his theories.[94] Yet by 1985, Goldenberg advocated a complete abandonment of Jungian theory in favor of Freud, based on her view of Jung's archetypal theory. Falsely equating archetypes with Platonic forms, she interprets them as "perfect" and "vastly superior" to actualized reality, including the flawed body.[95] She describes archetypes as "unchanging and unchangeable . . . transcendent ideals" while our "'images,' i.e., our experiences, are only inferior copies."[96]

I will not present here Goldenberg's reasoning as to why mind-body dualism is dangerous, as I have no quarrel there, but I will show in chapter 4 that her charge of dualism is misplaced. Goldenberg interprets archetypes as "determining" of human thought patterns, as a kind of controlling external deity, and this sense of the archetypes as oppressive colors much of her writing. Demaris Wehr picks up this notion when she describes Jung's psychology as "contextless," and one in which "Archetypal factors that transcend time and space (and thus transcend context) are seen as the main shaping forces in individual personality."[97] While viewing archetypes as "context-less," some feminists conflictingly view Jungian psychology as lacking in "awareness of the political dimension of symbols" and therefore tending to "reinforce the status quo" and supporting the "gender-based social order from which it sprang."[98] In summary, feminist critics accuse Jung and Jungians of being foundationalists or essentialists, of separating mind from body and placing all reality in a disembodied "psyche," and of describing an archetypal reality that is universal, ahistorical, and divinely coercive. Moreover, Jung has also been criticized for being venerated and, even more alarmingly, as anti-Semitic and a Nazi sympathizer. Is it possible to wade through these critiques and reclaim any of his work for the express purposes of this project?

Archetypal Theory

To see Jung's archetypal reality as representing a transcendent realm of "ideal" forms of perfection that carry a divine caveat insistent upon the universal actualization of predetermined behaviors is to simply misread his theory. As will be shown in various sections throughout this work, Jung, in his later writing, more clearly distinguished between archetypes and archetypal images: while the archetypes themselves are abstract and transpersonal, they are not "ideal." Archetypal images, on the other hand, are contextual—either personally or culturally. Neither the archetypes themselves nor the images are deterministic, but the images certainly carry the pressure of history and can feel "sovereign," due both to their numinosity and to the sense that they are encountered as an objective *other* in the psyche.

We might better understand archetypal theory as reflecting the human tendency to collect experiences and form images around a behavioral theme, such as what it means to be a mother, a father, a woman, a man, or even just a unified self. For presumably the entire existence of humanity in its modern form, we have understood there to be such categories as *mother*, *father*, etc., even while each culture or epoch has defined the behavior of each category for itself. Specific definitions may evolve but *the need to define what it means* to act like a "mother" is universally human. The images and experiences that are collected around such a center are personal, cultural, historical, and contextual, but the *tendency* to categorize and define human behavior in this way is universal.

The fields of evolutionary psychology and neuropsychology may end up supporting Jung's theories in an interesting—and probably unintentional—way. Evolutionary psychology argues that it would make sense that there are behavioral structures in the brain that have co-evolved along with the physical structures that are required to carry out adaptive behaviors. Lee Kirkpatrick describes these as being species-specific, but universal to that species.[99] On the other hand, it is the interaction of those structures with particular environments or contexts that produce the variations and diversity of forms of behavior that we witness. From my perspective, it seems that if there were not some kind of inherited predispositions of behavior that were particular to humans, then it would be necessary for every individual born to repeatedly re-invent basic human behaviors. That seems to be incredibly inefficient from an evolutionary perspective. Jung was an empiricist who described what he found in the experiences of his patients and who refused to speculate on any transcendent reality that might be behind the images. He urged us to remember that the archetype in and of itself is "irrepresentable," but its effects enable us to visualize it via the archetypal image.[100] Jung theorized on causes only after observing the effects.

Far from being disembodied, Jung saw the archetypes as being inherited with brain structure in the depths of the psyche. For him, not only is the psyche not separate from the body, but I will show later that it is not even separate from the rest of nature. When Jung uses terms like "transcendent" or "beyond the psyche" to describe the archetypes, I believe he means that they transcend the *individual* in the sense that they are *transpersonal.* They "go beyond" the individual psyche and the individual culture—while still being grounded within them—and he believed this was true because of the "mythologems" and symbols that spontaneously arose across cultures. As Frey-Rohn writes, Jung believed archetypes to be motifs that organize psychic elements into images that can be recognized by the effects produced by them. They are preconscious and arise with organic life, forming the structures of the psyche in the same way that a "crystal lattice" forms in a saturated solution.[101] Archetypes are "irrepresentable" in the same way that the quality of "dog-ness" (the generic concept that we hold in our minds) is not representable in its basic *formal* concept, but only in the endlessly varied images of actualized dogs. Or, as Rowland notes, while the concept "vase" may be inherited, specific vases that appear in a dream will be imaged according to the dreamer's personal experience. "Vase" is the archetype, while the specific characteristics are the image.[102]

A characteristic of archetypes that does not seem to be generally recognized by Jung's critics is, as Rowland describes, that they are bipolar; they contain their own opposites. In other words, the mother archetype may be manifested as either a nurturing or devouring female form, depending on the individual's ego needs. Not only that, but they are also androgynous, encompassing both genders.

> [A]rchetypes can represent themselves as good or evil, animal or human, divine or demonic, high or low. Their bipolar nature reflects Jung's intuition that the tension of the opposites underpins the psyche. He borrowed the Greek term,

> *enantiodromia*, to signify his view that everything eventually turns into its own opposite. If that is so, then archetypes must be continually re-imaging, or imagining the subjectivity of the conscious ego.[103]

Though Goldenberg interprets the psyche as being disembodied along with the archetypes, Lauter and Rupprecht argue that Jung saw body and psyche as inseparable,[104] and Frey-Rohn notes that he coined the term *psychoid* to describe the characteristic of the archetype as being both psychic yet also connected to matter.[105] The psychoid basis of the archetypes may be compared to the somatic and neural basis of the instincts. The archetype is a bridge between psyche and matter, according to Charles R. Card.[106]

Nazism and Anti-Semitism

As to the charges that Jung was anti-Semitic and a Nazi sympathizer, Rowland concludes that while there is some evidence of "culpable anti-Semitism and a morally flawed participation in Nazi culture," she does not believe Jung was a Nazi who supported Nazi policies.[107] A helpful perspective comes from Gerhard Adler via an interview conducted by the Jung Institute of Los Angeles for the making of their documentary "Remembering Jung." In the interview, Adler, the Jewish co-editor of the entirety of Jung's *Collected Works*, notes the close working relationships that Jung held with several other Jewish colleagues, including Aniela Jaffe, editor of Jung's autobiography, Erich Neumann, James and Hilde Kirsch, Jolanda Jacobe, and Max Zeller. Adler insisted that he did not believe that Jung was anti-Semitic. The claim of Nazism, on the other hand, he describes as "more complicated." At the start of the Nazi period, according to Adler, Jung was convinced that there was something happening on an archetypal level that could be of some value, and subsequently produced the *Wotan* essay for which he attracted much criticism. During this same period, Jung accepted the presidency of the International Society of Psychotherapy, an organization run by Germans, for which he was also criticized and perceived to be a Nazi sympathizer. Yet Adler notes Freud's support of Kaiser Wilhelm II during World War I, concluding that psychologists can be "unrealistic" about politics and political power. Adler notes that when later confronted by Rabbi Leo Baeck, Jung admitted that he had "slipped up" regarding his *Wotan* essay.[108]

Gender Essentialism and Misogyny

Clearly, Jung was a man of his time, and displayed widespread views of women that are now considered misogynous but which were accepted in his era. It is true that he equated gender identity with bodily sex and expressed essentialist views of femininity and masculinity as innate. On the other hand,

Rowland sees this essentialism as tempered significantly by Jung's theory of anima and animus and by "his explorations of the cultural shaping of the feminine in literature and religion." She argues that his own view of the psyche and unconscious makes his essentialism less strident.[109] Despite his time-bound and limited perspectives on gender, Rowland claims that some of Jung's views on gender and the feminine, while not completely eliminating problem areas, have been seen as valuable by his "profeminist successors."

> These ideas include the exploration of 'the feminine' in symbols and myths, proclaiming the presence of the feminine and masculine in each gender, protesting at the harm done to psyche and culture through repression of the feminine, and an insistence on full individuation for women in analytic practice.[110]

Rejecting a "fixed opposition between essentialism and social constructivism," Rowland helpfully notes that if we claim that history wholly determines gender, then we are merely shifting the essence from biology to history, also an essentialist position. In her deconstructive approach, Rowland argues that the "innate essence/history binary on gender" still results in a "metaphysical residue." But, she notes, if we look at that binary through an archetypal lens, that metaphysical residue becomes a creative energy rather than a fixed identity. "Archetypal images," she writes, "are created in dialogue between biological inheritance and culture. As a metaphysical residue, archetypes remain radical, since they are also the irreducible unknowableness of the unconscious, making and undoing the ego's understanding of gender." When we view gender as a "creative dialogue with the unknowable, in which history and culture have a formative role," we can discover feminist versions of Jung.[111]

Within this project, I will not draw conclusions as to whether gender is a stable category. Instead, I assume all binaries to be dipolar rather than bifurcated. Like Rowland, I am interested in the value of Jungian thought as an "experiential and pragmatic means of aiding wounded [people]" and therefore see this work as feminist in nature.[112] A key point is that neither Whitehead nor Jung cast out or suppress "the other," but see the objective "other" as crucial to life. Rowland notes that when "crude essentialism" is discarded from Jungian thought, the system is more coherent.[113] Because the psyche is gender fluid, then psychological gender and bodily sex cannot be simply equated. Archetypes are androgynous, and their relationship to the ego is compensatory, meaning the unconscious will always produce "*contrasting notions* of the femininity and masculinity witnessed in material culture."[114]

Rowland also notes that whereas other psychiatrists and psychologists of his time saw the fantasies that arose from the unconscious as "pathological," Jung's "unconscious was a meaningful, healing place." The deep respect for unconscious processes he fostered was so strong that some of his own female patients, including Sabina Spielrein and Toni Wolff, moved through their illnesses and later became respected analysts. Rowland links some of Jung's "reductive misogyny" to Enlightenment notions of polarity and gender yet sees him as having "feminist credentials" because he was committed to reconnecting the feminine and the irrational (the unconscious) with religion and philosophy.[115]

Supporting the Status Quo

While it is certainly legitimate to point to the tendency of religious symbol systems to uphold the status quo, it hardly makes sense to place that in the lap of Jung, a religious iconoclast if there ever was one. He considered modern people to be "Bolshevists" regarding religious tradition and doctrine because they are invested in spiritual experimentation. For moderns, he argued, the scientific outlook cannot be reconciled to the religious outlook and Christian doctrines no longer hold the same authority spiritually or psychologically.[116] The reason that religion no longer has the same hold on modern people, Jung felt, was because "traditional religious symbols no longer mediate the transcendent factors they once did; they are no longer alive."[117] Jung and Whitehead both understood their respective systems to be the best they could devise based on the empirical knowledge they acquired and observed but both equally encouraged—and even expected—revision of their thought. Both understood religion and culture to be malleable and in need of constant examination and revision, and both prized the roles of novelty and creativity in the transformation of individuals and societal systems.

In response to Jung's critics, I have suggested that charges of mind-body dualism on the part of Jung are misplaced. At the same time, a synthesis with Whiteheadian thought in this area only strengthens even more the unity of mind and body. Critique of Jung's archetypal theory seems to be based solely on Jung's early theorizing rather than upon his later distinction between the archetype and the archetypal image. Still, as will be explored in detail in chapter 6, a synthesis of process thought and analytical psychology leads to an understanding of transpersonal reality as formally causative without being determinative. Jung's approach to Nazi Germany was certainly flawed, and he acknowledged that later. On the other hand, claims of anti-Semitism do not seem wholly legitimate based on Jung's close working relationships with—and professional encouragement of—several Jewish colleagues. His ideas on gender and sex are unquestionably flawed, and also timebound, as was the case with Whitehead, yet Jung's work remains experientially life-giving. Finally, the criticism that Jung supported the status quo seems somewhat misplaced, as is evident when his views of religion are considered as well as his understanding of the cultural and contextual nature of archetypal images. We must acknowledge that while the archetypes themselves are not determinative (see chapter 6), the images carry the weight of the historical past and are therefore compelling and authoritative. As a result, I strongly argue that criticisms of both men and their work should not prevent us from utilizing the rich resources that their thought provides.

LIMITATIONS AND PROJECT REQUIREMENTS

As a project that seeks to reveal the value-soaked, relational, and transformational nature of both cosmic and psychic reality and articulate a praxis for realizing those characteristics while fostering psycho-spiritual wholeness and flourishing, I argue here that there are clear gifts that Whiteheadian and Jungian systems of thought bring to the table. Moreover, the well-established practice of using dream work (explored in detail in chapter 5) for psychological growth also offers much. Yet each area also has its limitations.

As already discussed, Whiteheadian thought can be overly abstract and optimistic about the progressive evolution of individual and social forms. To those limitations, Jungian thought brings imaginal depth, intimate empirical observation of human behavior, and a respect for the destructive forces of the unconscious and the ever-present potential within human nature for evil. Jungian thought describes a transpersonal archetypal reality and the possibility of numinous encounter with the "Other" at the depths of experience, but has no metaphysical framework that can show how such formalism can exist, why it is necessary, and that it is, in fact, possible to encounter God at the depths of experience. Whiteheadian thought describes an event-based reality where transformative and novel possibilities offered by God for actualization are available in every moment yet offers no practical method for discerning those divine aims, let alone aligning with them. Jung's process of individuation can be understood, on the other hand, as a process through which one can distinctively embody novel possibilities through the archetypal Self's guidance.

Psychological and spiritual dream work enables individuals to begin to interpret the symbolic language of the unconscious and discern God's aims; such a practice could be seen as operationalizing process thought as well, but its reach has been somewhat limited to those who can access and afford psychological analysis. Jung's process of individuation furthered through a practice of dream work increases individual value, wholeness, and zest or enjoyment, but it has no philosophical or metaphysical framework to show how it facilitates real and healing encounters with the living God. Process thought, on the other hand, can provide dream work and the process of individuation a metaphysical-theological framework that shows a one-world reality, where God is immanent in the world and in the psyche, and makes coherent the whole system of the symbols of the Self, shows how there can be formal influence without determinism, how the pressure of the objective/historical past is real but that there is also freedom and choice, and how Jung's transcendent function can be seen as God's novelty and creative transformation. Said another way, process thought has been overly conceptual, and needs the imaginal to make it more compelling and persuasive. Jungian thought needs the conceptual frame to show how it is coherent in a one-world reality, friendly to science, and not dependent upon a supernatural God. Dream work lacks a metaphysical-theological framework and needs to be democratized as a spiritual practice that is more readily and easily accessible.

Although Whitehead approached his topic "through the logical relations of abstract symbolic language" and "Jung's approach was based on his extensive practical experience exploring the images produced in the psyche," Maxwell sees both as "entirely valid ways of understanding the complexity of experience." Even more, he sees them as "highly complementary to the point of being necessary to one another for the sake of completeness."[118] When Cobb claims that what Jung imagines as *depth* is the same as what Whitehead imagines as *past*, he acknowledges the generative possibilities in synthesizing the two, noting that our imaginations might be enhanced by a more fluid approach.[119] Keller also connects these two ideas with an "underworld passage" that, when undertaken, may reveal the deep intersection of Jung's psyche and Whitehead's cosmos.[120]

We can afford to lose no more time in making this "underworld passage." It might be that the very health of our people and our planet depends on it. In his concluding contribution to *The Archetypal Process*, James Hillman—having acknowledged his former pointed aversion to metaphysics—describes the deep change he experienced at a meeting in Cordoba where physicist David Bohm "admitted frankly and sadly that physics had released the world into its perishing." Through this encounter, Hillman came to realize that the nuclear threat of the end of the world arose from a "metaphysical catastrophe" and that his reluctance to engage at the level of metaphysics was no longer sufficient. He came to see that the soul must psychologically understand the cosmos and that its "paranoid restlessness" has to be satisfied at the metaphysical level by "ultimates of meaning."[121] Moreover, meeting internal needs is still not enough; Hillman further acknowledged that the existential crisis of the whole earth showed him that to decline to engage in metaphysics was to move us closer to "concretized nihilism."[122]

We cannot decline to engage in metaphysics, and so we must supplement Jung with Whitehead. We cannot effect a change in the popular imagination with dry conceptual language alone, and so we must supplement Whitehead with Jung. We cannot achieve a transformation of consciousness through beautiful theoretical and empirical ideas alone, and so we must supplement Whitehead and Jung with an embodied, transformational praxis wherein one can encounter primordial, transpersonal Reality that shows us that *we matter*, that *we belong*, and that *we can experience positive change*.

SUMMARY

Part One of this work tackled the problem of fragmentation in American society, demonstrating how we are divided societally, interpersonally, and intrapersonally, and lays blame for the bulk of this painful reality at the feet of our divisive but dominant worldview. Mind-body dualism and our dismissal of the nonrational and nonsensory has diminished human appreciation for what Jung called nondirected thinking and thereby limits our access to the vital resources of primordial experience and transpersonal reality. At the same time, the losses of transpersonal projection and ritual may result in the rise of ego inflation and the severing of communal bonds, and raises the seeming inability of the Church to address such problems in a way that still has relevance for contemporary society. Even if we could introduce more people to the better paradigmatic options that exist, such cognitive shifts are unlikely to effect any lasting change; no, only *an embodied transformational experience of wholeness* holds any hope for shifting human consciousness and behavior. In Part Two, I will present each of these resources in more detail: (1) the *theoretical* process thought of Alfred North Whitehead; (2) the *empirical* analytical psychology of Carl Gustav Jung; and (3) the *practical* resources of dreaming and dream work.

The process thought of Whitehead and the analytical psychology of Jung positively address the limitations and deleterious effects of a dualistic worldview, the fragmentary nature of human experience, the ability of humans to encounter a life-giving source of dynamism in their everyday lives, the inherent value of all beings and of diversity itself, the validity of non-sensory experience, and the relationship of mind to body. Even more importantly, both allow access to resources for positive change within everyday human experience that are transformative, liberative, and salvific. Their thought might be even more relevant today than it ever was, their work may provide resources for common flourishing, and a creative synthesis of the two systems is generative and offers new possibilities. By examining what I am calling resonances and contrasts between Whitehead and Jung as well as their critics and responses, I have prepared the ground for the next two chapters wherein I will introduce the foundations of Whiteheadian and Jungian thought to move us toward a compelling synthesis that (1) describes the depths of unconscious experience as the source of dynamism, value, and creative advance; (2) describes an integrated and relational reality that grounds both cosmos and psyche; and, (3) values multiplicity, diversity, and individual contributions of value.

Hoping to contribute something—no matter how small—to the efforts to move us toward individual and planetary health and wholeness, I thereby offer the following pages of integration, synthesis, construction, and transformation. In the remainder of this work, after demonstrating the value of a framework that synthesizes Whiteheadian and Jungian thought, I will show that when such a framework is combined with a practice that connects mind and body, reveals the relationality at the base of experience, and raises unconscious experience to consciousness, the result can facilitate the transformation of human experience in liberative and salvific ways. *Ultimately*, this project will show how a generative synthesize of these three strands of resources—theoretical, empirical, and practical—drawn from Whitehead, Jung, and dream research, allows the construction of: (1) a *relational-imaginal theory of dreaming*; (2) a theory of a *relational-imaginal God-Self in the human being*; and (3) a transformative *relational-imaginal praxis for psycho-spiritual wholeness and flourishing*.

Let us turn now to Alfred North Whitehead and discover how his *philosophy of organism*—what later came to be known as *process-relational philosophy* or *process thought*—describes an integrated, relational cosmos.

NOTES

1. Kalsched, *Trauma and the Soul*, 267.
2. Craig Chalquist, "Who Was Carl Jung and Why Should We Study Him and His Work?" *Pacifica Post* (blog), October 17, 2016, http://www.pacificapost.com/who-was-carl-jung-and-why-should-we-study-him-and-his-work.
3. Hosinski, *Stubborn Fact and Creative Advance*, 247.
4. Sheri D. Kling, "Whitehead's Metaphysics as a Cosmological Framework for Transpersonal Psychology," *The Humanistic Psychologist* 47, no. 2 (2019): 184, https://doi.org/10.1037/hum0000124.
5. Though it could certainly be argued that Whiteheadian thought is experiencing a resurgence in certain fields such as ecology, it is less well-known than Jungian psychology. On the other hand, it could be argued that the promise of both schools of thought is currently under-exploited.
6. David Ray Griffin, "Introduction, Archetypal Psychology and Process Philosophy: Complementary Postmodern Movements," in *The Archetypal Process: Self and Divine in Whitehead, Jung, and Hillman*, ed. David Ray Griffin (Evanston, IL: Northwestern University Press, 1990), 15.
7. Carol P. Christ, *She Who Changes: Re-Imagining the Divine in the World* (New York: Palgrave Macmillan, 2004), 228.

8. Susan Rowland, *Jung: A Feminist Revision* (Cambridge, UK; Malden, MA: Polity Press, 2002), 158.

9. Loomer, "The Size of God," 29.

10. David Ray Griffin, ed., *The Archetypal Process: Self and Divine in Whitehead, Jung, and Hillman* (Evanston, IL: Northwestern University Press, 1990).

11. Steve Odin, *Process Metaphysics and Hua-Yen Buddhism: A Critical Study of Cumulative Penetration vs. Interpenetration* (Albany, NY: State University of New York Press, 1982).

12. Chae Young Kim, "A Comparison of Alfred North Whitehead's and Carl Gustav Jung's Idea of Religion: Special Reference to Their Lectures on Religion," *Journal of Dharma* 27, no. 3 (July 1, 2002): 417–28.

13. Grant Maxwell, "Archetype and Eternal Object: Jung, Whitehead, and the Return of Formal Causation," *Archai: The Journal of Archetypal Cosmology* 3 (Winter 2011): 51–71.

14. Scholars in the field of transpersonal psychology such as Richard Tarnas, Stanislov Grof, and John Buchanan have also drawn from Whitehead's work. My own exploration of Whitehead's thought as a framework for transpersonal psychology appeared in a 2019 issue of *The Humanistic Psychologist* focused on transpersonal psychology and scholars from both fields gathered in Claremont, California in March of 2019 to explore potential fruitful collaboration on the topic of exceptional experience and ecological civilization.

15. Griffin, "Introduction, Archetypal Psychology and Process Philosophy," vii.

16. Kling, "Whitehead's Metaphysics as a Cosmological Framework for Transpersonal Psychology," 185–86.

17. Slusser, "Jung and Whitehead on Self and Divine," 77.

18. Heisig, "The Mystique of the Nonrational and a New Spirituality," 183.

19. J'nan Morse Sellery, "The Necessity for Symbol and Myth: A Literary Amplification," in *Archetypal Process: Self and Divine in Whitehead, Jung, and Hillman*, ed. David Ray Griffin (Evanston, IL: Northwestern University Press, 1990), 107.

20. Sellery, "The Necessity for Symbol and Myth," 99.

21. Robertson, *Jungian Archetypes*, 139.

22. Pittenger, *The Lure of Divine Love*, 16–17.

23. Loomer, "The Size of God," 23.

24. Hosinski, *Stubborn Fact and Creative Advance*, 84.

25. Hosinski, 42–43.

26. Robertson, *Jungian Archetypes*, 139.

27. Slusser, "Jung and Whitehead on Self and Divine: The Necessity for Symbol and Myth," 88.

28. Morton T. Kelsey, *Encounter With God: A Theology of Christian Experience* (New York: Paulist Press, 1988), 106.

29. Robertson, *Jungian Archetypes*, 140.

30. Faber, *God as Poet of the World*, 2.

31. Alfred North Whitehead, *Adventures of Ideas*, Paperback (New York: The Free Press, 1933), 180.

32. June K. Singer, *Boundaries of the Soul: The Practice of Jung's Psychology*, Revised (New York: Anchor Books, 1994), xiii.
33. Hosinski, *Stubborn Fact and Creative Advance*, 229, 232.
34. Pittenger, *The Lure of Divine Love*, 14.
35. Tacey, "The Challenge of Teaching Jung in the University," 16.
36. Young-Eisendrath and Hall, *Jung's Self Psychology*, 18.
37. Young-Eisendrath and Hall, xv.
38. Faber, *God as Poet of the World*, 22.
39. Griffin, "Introduction, Archetypal Psychology and Process Philosophy," 4–5.
40. Kim, "A Comparison of Alfred North Whitehead's and Carl Gustav Jung's Idea of Religion," 418.
41. Alfred North Whitehead, *Religion in the Making*, Reissue (Cambridge: Cambridge University Press, 1927), 87.
42. Faber, *God as Poet of the World*, 8.
43. Rowland, *Jung*, 139.
44. Rowland, 139.
45. Heisig, "The Mystique of the Nonrational and a New Spirituality," 179.
46. Griffin, "Introduction, Archetypal Psychology and Process Philosophy," 9.
47. Griffin, 7, 11.
48. Rowland, *Jung*, 28.
49. Elizabeth M. Kraus, *The Metaphysics of Experience: A Companion to Whitehead's Process and Reality* (New York: Fordham University Press, 1979), 3.
50. Kim, "A Comparison of Alfred North Whitehead's and Carl Gustav Jung's Idea of Religion," 418.
51. Kim, 421.
52. Kim, 423.
53. Kim, 423.
54. Jung, *Modern Man in Search of a Soul*, 67. This sense of continuity with the past is also resonant with Whitehead's understanding of the effect of the past on the concrescence of actual entities.
55. Kim, "A Comparison of Alfred North Whitehead's and Carl Gustav Jung's Idea of Religion," 425.
56. Stanley R. Hopper, "Once More: The Cavern beneath the Cave," in *The Archetypal Process: Self and Divine in Whitehead, Jung, and Hillman*, ed. David Ray Griffin (Evanston, IL: Northwestern University Press, 1990), 112.
57. Hopper, "Once More," 112.
58. Keller, "Psychocosmetics and the Underworld Connection," 143.
59. Kelsey, *Encounter with God*, 106.
60. Robertson, *Jungian Archetypes*, 142.
61. Rowland, *Jung*, 24.
62. Robertson, *Jungian Archetypes*, 141.
63. Hillman, "Back to Beyond," 219.
64. McGehee and Thomas, *The Invisible Church*, 113.
65. C. G. Jung, *The Basic Writings of C. G. Jung*, ed. Violet Staub De Laszlo, Reprint (New York: Modern Library, 1993), 584.

66. Rowland, *Jung*, 25.

67. Harold Coward, "Taoism and Jung: Synchronicity and the Self," *Philosophy East and West* 46, no. 4 (1996): 488, https://doi.org/10.2307/1399493.

68. Coward, "Taoism and Jung," 488.

69. Slusser, "Jung and Whitehead on Self and Divine," 86.

70. Heisig, "The Mystique of the Nonrational and a New Spirituality," 181.

71. Slusser, "Jung and Whitehead on Self and Divine," 86.

72. Alfred North Whitehead, *Process and Reality*, ed. David Ray Griffin and Donald W. Sherburne, Corrected (New York, London: The Free Press, 1979), 52.

73. Alfred North Whitehead, *Symbolism: Its Meaning and Effect*, Revised (New York: Fordham University Press, 1985), 60.

74. Keller, "Psychocosmetics and the Underworld Connection," 142.

75. Whitehead, *Process and Reality*, 183.

76. Slusser, "Jung and Whitehead on Self and Divine," 85–86.

77. Walter Shelburne, *Mythos and Logos in the Thought of Carl Jung: The Theory of the Collective Unconscious in Scientific Perspective* (Albany, NY: State University of New York Press, 1988), 4.

78. Hosinski, *Stubborn Fact and Creative Advance*, 248.

79. David Ray Griffin, "A Metaphysical Psychology to Un-Locke Our Ailing World," in *The Archetypal Process: Self and Divine in Whitehead, Jung, and Hillman*, ed. David Ray Griffin (Evanston, IL: Northwestern University Press, 1990), 247.

80. Christ, *She Who Changes*, 14–15.

81. Anil Kumar Sarkar, *Whitehead's Four Principles from West-East Perspectives: Ways and Prospects of Process-Philosophy* (Patna: Bharati Bhawan, 1974), 113.

82. William D. Dean, "Introduction: From Size to Integrity," in *The Size of God: The Theology of Bernard Loomer in Context*, ed. William D. Dean and Larry E. Axel (Macon, GA: Mercer University Press, 1987), 8. Dean attributes this quote to Loomer's lecture at the University of Montana called "Notes on Beauty as a Design for Life."

83. Griffin, "A Metaphysical Psychology to Un-Locke Our Ailing World," 247.

84. Lucinda A. Huffaker, "Feminist Theology in Process Perspective," in *Handbook of Process Theology*, ed. Donna Bowman and Jay McDaniel, Annotated (St. Louis, MO: Chalice Press, 2006), 186.

85. Huffaker, "Feminist Theology in Process Perspective," 187.

86. Pittenger, *The Lure of Divine Love*, 12.

87. Monica A. Coleman, *Making a Way Out of No Way: A Womanist Theology* (Minneapolis, MN: Fortress Press, 2008), 78.

88. Coleman, *Making a Way Out of No Way*, 80.

89. Coleman, 79.

90. John A. Sanford, *Evil: The Shadow Side of Reality* (New York: The Crossroad Publishing Company, 1986), passim.

91. Goldenberg, "Jung after Feminism," 53.

92. Goldenberg, 53–54.

93. Goldenberg, 53, 55.

94. Goldenberg, 55–56.

95. Naomi R. Goldenberg, "Archetypal Theory and the Separation of Mind and Body: Reason Enough to Turn to Freud?" *Journal of Feminist Studies in Religion* 1, no. 1 (Spring 1985): 55.

96. Goldenberg, "Archetypal Theory and the Separation of Mind and Body," 61–63.

97. Demaris S. Wehr, *Jung & Feminism: Liberating Archetypes* (Boston: Beacon Press, 1987), 14.

98. Wehr, *Jung & Feminism*, 22.

99. Lee A Kirkpatrick, "Evolutionary Psychology: An Emerging New Foundation for the Psychology of Religion," in *Handbook of the Psychology of Religion and Spirituality*, ed. Raymond F. Paloutzian and Crystal L. Park (New York: The Guilford Press, 2005), 101–19.

100. Wehr, *Jung & Feminism*, 51–52.

101. Liliane Frey-Rohn, *From Freud to Jung: A Comparative Study of the Psychology of the Unconscious* (Boston: Shambhala, 2001), 97.

102. Rowland, *Jung*, 30. Another writer who has made significant contributions to a feminist understanding of archetypal theory is Roberta K. Rigsby and her article "Jungians, Archetypalists, and Fear of Feminism," *Continuum*, vol. 3, 1994.

103. Rowland, *Jung*, 30.

104. Estella Lauter and Carol Schreier Rupprecht, "Feminist Archetypal Theory: A Proposal," in *Feminist Archetypal Theory: Interdisciplinary Re-Visions of Jungian Thought*, ed. Estella Lauter and Carol Scheier Rupprecht (Knoxville: University of Tennessee Press, 1985), 224.

105. Frey-Rohn, *From Freud to Jung*, 98.

106. Charles R. Card, "The Archetypal View of C.G. Jung and Wolfgang Pauli," *Psychological Perspectives* 24, no. Spring–Summer 1991 (1991): 26.

107. Rowland, *Jung*, 12.

108. Suzanne Wagner, *Remembering Jung: Conversations about C. G. Jung and His Work*, DVD (Los Angeles: Bosustow Video Production, 1986).

109. Rowland, *Jung*, 32.

110. Rowland, 67.

111. Rowland, 108.

112. Rowland, 68.

113. Rowland, 41.

114. Rowland, 39–40.

115. Rowland, 61.

116. Jung, *Modern Man in Search of a Soul*, 232.

117. Stein, "Jung's Green Christ," 3.

118. Maxwell, "Archetype and Eternal Object," 53.

119. John B. Cobb Jr., "Eternal Objects and Archetypes: A Response to Stanley Hopper," in *The Archetypal Process: Self and Divine in Whitehead, Jung, and Hillman*, ed. David Ray Griffin (Evanston, IL: Northwestern University Press, 1990), 127.

120. Keller, "Psychocosmetics and the Underworld Connection," 134, 136.

121. Hillman, "Back to beyond," 215–16.

122. Hillman, 216.

Part Two

INTEGRATION

THEORETICAL, EMPIRICAL, PRACTICAL

Chapter 3

Theoretical

An Integrated, Relational Cosmos

INTRODUCTION

Whereas Part One concentrated on Fragmentation, Part Two focuses on Integration. Chapters 3 and 4 introduce the foundations of Whiteheadian and Jungian thought so as to move us toward a generative synthesis that (1) describes the depths of unconscious experience as the source of dynamism, value, and creative advance; (2) describes an integrated and relational reality that grounds both cosmos and psyche; and, (3) respects and fosters multiplicity, diversity, and individual contributions of value. In this chapter, we traverse the wounding and healing power of worldviews and the importance of Whitehead's accomplishments. We will then dive deeply into the ontological foundations of his philosophy of organism so that we may understand his one-world ontological theory and the process he conceived of as the way in which everything becomes and actualizes its instance of existence. Then we will unpack how the dead past and living immediacy are both part of the beginnings of experience, and how Whitehead conceptualized subjects, objects, perception, internal relations, and the relationship between mind and body. Finally, we will explore his descriptions of transpersonal reality and God, and how multiplicity, flux, value, and transformation are inherently and unavoidably part of our world.[1]

WORLDVIEWS: WOUNDING AND HEALING

Can a worldview wound? Alternatively, can a worldview heal? There is little doubt that our thoughts both shape and are shaped by our experiences. In the same way that some say our "biography becomes our biology,"[2] it may be that our worldview becomes our world. In a damning opinion piece published online by *The Guardian*, George Monbiot blames neoliberalism for the "plagues of anxiety, stress, depression, social phobia, eating disorders, self-harm and loneliness" that humans now experience. Pointing to the negative effects of media—both broadcast and social—he notes that humans, "the ultrasocial mammals, whose brains are wired to respond to other people, are being peeled apart . . . Though our wellbeing is inextricably linked to the lives of others, everywhere we are told that we will prosper through competitive self-interest and extreme individualism."[3]

We are suffering. We are fragmented; and the proof lies in our politics, in our racism, in our pollution of the earth, in our loneliness and alienation from each other and from ourselves, and in the disconnection we feel from our own bodies. In many ways, this reality has come to be because of the story—the worldview—that we are telling ourselves. The main characters in that narrative include

- The *substance metaphysics* that tells us that the world is ultimately made up of dead, inert bits of "stuff" that are passively pushed around by causal forces beyond their control, displacing any sense of freedom or choice, leaving us impotent in the face of oppressive forces;
- The *dualism/materialism* that separates mind from body and fact from value, displacing all meaning and value from the world and placing it all within the atomistic self that has only external relations to other beings, thereby leaving us incredibly alone in an uncaring universe;
- The *mechanistic view of the world* that tells us not only that soul is separate from body, but that there is no such thing as soul, thereby displacing all sacredness and subjectivity from humans, animals, and the world itself, leaving us to despoil the planet for its resources and turning us from beings with dignity, integrity, and inherent value into consumers that exist solely to use and abuse whatever is at our disposal; and,
- The *patriarchal view* that preferences male over female, mind over body, rationality over feeling, *Logos* over *Eros*, and *power* over *relationship*.

Yet the characters in this dominant—and dominating—narrative cannot explain the very foundations of our existence: the way our minds and bodies interact, the purposive nature of our lives, the meaning that comes with relationship, the power of both aesthetic and non-sensory experiences, or even the relationship between the knower and the known. Still, their scathing power wreaks havoc on our human spirits and interpersonal bonds and brings us to the brink of ecological disaster.

A Worldview for Wholeness

The point of metaphysics, writes Thomas Hosinski, "is to discover the structure of reality,"[4] or, per Susan Mattingly, to account for "the unity and systematic character of our experience, while at the same time doing justice to its multiple dimensions."[5] Stated similarly by Roland Faber, the goal of metaphysics is to show how "all spheres of reality, all levels of experiences, and all modes of cognition" are part of the same "coherent context" even while being "differentiated" and diverse.[6] If this is so, then we might ask ourselves if the divisive worldview that has dominated Western culture is the only way we can approach and interpret the cosmos we inhabit.

Mary S. Poplin of Claremont Graduate University argues that there are four primary worldviews at work globally: naturalism, humanism, pantheism, and Judeo-Christian theism.[7] In this project, I will argue that a process-relational worldview offers the most compelling resources for a project focused on wholeness and transformation. As Coleman notes, process thought "offers a description of reality as a whole, including atoms, amoebas, dolphins, humanity and God. More specifically, process theology explains the constant sense of change in the world and how we exist in the midst of stability and instability."[8] Rather than giving us either only Leibnizian "windowless monads" or a "billiard ball universe of blindly interacting, qualityless particles," Whitehead offers us a metaphysical "intertwining" of all things.[9]

Those of us who are theologically inclined have the additional task of showing how God interacts with and influences that "sphere of reality" within which humans find themselves. In his book *The Shape of Practical Theology*, Ray S. Anderson relates a conversation he had early in his ministry with a congregant who told him that

> [I]t was easy to agree to the omnipotence of God—that [God] could do everything—but what was of more immediate concern was whether God could do anything in particular. If it is important to know and believe that God is omnipresent—that [God] is everywhere present—one could readily assent, but what one really longed for was to discover God present in the small space of one's personal life.[10]

Drawing from James E. Loder's "transformation theory," Eolene Boyd-MacMillan describes a movement of the human spirit in which it is transformed through encounter with God.[11] It is my own deep conviction that any theology that does not help people to experience transformative encounters with God is a worthless theology. Moreover, the only theology that will have living relevance for contemporary society in the United States is one that reflects the diversity, complexity, and depth present in human experience and offers something of value to that experience.

Worldviews, then, can either be wounding or healing, divisive or connective, nourishing or devouring. While Monbiot may view neoliberalism as the guilty "homewrecker" that breaks the social bonds necessary for the human animal's flourishing, it is also imperative to recognize the deleterious effects of substance metaphysics, dualism, materialism, mechanism, and patriarchy. Few of us give any thought to the worldview that lies at the bedrock of our way of moving through the world, and even fewer of us spend our time reflecting on metaphysical philosophy. Yet if metaphysical reflection helps us discover the structure of reality and offers a way to understand all of experience as having a coherent wholeness that still honors diversity, then *we cannot ignore metaphysics*. Theologically, we also cannot ignore the need for an understanding of how God interacts with our world. If a compelling worldview can counter the dominant destructive narrative, then I offer process metaphysics as an alternative worldview for wholeness. We can begin to understand this claim by grasping the ontological foundations of process thought.

ONTOLOGICAL FOUNDATIONS

For a worldview to have any hope of healing our fragmentation through recognition of a coherent context of wholeness, then it must show how we are all part of one interrelated world where everything has value. In Whitehead's philosophy there is no hidden world that is more real, no first causes that "float into the world from nowhere."[12] As Faber explains, Whitehead sought to reunite experience and reality,[13] a "volatile" perspective that is the source of both its "theological attractiveness and the hostility directed toward it." Whitehead, he writes, shows us that (a) descriptions of *all* experience, including religious, must have the same "inner integrity," (b) *every* experience must make sense within the context of one world, (c) all experiences are "mutual transitions" from matter to mind or knowledge to reality, and, (d) "Nothing isolated from experience can be real . . . ."[14]

Whitehead's foundational ontological principle states that metaphysical explanations must refer to something actual and so we "must appeal only to actual things that are experienced."[15] As I have noted elsewhere, his cosmology describes a relational reality within which God is encountered as immanent and all things have value.[16] Because actualized reality is always in the process of becoming, the experiential units of reality can choose in every moment what they will become, and therefore, no matter how painful one's past or present, complex individuals have the capacity—within possibilities that are relevant to one's immediate reality—to move forward in a way that is novel and positive. In this one reality, God seeks to lure every entity toward its highest enjoyment and greatest intensity of experience, and so, again, no matter what one has experienced in one's past, every moment is afresh with possibilities that can lead toward more wholeness, more enjoyment, more zest for life, and more harmony and peace.

Whitehead describes four principles at work: (1) the *spatio-temporal process* of forming and perishing entities; (2) *eternal objects*, or the spectrum of available possibilities; (3) *God*, the dipolar entity that envisions value, offers relevant possibilities in the form of eternal objects, and receives the actions of the world, holding them in divine memory and responding with compassionate and redemptive love; and (4) *creativity*,[17] the active principle that results in there being something rather than nothing.[18] Sarkar describes this as "a continuity of *objective immortalities* or an emergence of *possible forms* in the midst of other possible forms. What is suggested here is not a world of *static existence*, but a world of *possible existence*—existence by continuous elimination of the possibles."[19] This reality is neither static nor linear; all four principles are in a constant dance between perishing and abiding.[20]

According to Heraclitus, we cannot step into the same river twice. Similarly, in Whitehead's philosophy of organism, reality is not static, but an adventure where dynamic creativity is always at work and momentary unities arise and then perish to influence the next momentary unity that is forming.[21] The process universe "is alive and changing, continually co-creating new possibilities of life . . . . For process philosophy, change, freedom or creativity, and embodiment are interconnected. Everything in the world is in process."[22] While the ordered past is made up of "stubborn" facts,[23] possibilities for novel futures are also given; neither novelty nor order have the final word. Reality is ultimately characterized as relational, concrescing, and creative.[24]

Whitehead's Ontological Theory

There are many reasons why Whiteheadian thought provides such rich resources for a project that seeks to foster transformation, but the primary reason is due to Whitehead's prioritization of *experience*. In his *ontological theory*, Whitehead hypothesizes that at their most basic level, *occasions of experience* form the same way whether they are part of a living human or animal, or even a non-living entity. The only difference is that higher order beings experience more complex phases within the same basic process. Whitehead begins with human experience; furthermore, he insists that we can extrapolate from human experience to understand the workings of the entire cosmos. Pittenger reminds us that we can relate our experience to the greater evolutionary process, and that although some aspects of human experience are unique, "*We belong to the world that has produced us.*" Therefore, what we learn about ourselves informs us of the qualities of the world, and what we learn of the world, informs our knowledge of human experience.[25] We experience ourselves as envisioning, decision-making individuals, who choose from various options, who respond to the stimuli of our world, and who connect with the others around us.[26]

While I may experience myself on a moment-to-moment basis as a subject, each moment is actually "the child of the past."[27] As Hosinski notes, there is a continuity to our experience as it flows from past to present and we know ourselves to be individuals with goals and purposes. Each of us is a "unique center of feeling" that experiences value, freshness, and creativity.[28] Whitehead asserts that human experience is "entirely dominated" by the relationship between insight, purpose, and conduct[29] and purposes always aim at the realization of value. As Hosinski argues, our experience of value requires that we have the capacity to discern and judge the values inherent in the actual situations that we encounter and in any alternatives that we may envision. In other words, human experience rests upon four presuppositions:

(1) There are *real alternatives* available to us in every moment.
(2) We can discern their *value* for us in the present.
(3) We *select* from those alternatives based on perceived value.
(4) Individual subjects possess the *freedom to choose* from among real alternatives.[30]

One of the most controversial aspects of Whitehead's metaphysics is his proposal that every occasion of actualized existence is subjective in nature. That is, each occasion is a "center of becoming" with its own subjective unity and a degree of active "self-construction."[31] Whitehead is in agreement with modern physics that also seems to propose that all actual things are, at their most basic, occasions of experience rather than static substances.[32] We do not live in a "billiard ball" universe that can be adequately explained by scientific materialism as a universe of dead matter being controlled by predetermined laws. Such a view necessarily makes human freedom either an aberration or an illusion. Christ writes that rather than seeing all matter as "dead," Whitehead and Hartshorne actually saw it all as "alive" because even the smallest atomic particles can *prehend* or "feel the feelings of others."[33]

The Process of Concrescence

To understand the creative advance of both atomic particles and humans, then, we must dive into the details of Whitehead's hypothesized process of concrescence—the process by which anything actual comes into being. To show how entities both obtain their qualities and why there is not random chaos, Whitehead introduces his process of *objectification*, a "relationship between actual entities in which the development of one is in some sense dependent upon the other."[34] Within that process, entities are internally related to other entities and to God, upon whom they rely for their formation.

Here it is important to note that Whitehead imagined every occasion to be *dipolar* in nature; entities have a *mental* pole, through which they experience *conceptual* possibilities for the future as well as qualitative or aesthetic value, and a *physical* pole through which they experience other actual entities from their immediate past in an *objective* way.[35] Because there is both "determinateness" that enters each forming entity from the actual world in its "physical inheritance"[36] and "indeterminateness" that comes due to the nature of conceptual possibilities and values or "the basic operations of mentality,"[37] Whitehead describes the world as *bipolar* or *dipolar*. As I have previously noted, unlike the dualistic bifurcation of the mental and the physical in a Cartesian worldview, "Whitehead's dipolar aspects are like the opposite poles of a battery or magnet; they are necessarily together."[38] It is through this polarity that "novel determinateness of feeling" enters into the actual world.[39] Each entity integrates its physical feeling of the determined actual past world with its mental grasp of conceptual possibilities for the future.[40] This integration results in a unity of experience and self-formation that Whitehead calls *concrescence* and it can be considered both a spatial and a non-spatial process.[41]

While we can think of the process by which entities form as having distinct phases, Whitehead believed that such distinctions are an abstraction from both the actual simultaneity of the phases and their continuity with previous and future occasions of experience. Therefore, for purposes of explanation only, the basic core process can be described as an *initial (receptive)* phase, a *responsive* phase, and an *integrative* phase.[42] Higher order occasions (such as sensate living organisms) also experience supplemental phases, which will be discussed later.

The Initial (Receptive) Phase

An entity or moment of experience begins with that entity's *initial aim*—this is "its thrust at being, its urge to make of itself something actual, its living dynamism of creativity that kick starts it into existence."[43] As the concrescing subject progresses, it claims the initial aim as its own *subjective* aim, using it to fuel its own self-creation. Its urge to make some possibility *actual* is what Whitehead called the occasion's *subjective aim at satisfaction*. According to Hosinski, we may think of this as the occasion's "drive" or its desire "to make something of and for itself."[44] Because the fullness of experience is always greater than mere thought about it, Whitehead only claims to show how concrete uniqueness is possible, not to fully explain its undeniable existence.[45]

The *initial stage* of the actual occasion's aim is "an endowment" first conceived of by God. The initial aim is the very "immediacy" that constitutes the entity's desire for its own self-constitution. At any given moment's arising, the initial aim is the best possibility envisioned by God for that moment, but the outcome is not determined by God because every entity chooses for itself what values it will realize. Actual entities have agency and the consequences of such freedom may, indeed, be tragic: "The initial aim is best for that *impasse*. But if the best be bad, then the ruthlessness of God can be personified as Ate, the goddess of mischief. The chaff is burnt."[46] The best for the impasse is the best for current conditions, and in this stage, the possibilities appropriate for each entity are bound by the facts of the immediate past that are experienced *objectively*. Visions for possibility are heavily contextualized and relevant.

In Whitehead's philosophy, experience moves from the past objective world to the subjective present.[47] The past is given as a physical "inheritance" and is at the same time actively received by the forming subject of experience. Here, something real is moving from past to present, and to indicate the active nature of such receiving, Whitehead terms it *prehension.*[48] By this he means a type of apprehension through which things are seized or grasped in a way that may or may not be *cognitive* but is certainly *unified* by the perceiving entity.[49] In fact, Les Muray relates Whitehead's term "to prehend" to the psychological term "to internalize."[50] If the process ended with this initial phase, there would be no change, evolution, or growth, only repetition of the past. We know there is more—that we respond to what is given, that we imagine hopeful futures, and that we can choose to move toward those imagined futures in novel ways. It is therefore in the *responsive* and *integrative* phases of concrescence that novelty and uniqueness come into play.

The Responsive Phase: Possibilities and Purposes

In the initial phase of concrescence, we see how the objective past flows into the present moment, and how the forming moment grasps or prehends the past. While the past is already a *fait accompli*, when forming in the present a momentary event can either repeat, or conform to, its past, or it can entertain other possibilities. While the past is prehended physically, Whitehead argued that potentials are entertained in the mental pole of each occasion because possibilities are not physically actual;[51] therefore, such possibilities are experienced as *conceptual prehensions*.[52] Concrescing entities must be perceiving *something real*, some object or datum that is entertained as possibility or value; Whitehead referred to these conceptually prehended objects as *eternal objects*.

Eternal Objects

While *creativity* can explain the reason there is anything at all, eternal objects explain "*what* things are" and what ingredients characterize those things.[53] Mattingly considers the doctrine of eternal objects to be "central" in Whitehead's system.[54] It shows why things have a "definite nature" and what the relationships between things are.[55] Eternal objects are formal elements that function both objectively and subjectively: as *objective*, they are "forms of dynamic, extensive relationships" and as *subjective*, they are "forms of feelings" and it is the oscillation between them that "rhythmically" advances the creative process.[56] Eternal objects are both *real* potentials and *pure* potentials;[57] they are *real* in that they can be conceptualized before being actualized, and they are *pure* because they are not necessarily referent to anything actual in the temporal world.[58] We see this clearly when we think of colors or numbers. "Redness" or "threeness" can be observed in specific, actual things that display the color or quantity but we can also think of "redness" or "threeness" in a general way that is not limited to any of the instances in which we observe it. As Lee describes, actual entities have forms of definiteness, and those definite characteristics are due to eternal objects. While eternal objects in and of themselves are not actual, but purely potential, they are objects that participate in experience. Without eternal objects, we would see nothing truly new in the world, just the rearrangement of existing actualities.[59]

Eternal objects are conceptual because they operate as possibilities[60] and are "indifferent to any temporal exemplifications."[61] As I have noted, they both transcend all individual occasions (thereby participating in the eternal) and are only actualized in individual occasions (participating in the temporal). They are not an "ideal, ultimate reality" but are abstractions that gain reality "solely in events and event nexuses."[62] Because an eternal object can be "realized in many events" given the right conditions, they transcend "the singularity of every event." They are not the "essence" of events; rather, they "make it possible for events to become what their 'essence' is."[63] Eternal objects are envisaged within the actual entity of God. They cannot coerce anything into being—in and of themselves they possess no causal force—but depend upon real entities for embodiment.[64] They are the "timeless ground of the actual world" that must be "grounded in an event."[65] We consider eternal objects to be "eternal" in part because they are inexhaustible, meaning they cannot be used up in any given actualization.[66] Forms may be used repeatedly; they are "essentially indeterminate" regarding their ingression into the world's entities.[67]

Odin describes eternal objects as aesthetic "value-patterns," and as "basic organizational patterns" that initiate every occasion.[68] Lee understands them to be God's "envisagement of the structure of possibility" and describes the universe as "reasonably together" because there are "patterns of assemblage" that are demanded by "the creative advance of the universe." Such order is required in each actual entity and grouping of entities.[69] At the same time, Whitehead writes that eternal objects function "in the guise of subjective novelty meeting the objective datum from the past."[70] Here again, it is critical to remember that neither the order nor the novelty is determined ahead of time by God; "each act of becoming is a free act" that arises *with* the moment itself "as a result of which the texture of reality is modified."[71]

How are eternal objects presented to forming moments of experience? Whitehead believed that eternal objects *ingress*—or enter—into occasions through the internal presence of other entities—either past entities or God. As Ballard describes it, subjects "feel" or "absorb" other entities physically or they may "include or absorb" eternal objects through the mental pole[72] as a conceptual prehension of God's initial subjective aim for that occasion. The objects perceived by forming subjects—whether they are physical objects of the past or conceptual objects of potential futures—are *qualitative* elements with "complex location," meaning that they are "shared by the datum and by the percipient event"; they are what Mattingly refers to as "extensively relational" because they "cannot be divested of their spatial and temporal reference."[73] Said more simply, the same "redness" or "threeness" is present in the object being perceived, the eye that is capturing the sense data, and in the mind that is interpreting the sense data as having those qualities. Eternal objects are also partially responsible for the fact that we experience permanence in the world because the same form or eternal object is present in successive entities. While often compared with Plato's *Ideas*, Krauss argues that eternal objects "are not inert forms waiting to be appropriated" but "have the unrest of the Platonic Eros" and act as persuasive "lures for feeling."[74]

Eternal objects function in a relational[75] way, determining both the datum and what Whitehead calls the *subjective form*—the emotion and purpose—of what is prehended.[76] Prehended objects, then, carry feeling. When a feeling has the "datum" of an eternal object, it is known as a "conceptual feeling" and it is then a determinant of the character of the concrescing entity.[77] Subjective forms are the "how" of any prehension and the subjective forms of conceptual prehensions are a *valuation*, or an emotional or aesthetic response to the perceived worth of the eternal objects being prehended by the subject.[78] The responsive phase is also marked by what Whitehead termed *appetition*, meaning an urge or drive to form a subjective experience that is unique to that subject.[79]

The Integrative and Supplemental Phases

The third stage of concrescence—the final stage for most simple occasions of experience—is known as the *integrative* phase. In this phase, the physical feelings of the first phase are integrated with the conceptual feelings of the second phase.[80] At this point, the subject reaches the determination of its subjective aim in its final decision. Its purpose is complete, and it has reached its terminal phase, that of satisfaction. Sadly, the satisfied subject cannot linger in any golden haze of glory, but immediately perishes and becomes objective data—what Whitehead called a *superject*—to be prehended by future forming occasions.[81] This word—*superject*—literally means to be "thrown beyond," and Whitehead uses it to convey the sense of the present moment's *objective immortality* in future events.[82]

In more complex organisms, Whitehead imagined that experience did not terminate at the end of the integrative phase as it does with simpler occasions. Rather, he proposed that experience could progress to include what he called *propositions*, *propositional feelings*, and *intellectual feelings*. These supplemental phases produce another object that may be grasped, or prehended, by the subjective center of experience. He calls this new datum a *metaphysical proposition* and its purpose is not to express truth or falsehood, but rather to influence the concrescence of actual entities through persuasive feeling.[83] "Feeling," "emotion" and "purpose" are important to the process of concretion, and that which is a "datum for feeling has a unity as *felt*."[84] Whitehead stresses the importance of feeling when he writes, "It is an essential doctrine in the philosophy of organism that the primary function of a proposition is to be relevant as a lure for feeling."

When a subject feels a proposition worthy of influencing its self-creation, that proposition has become the occasion's "subjective aim."[85] In simpler occasions, Hosinski explains, the integrative phase forms what is called a "comparative feeling," where the eternal object or possibility is integrated with the definitive facts of physical prehensions. Yet simple occasions do not feel such integration as a proposition, nor do they have the capacity for real novelty. Whitehead believed that it is conformal feeling with the past that can explain the continuity and connectedness in our world; but what, Hosinski asks, can explain novelty and the world's amazing diversity?[86] While novelty begins to be possible only for "higher level" occasions, metaphysical propositions can be "felt" even by occasions that that do not possess consciousness or language. This occurs at what we may identify as an *affective* or unconscious level—prior to any rational judgment—where the occasion is acting through an emotional desire for value.[87] We can understand this more clearly when we think of our own reaction to especially beautiful artistic expressions. The potentialities of eternal objects are abstract while lacking concreteness and the actualities of occasions are concrete without indication of unrealized potentialities.

Propositions are *relational*, in that they are present in both past and forming occasions who share the same actual world; if a proposition conforms to the actual world of the concrescing occasion, it is considered "true." Yet it is only those propositions that *do not* conform to the concrescing occasion's actual world—those considered "false"—that make novelty possible. True propositions that successfully lure an occasion to actualize them result only in repetition. A false proposition may serve as an effective lure toward possibilities.[88]

As already discussed, metaphysical propositions do not require rational judgment or consciousness to be entertained, and so the process of concretion can yet include another "sub-phase" in which metaphysical propositions are raised to the level that Whitehead called *intellectual feelings*. A *propositional feeling* is felt as the contrast between potential and fact and it is integrated *unconsciously* according to its affective value or attractiveness for the concrescing subject.[89] When an occasion of experience becomes *aware* of the contrast between what is and what is possible, what is evoked is an *intellectual feeling* that reflects the contrast between fact and theory.[90] While such knowledge is not yet *rational*, it is the data that initiates rational thought.[91] Within this world, then, we are assured that when we sense meaning and significance in our experience it is reflective of a reality within which meaning and experience *are possible*. As Pittenger argues, process thought always seeks to describe the fullness of human experience at both the cognitive and feeling levels.[92]

Here we have seen the radical alternative that process metaphysics offers to the dominant dualistic and mechanistic worldview and its disregard for the nonrational. Whitehead's system explains the nature of reality as one coherent context that does not require interventions by a transcendent, supernatural God; moreover, it does not narrow human experience to exclude freedom, purpose, and value. In this section, I have described Whitehead's ontological theory and the process of concrescence. We have seen how everything in existence has internal relations to everything else; even more importantly, I have shown how Whitehead's cosmos is inherently relational, value-seeking, and how dipolar entities experience the world through both mentality and physical feeling. Now let us return to the very beginnings of experience and the way in which Whitehead integrates the presence of the dead, factual past with the living immediacy and possibility of the present moment.

THE BEGINNINGS OF EXPERIENCE: DEAD PAST AND LIVING IMMEDIACY

As described earlier, the process of concretion begins with the internalization or prehension of both the objective past world and the living immediacy afforded by God through that entity's initial subjective aim. By using the term prehension, Whitehead asserts that there are internal relations between the subject and its world.[93] The reason he can claim such internal relations is because of what Whitehead does with perception. In his system, both the past world and the initial aim are prehended through the mode of perception that Whitehead termed *causal efficacy* (discussed later in more detail) and therefore enter physically and unconsciously into the new occasion. Joseph Petek describes causal efficacy as a "deep non-conscious sense of causal relatedness, common to all entities."[94]

Because of this relationship between dead, objective past and living immediacy and aim, every occasion of experience is both subject and object. The inexorable flow of process is the many (the diverse past world) becoming one (integrated in the subject) and increasing by one (as the subject perishes and becomes objective data and past fact for the next concrescing moment.[95] With Hosinski, we must ask: "If subjectivity 'perishes' in 'decision,' then how does the *living immediacy* of subjective experience begin?" It cannot arise from a "dead" past, nor can it be self-created or randomly appear "out of the blue."[96] The answer is that living immediacy arises when a forming entity grasps its own subjectivity by "feeling God's conceptual feelings," by encountering God within itself.[97] Every actual entity in its beginnings encounters—and is internally related to—both the objective past and God as "other" within its own constitution. Steve Odin links this to Jung's description of the "depth-dimension" of our own experience, or what Jung named "the archetypal imagination." He comparatively views God-in-process as the "imaginative experiential synthesis" of the collective unconscious wherein antecedent pluralities are formed into a new unity. God as this primordial, provider of "normative aesthetic value patterns" organizes "the manifold of causal feelings into harmonic contrasts, thus producing maximum depth of emotional intensity in each occasion of experience."[98]

Subjects, Objects, and Perception

Descartes believed thought precedes being. John Locke, David Ray Griffin notes, pressed for a "mechanical philosophy" in which nature possessed only the quantitative properties necessary for mechanistic interactions; any other aesthetic or purposive qualities were located in the human soul and projected onto the natural world.[99] Once value and creativity were removed from both the human and the rest of the world, all questions of ultimate reality that could not be answered through sensory perception were dismissed entirely.[100] Such mechanistic-materialistic thinking forms the unquestioned basis of our culture and the idea that mind or spirit acts upon matter is "unthinkable."[101] Within such a worldview, not only are claims of revelation and religious experience problematic,[102] but even the very existence of an objective world are no longer tenable.[103] While sensate materialists dismiss anything not perceived by the senses, Whitehead argues that "In human experience, the most compelling example of nonsensuous perception is our knowledge of our own immediate past."[104]

Though our cultural worldview appears not to have noticed, within the past century classical physics and the mechanistic view of nature have collapsed due to the emergence of quantum physics, relativity theory, and other new insights.[105] As a result, our understanding of subjects and objects has been upended. As Sherburne notes, "For Kant, the world emerges from the subject; for the philosophy of organism, the subject emerges from the world."[106] Understanding the relationship of subjects and objects is key to understanding Whitehead's metaphysics. As I have explored elsewhere,[107] there would be no "solidarity of the universe" and no interconnected web to which we might belong if "prehending subjects and prehended objects form exclusive sets of entities" that are unrelated.[108] We are part of a relational web because subjects are also objects and objects are also subjects; this is true without each entity losing its own identity.[109] In Whitehead's philosophy, "subjectivity and objectivity, mind and matter, cognition and being must be viewed as being *essentially* the same."[110] Rather than a cosmos marked by monism, Whitehead describes reality as a "dynamic rhythm of transition" that perpetually moves from object to subject to object in an "ecological unity" that is "irreducibly pluralistic."[111]

For Whitehead, there is an *internal relationship* between knower and known and the basis for the possibility of knowledge lies in the relatedness of the elements of our experience. In order to understand Whitehead's views on internal relations, we must understand how he approaches perception and causation. These relate to truth and error, as much of philosophy has concerned itself with making sense of the relationship between epistemology and ontology. As Whitehead writes, "An adequate account of human mentality requires an explanation of (i) how we can know truly, (ii) how we can err, and (iii) how we can critically distinguish truth from error."[112] As Steven Shaviro points out in his exploration of Whitehead's *Symbolism*, the question of error comes into play because philosophy "is deeply concerned with the unreliability of immediate experience—or of the body and the senses" and considers sense perception "delusional."[113]

What is happening and what information is given in sense perception? Whitehead defines sense perception as "our immediate perception of the contemporary external world" that includes such qualities as color, shape, size, sound, taste, etc.[114] Sensory data is precise but it lacks any information on value, duration, extension, or the relationships between those qualities. Whitehead disagreed with the prevailing view that multiple qualia are perceived as discrete, abstract qualities that are then—truly or falsely—assembled by the perceiver's mind into a subjective interpretation. He showed that we actually perceive more than what is transferred by sense data; in fact, the very action of sensory perception relies on functioning bodily organs. Whitehead writes that

> [W]e see the picture, and we see it with our eyes; we touch the wood, and we touch it with our hands; we smell the rose, and we smell it with our nose; we hear the bell, and we hear it with our ears; we taste the sugar, and we taste it with our palate.[115]

Our sensations are more correctly viewed as inherited feelings of the workings of the body that are perceived by the self, or presiding occasion in our brain.[116] In other words, the data captured in hearing, seeing, touching, smelling, etc., is collected by the body prior to the grasping of that data by the mind. The world that is perceived as contemporary is actually based on data gathered in the millisecond prior; the unity we experience with our bodily conditions and our immediate past are instances of nonsensuous perception.[117] For Loomer, "Sense perception is an abstract version of physical experience."[118] Whitehead insists that there must be two modes of perception: *presentational immediacy* and *causal efficacy*. What we typically think of when we refer to "sense perception" is what Whitehead calls *presentational immediacy*. The physical, non-sensory perception of the past world is what Whitehead referred to as perception in the mode of *causal efficacy*.

Of the two modes of perception, causal efficacy is the deeper and more primordial. While presentational immediacy operates in "high-grade organisms," causal efficacy is ubiquitous, witnessed in the conformation each present moment has with its immediate past, and the resulting unification of the world.[119] According to Shaviro, "Without this conformation of the present to the past, this physical experience of causal efficacy, the clarities and intensities of presentational immediacy could not even arise for us in the first place. Even our most clear and distinct perceptions are grounded in a deeper sense that is 'vague, haunting, unmanageable.'"[120] It is critical to understand that in the mode of causal efficacy, Whitehead shows how the past world is being directly perceived as causally efficacious for the present moment. As Hosinski instructs, causation is not something produced by a reflecting subject examining sense data but is directly perceived unconsciously through causal efficacy before being reflected upon.[121] In this mode, real objects touch or physically penetrate other real things; causal efficacy is both "a mode of perception and an actual physical process."[122]

It is also in the mode of causal efficacy that value is transferred and by which we aesthetically perceive the relationships between things.[123] While sensory images are devoid of information about relations, aim, purpose, or intrinsic value, these parts of our experience should not be disregarded.[124] Again, we must be able to make sense of all human experience within one coherent context. Whitehead argues that our sensory perceptions of spatial, physical occasions via the body and our non-sensory perceptions of non-spatial mental occasions are *essentially related* or correspondent to each other.[125] The relating of data given in the mode of presentational immediacy to data given in the mode of causal efficacy is what Whitehead called *symbolic reference*. In fact, it is in the relating of the two kinds of data that error arises. What we perceive via causal efficacy is "infallible" because it is direct experience.[126] Whitehead uses the example of the dog in Aesop's fable who drops a piece of meat in the water in an attempt to grab its reflection to illustrate how error arises in symbolic reference.[127] Shaviro notes that the dog did, in fact, perceive meat to be in the water, but misunderstood it to be edible.[128] The topic of symbolic reference will come up again in chapter 7.

As I have previously written, Whitehead's theory of perception relates us directly to the world, describes a world that has intrinsic value, and shows us that human experience, at its deepest level, is nonsensory and nonrational.[129] Whitehead invites us into a world where feeling, emotion, and aim are primary and the soul is embedded in nature.[130]

Relations

The primary reason that process thought is considered *relational* is because it describes an interdependent reality wherein actual entities are formed internally by their relationships to others. Yes, each entity enjoys freedom to decide what it will ultimately become—what value it will attain—but an entity's process of concrescence is never fully *sui generis*. Every subjective entity:

(1) is initiated by God's incarnation of God's self as that entity's "living immediacy"[131] and initial aim—the reason the entity's self-causation begins;[132]
(2) emerges from the objects it prehends—or internalizes—in its initial phase;
(3) prehends physical data from the objective past and conceptual data in the form of eternal objects; and
(4) upon its satisfaction becomes an objective datum that is available to be internalized, and will therefore be related to, subsequently forming entities in its future world.

No entity, society of occasions, or individual can claim that it is entirely self-made or that it stands independent of the rest of the world. Such a concept is ludicrous.

Although there is a unity experienced by every occasion in its forming, as it completes the concrescent integration of all its relationships and decides what it will be that unity does not endure; it is experienced as immediacy and momentary in duration.[133] As soon as occasions form, they perish, and so have no history and no future. Yet an *event* is comprised of an "historic route of successive occasions"[134] which enjoys a certain kind of unity. When we point to a thing or a person, we are actually identifying what Whitehead called a "society" or "nexus"—an "enduring group" with shared characteristics.[135] Such assemblies of occasions dominate our conscious experience. Even though they are not completely "real" in the way that actual occasions are, societies of occasions are what endure while actual entities are continuously perishing. Societies of occasions reveal the social character of the world.[136]

If Whitehead is correct about perception in the mode of causal efficacy and the ingression of past entities into forming entities, then the universe is "intersubjective,"[137] an "inter-locked community,"[138] and a "universal web of interconnected events"[139] that are in "an ever-renewing relational process."[140] While this web of events can appear to be "enduring"[141] and self-sustaining, with "patterns of assemblage,"[142] such appearance "enshrouds the unfathomable or inexhaustible mystery" of our world.[143] We are not self-sustaining monads with only external relations to others. Rather, we are "dependent" beings who can neither explain ourselves nor keep ourselves in existence; we require others to become ourselves.[144] Not only do we depend on our daily "proximate realities" of food, water, shelter, and family, but at the deepest level of existence we depend on the creativity and sustenance of the cosmos itself.[145] "To pretend that we are independent," writes Pittenger, is "vainglorious nonsense."[146]

The Unity of Body and Mind

While Enlightenment thinking viewed mind and body as separate and qualitatively distinct, Whitehead thought this Cartesian bifurcation to be an "arbitrary disconnection"[147] that was "disastrous,"[148] "incoherent,"[149] and a "tremendous fraud."[150] Such a separation calls into question the unity we feel with our own bodies. Whereas Aquinas saw mind as informing the body, Whitehead reminds us that "all the life in the body is the life of the individual cells . . . . So what needs to be explained is not dissociation of personality but unifying control" or the sense of a "presiding personality."[151] Our personality is a "strand of 'presiding' or 'directing occasions'" that is supported by the "complex living society" of the body and both are in constant "interplay."[152] As I have stated in an earlier chapter, my sense of unity with my personal past and my body's perpetuity reveals that my *route of occasions* holds together in a way that gives me character and individuality.[153]

In process thought, subjective experiences give us insight into reality and therefore cannot be dismissed. Mind and matter are not two distinct substances; in fact, Whitehead equates the energies of physics and emotion.[154] Pittenger reminds us that human goal orientation and the creative movement of evolution in the universe are intimately related; human life and the natural world cannot be understood apart from one another. Human life is part of the cosmic process and therefore the cosmic process is itself disclosed in human life.[155] Any bifurcation of our emotional and physical selves or even of humans and nature is, therefore, a "false disjunction." We can alternatively embrace a "unified world view" that makes possible "a coherent and consistent grasp of life *and* of nature, of human life *and* of the world."[156]

From Whitehead's theory on how entities form, we learn that from successive occasions emerges the unity of an event, and from successive events emerges the unity of a society of occasions. But how do we understand the personal unity of the self? Moreover, how do we understand the unity we experience between that mental self and the physical body that supports it if both are made up of continuously emerging and perishing "drops of experience"? Loomer attributes our assumptions of an enduring self that secondarily experiences the flux of embodied experience to the substantialist tradition in philosophy and theology.[157] Yet, this notion that there is a "more real" substratum that undergirds experience dashes any hopes of an integrated cosmos. Instead, Whitehead argues that there is nothing more real than actual occasions. Events occur in the lives of other events, and the enduring person or self is what he called the "historic route of such occasions."[158]

My self-identity is a "special strand of unity within the general unity of nature." It is a point of focus within the whole that reflects the same "general principle which guides the constitution of the whole." This is the "object-to-subject structure of experience" or the "vector-structure of nature" wherein the past "energizes" in the present.[159] Whitehead's cosmology describes an "overarching scheme of relational possibility" in which actual entities or occasions of experience "particularize the extensive continuum, rupture it, specify its generality from their perspective."[160] Every occasion, therefore, has its own perspective and experience while being in relation to the whole interconnected matrix of events. My momentary present "ruptures" the extensive continuum from my perspective and my historic route of successive perspectives give me my sense of self-identity. My personal life is only my unique stance within the wider continuum.[161]

Yet we are not just rational, cognitive selves. In every moment, every human subject inherits both its bodily feelings and its immediate past.[162] For Mesle, it is not the "fleeting moments of reasoning" that make up the bulk of our experience; rather, it is "the mind/soul/self/psyche" that is the "flow of the body's experience or feeling" that predominates.[163] In fact, reason is a rarity; the majority of experiencers in the natural world swim mostly in that "great ocean" that is the "flow of felt emotion" on which rationality floats precariously.[164] As noted earlier, our sense perception depends on the prior functioning of our bodies. According to Hosinski, while we may "see 'with our eyes,' hear 'with our ears,' feel 'with our hands.' . . . These are vague feelings." Without eyes, ears, and an epidermis carrying out their essential functions, we would have no visual sense data, auditory sense data, or touch sense data.[165] Though we typically do not give it any thought, each time my brain joins the images it produces to the physical sensations that my eyes and nervous system generate in my capacity for vision, I am experiencing my bodily feelings and past occasions as unified.

Our sense experience reflects the unity of self and body, yet our body inherits its physical conditions from its physical environment[166] and lies "in the field of nature" in a way that is "distinct from our personal existence." For Whitehead, the body "is part of the external world continuous with it," and is as much a part of nature as any river, mountain, or cloud. In fact, he argued that we "cannot define where a body begins and where external nature ends" yet our personal bodily unity is a foundational experience.[167]

We know that we experience an "interplay" between the "innumerable inheritances" that have been physically generated by the functioning of our nervous system, our visceral and circulatory systems, etc., as well as the "emotions, hopes, fears, inhibitions, sense-perceptions" that arise from our body and our cognitive functioning.[168] Whitehead writes that it is impossible to determine the molecules that mark the end of the brain and the beginning of the body or even the end of the body and the beginning of the external world. No, brain is continuous with body is continuous with world. Neither is our "animal body" different in principle from the past actual world; we might say, "the actual world is mine."[169] Cobb and Griffin reference the same idea expressed by Pierre Teilhard de Chardin who writes that rather than the common view that the body is a small, detached part of the universe, we actually contain the entire Universe within ourselves.[170]

Whitehead embraces the dominant scientific view that our conclusions about the living body must be based on what we know to be true about other, non-living aspects of the physical world and then radicalizes it by insisting that the reverse must also then be true. In other words, we must also draw our conclusions about the rest of the physical world based on what we know to be true about the human body.[171] What we know about the human body is that there is an intimate interplay between the physical and the mental and between the objective past and the subjective present. Bruce Epperly reminds us that although they "differ quantitatively in terms of richness, complexity and novelty of experience," mind and body "are similar in kind . . . the notion of unfeeling matter is an abstraction, the result of the apparent stability of physical objects."[172]

Anytime we isolate something in nature for examination, we focus our perception on the "foreground" item in relief against a now diffuse "background" of the environmental relationships within which that thing exists. Theologian-turned-philosopher Alan Watts uses the example that we cannot fully describe a human being walking without referring to the ground or spatial location within which that activity is occurring.[173] It is a misperception to believe that the thing being studied exists independently of the web of relationships in which it is enmeshed. According to Faber, the bifurcation of bodily nature and mind is a "fundamental error" because "it views that which appears within thought (causal particles void of relation) as concrete nature."[174] Robertson agrees that isolating any part from the unity of the world for scientific study is a "game" that we have been playing since the Renaissance.[175] To be actual is to be embodied and embedded. According to Christ, Hartshorne believed that without bodies we would be "just gibberish" and that the mind and the body "are an irreducible continuum." Naming Hartshorne's perspective "pansomatism," Christ describes all bodies as the location of feeling.[176] Similarly, Epperly refers to our cosmos as "psychosomatic" and "panexperiential" because mind and body are "dynamically interconnected" and actually "interpenetrate one another," with mind "constantly shap[ing] the body even as the body continuously conditions the mind."[177]

In this section, I have shown how a small but significant change to one part of our existence—the way we view perception—can create seismic shifts. These ripple out aftershocks in all directions of the human experience and radically change the way we understand our relationships with everything in our world, from the deeply intimate experience of our own bodies to our inner experience of God. Now we will move from the most intimate workings of each entity's inner experience to the way that we encounter transpersonal reality, the nature of God, and the necessary role that Whitehead understands God to play in the cosmos.

TRANSPERSONAL REALITY: DIPOLAR GOD, MUTUAL IMMANENCE, AND NOVELTY

The presence of value, belonging, possibility, and choice at the foundation of human experience is crucial to any metaphysical and *practical* theology that seeks to offer transformative potential to humans suffering from the crippling effects of adverse childhood experience or any of the other myriad negative aspects of embodied life. Equally important is to see in our moment-to-moment experience where and how we encounter God—understood by most religious traditions as the primordial mystery at the base of all life—and how we can discern the best from among the many alternatives available to us. These aspects of life must either be universally available to all persons equally—as a *transpersonal reality*—or it is meaningless to speak about them at all. We have already examined how the loss of transpersonal projection can cause individuals to identify too closely with the powerful, unconscious energies of life, resulting in ego inflation and disconnection. As well, it is by this transpersonal reality that truly novel possibilities for actualization are offered.

In process thought, unlike in some classical Christian thought, a sure future does not yet exist; it has not already been determined in advance by God. As Mesle muses, "We are all on the verge of falling forward into nothingness; but, in each moment, the world becomes anew, and the creative advance continues."[178] The creative advance within our "ecological universe of moving relationships"[179] is characterized in three ways: (1) as *creativity*, or the "pure happening" of becoming and perishing; (2) as the *sphere of forms*, or the "pure longing for the unrealized and toward that which is new"; and (3) as *God*, that "concrete event within the process of processes" which "integrates creativity and forms."[180] In the philosophy of organism, God is necessary, dipolar, and mutually immanent within, and available to, the world in every moment.

A Dipolar God

God, like every entity in the philosophy of organism, is dipolar—both creative and responsive[181]—with a mental and a physical pole, or what Whitehead calls God's *primordial nature* and *consequent nature*. God's *primordial* nature is *transcendent* in that it is "nontemporal, eternal, and thus 'out of time,' transcending the temporal world while being essential for the processes of the temporal world."[182] It is also "infinite," "free," "conceptual," and "unconscious." For Whitehead, God as primordial is "the unlimited conceptual realization of the absolute wealth of potentiality" and does not precede creation but is "*with* all creation."[183] For Lee, God's primordial nature sustains the world's potentiality.[184] As primordial, God is the "lure for feeling, the eternal urge of desire"[185] or the "Cosmic Lover" who comes to the world as a "luring, attracting, enticing, inviting, soliciting" presence that "persuasively but not coercively" demands a response of love from creation.[186]

As God's primordial nature is only conceptual, it is therefore "deficiently actual," and if that were all there was to God, then God would be a "truncated subject."[187] Yet God also possesses a *consequent* nature that is "temporal," "determined," "actual," "physical," and "conscious." Here, God *receives the world* and transforms it;[188] here, the love of the world and of God flow back and forth, and God is the world's companion in its suffering.[189] As consequent, God takes what the world does and shapes it into a harmonious whole.[190] Whitehead poetically writes,

> The consequent nature of God is his judgment on the world. He saves the world as it passes into the immediacy of his own life. It is the judgment of a tenderness which loses nothing that can be saved. It is also the judgment of a wisdom which uses what in the temporal world is mere wreckage . . . [God] does not create the world, he saves it: or, more accurately, he is the poet of the world, with tender patience leading it by his vision of truth, beauty, and goodness.[191]

There is a dialectical relationship of contrasts between God and the world wherein "God's primordial unity acquires multiplicity in God's consequent nature, and the world's multiplicity acquires a consequent unity in God."[192] Moreover, God prehends the physical world from which each subject will emerge and then makes available in an ordered way possibilities that specifically fit that subject and its contemporary world.[193] In God's own process of concrescence, God conceptually offers possibilities, physically prehends and *feels* the world, is aware of the contrast between propositions and facts, weaves God's own physical feelings together with God's primordial vision,[194] and returns possibilities to the world. It is here where the value that the world has achieved is preserved[195] and held eternally in God's memory.

A Necessary God

For Pittenger, human beings naturally seek a reference that transcends the self and its world in order to make sense of our experience; we yearn to possess something that is inexhaustible, "mysteriously beckoning us toward ultimacies."[196] Throughout history, humans have called this transcendent referent God, defined by Cobb as "*a unitary actuality which is supremely worthy of worship and/or commitment.*"[197] Process theologians generally see this reality as an agency within embodied experience and not as a coercive being that occasionally disrupts the world from outside it. God "makes things make themselves" and for Pittenger, this insight holds together the secular and the religious in a way that provides "cosmic refreshment and companionship."[198]

Whitehead's God is essential to the workings of the cosmos[199] because if God is not the initiator of all occasions, we cannot explain "that what cannot be, yet is."[200] Whitehead's argument for God asserts:

- The living subjective moment cannot arise from the past world of objective "dead" fact but requires "living immediacy" to begin its forming;[201]
- The presence of genuine novelty requires the infusion of possibilities that are not just repetitions of forms already actualized;[202]

- It would be impossible for forming occasions to entertain all possibilities an unlimited universe might realize in any given moment without some kind of restriction;
- Our world displays order and value, rather than the chaos that would exist without such restriction;
- God must then be the "ground of order and value" that "selectively limits" possibilities and allows the experience of value within possibilities by providing its standard.[203]

If there is a God—a transpersonal reality that seeks our good and offers us novel possibilities—then how can we understand the painful aspects of our reality? How do we makes sense of the ongoing flux and change—and the creative diversity that we witness? Is there a point to all of it? Is there value to this world? Must a painful past be a life sentence or are there really possibilities for transformation?

Multiplicity and Flux

To be human—to be *embodied*—is to be part of a world of perpetual perishing and creation, of beauty and terror, of joy and sorrow. Although this is a painful reality, the multiplicity and flux that we see in the world is inevitable because of the *creativity*—what Bracken calls the "divine matrix"[204]—at the heart of reality. In Whitehead's scheme, creativity is both the "*ground* of events" and the "*ultimate principle* of cosmology" responsible for the fact that anything comes to be in existence at all. Faber describes it as a principle of both "*spontaneity* and *causality*."[205] Nontheistic process thinkers often describe *creativity* as being "ultimate" in the same way that theistic thinkers describe God, but A.H. Johnson provides key insights into the relationships between God, creativity, the "many" and the "one." He notes that creativity is ultimate not in the sense of having a "concrete character" or of being "an external agency with its own ulterior purposes," but only in the sense that nothing can be actual without exemplifying it. In fact, "creativity," "many," and "one," are all "ultimate" eternal objects because all are exemplified in every actuality. Creativity is a "characteristic of self-causation" and is only "saved from being a 'nonentity'" because God's primordial nature "envisages" it.[206]

In a sense, we can say that creativity is one reason for the flux and perpetual perishing we see in the world, yet creaturely freedom is also part of the story. We must remember that in Whitehead's process of concrescence, it is the individual entity that finally decides what it will be, what value it will (or will not) actualize. The presence of God's initial aims does not negate the freedom of actual entities that maintain their agency within relevant possibilities. No outcomes are predetermined by God or coerced into being by God. Therefore, as Christ argues, God's power is never dominating "power over," but always cooperative "power with," grounded in relationship and mutuality. "Goddess/God is the one for whom no individual in the universe ever becomes merely an 'it.'" God's role, she writes, is that of encourager or "mother" and nothing in the world is solely the result of a single will, "not even that of Goddess/God. Because the world is co-created, everything that happens does not happen according to divine will."[207]

We live, love, feel, and strive within a dynamically undulating and dipolar *but not bifurcated* mystery that is "both physical and mental . . . transient and persistent; it is fact and value together," because even timeless and immortal value has no meaning apart from the world of fact.[208] In other words, a world without fragmentary, multiplicitous, perpetually perishing aspects would be a world in which no value could be experienced as real because it would have no specificity. From this perspective, we may begin to glimpse that it is not only worldviews that can be wounding or healing: reality itself may carry both properties. How can a reality that allows for differentiation avoid wounding? How can a reality that intimately receives and feels everything the world gives and offers novel possibilities for positive change avoid healing? In a cosmos where differentiation and unity dance in constantly fluid motion, we may conclude that wounding and healing are dipolar dance partners, inextricably bound.

Value

According to Hosinski, Whitehead's ontological theory—that every occasion of any type is formed in the same way—allows us to embrace value and aesthetics at the base of experience. When we connect value and fact as fundamental aspects of every occasion, we can retain the insights of both the scientist and the poet.[209] Whitehead's theory, rather than placing all value and aesthetic qualities only in the individual, subjective realm, places them squarely within objective, embodied experience itself.

There are no inert substances at the base of things that endure unchanged through time. We recognize this empirical truth immediately when we think about the way in which an oak tree is no longer the acorn from which it began, and an adult human is no longer the infant. We are people-in-process, gaining and losing cells, growing and changing, living out the dance between order and chaos in every moment. For Whitehead, every actual entity is

> [A] drop of process, a pulse, a throb of existence, an event, a happening of value which sacrifices its immediacy in the instant it is gained, in the same

> manner as any "now" loses its nowness to a subsequent "now" . . . . What is permanent in the Whiteheadian scheme is not, therefore, some underlying stage upon which accidental change is played, but rather the value achieved, the world-unification effected by and in an entity whose self-creative process is the growing together of the public world in the privacy of a perspective. . . . To exist in the Whiteheadian sense is to self-actuate, to create a moment of "for-one's-self-ness," to be now.[210]

According to Kraus, the "foundational insight" of Whitehead's philosophy is expressed as two inseparable ideas: that value achievement is ongoing and that value attained is permanent.[211] Neither *being* nor *becoming* can therefore be preferenced; what is most real is the *value attained* in their dynamic dance. It is this value that every moment seeks to attain within its momentary existence and is what is passed along to the next moment.

Transformation

The creative dance of becoming inherently entails flux, perishing, and loss. This is the wounding reality of embodied existence. Therefore, all of us have things in our past that are painful. Yet many of us find ourselves thinking or behaving in ways that prevent our own flourishing because "old habits" or old patterns of thinking "die hard." For those of us who fight those battles, process thought provides a hopeful vision of reality because it promises that novelty or positive change—aligned with God's aims—is possible in every moment. We are embodied beings who change and change each other within our very aliveness.[212] In process theology, God is not the one who sanctions the status quo; rather, God is the "basic source of unrest in the universe" luring us toward value and novelty. As Whitehead notes, "The pure conservative is fighting against the essence of the universe."[213]

The process God stimulates us to seek and achieve the new when the existing is no longer sufficiently enjoyable or zesty.[214] The reason for being is to experience enjoyment, intensity, and adventure while maintaining some stability; therefore, God seeks novelty as much as order. In describing why God seeks intensity through novelty, Whitehead writes, "the origination of conceptual novelty" is "the primary meaning of life."[215] Ultimately, the creative purpose of being and becoming is to aim at contrast in order to achieve maximum intensity of feeling.[216] Living occasions are distinguished by their capacity for realizing flashes of such imaginative novelty.[217] At the same time, we must understand that neither order nor novelty are "intrinsically good" but are only "instrumental" to the "one intrinsic good" or "absolute end" which is "the enjoyment of intense experience."[218]

SUMMARY

In this chapter, I have shown that Whitehead's philosophy of organism: (1) describes the depths of unconscious experience as the source of dynamism, value, and creative advance; (2) describes an integrated and relational reality that grounds both the world and the individual; and, (3) respects and fosters multiplicity, diversity, and individual contributions of value. We can recognize now that process thought describes a world where everyone matters, everyone belongs, and everyone can experience positive change. We are part of a cosmos wherein we can encounter God as a transpersonal reality to whom we are internally related, who feels everything the world is and does, and who offers us possibilities for realization that are novel and will increase our enjoyment and zest for life. If this is all true of our outer world, what of our inner psyche? Is there a system of thought that shows our psychological selves as integrated and relational as well? This is our destination in the next chapter on Carl Gustav Jung and his analytical psychology.

NOTES

1. In this chapter and later discussions of Whitehead's thought, I draw most heavily from Whitehead's own work and the writing of Thomas E. Hosinski, CSC, a professor emeritus of the University of Portland. Though there are numerous Whiteheadian scholars whose work I admire and that I include herein, I find Hosinski's presentation of Whitehead's metaphysics to be eminently rich while still being accessible.

2. This is an idea that has been discussed by such authors in the self-help movement as Caroline Myss and Donna Jackson Nakazawa.

3. George Monbiot, "Neoliberalism Is Creating Loneliness. That's What's Wrenching Society Apart," *The Guardian*, October 12, 2016, https://www.theguardian.com/commentisfree/2016/oct/12/neoliberalism-creating-loneliness-wrenching-society-apart?CMP=share_btn_fb.

4. Hosinski, *Stubborn Fact and Creative Advance*, 43.

5. Susan Shotliff Mattingly, "Whitehead's Theory of Eternal Objects" (PhD, Austin, TX, University of Texas at Austin, 1968), ix.

6. Faber, *God as Poet of the World*, 22.

7. Mary Poplin and Dallas Willard, *Is Reality Secular?: Testing the Assumptions of Four Global Worldviews* (Downers Grove, IL: IVP Books, 2014), passim.

8. Coleman, *Making a Way Out of No Way*, 45.

9. Kraus, *The Metaphysics of Experience*, 2.

10. Ray S. Anderson, *The Shape of Practical Theology: Empowering Ministry with Theological Praxis* (Downers Grove, IL: IVP Academic, 2001), 12.

11. Eolene Boyd-MacMillan, "Loder and Mystical Spirituality: Particularity, Universality, and Intelligence," in *Redemptive Transformation in Practical Theology: Essays in Honor of James E. Loder Jr.*, ed. Dana R. Wright and John D. Kuentzel (Grand Rapids, MI: Wm. B. Eerdmans Publishing Company, 2004), 385.

12. Hosinski, *Stubborn Fact and Creative Advance*, 20.

13. Faber, *God as Poet of the World*, 22.

14. Faber, 22.

15. Hosinski, *Stubborn Fact and Creative Advance*, 20.

16. Kling, "Whitehead's Metaphysics as a Cosmological Framework for Transpersonal Psychology," 186.

17. Sarkar, *Whitehead's Four Principles from West-East Perspectives*, iii.

18. Faber, *God as Poet of the World*, 76.

19. Sarkar, *Whitehead's Four Principles from West-East Perspectives*, iii.

20. Sarkar, iii.

21. Faber, *God as Poet of the World*, 76.

22. Christ, *She Who Changes*, 45.

23. Whitehead, *Process and Reality*, xiv.

24. Faber, *God as Poet of the World*, 23–24.

25. Pittenger, *The Lure of Divine Love*, 10–11.

26. Kling, "Whitehead's Metaphysics as a Cosmological Framework for Transpersonal Psychology," 197.

27. Hosinski, *Stubborn Fact and Creative Advance*, 73–74.

28. Hosinski, 74.

29. Alfred North Whitehead, *The Function of Reason* (Boston: Beacon Press, 1958), 13.

30. Hosinski, *Stubborn Fact and Creative Advance*, 75–76.

31. Hosinski, 57.

32. Hosinski, 57.

33. Christ, *She Who Changes*, 55.

34. Mattingly, "Whitehead's Theory of Eternal Objects," 59.

35. Hosinski, *Stubborn Fact and Creative Advance*, 84.

36. Whitehead, *Process and Reality*, 108.

37. Whitehead, 33.

38. Kling, "Whitehead's Metaphysics as a Cosmological Framework for Transpersonal Psychology," 192.

39. Whitehead, *Process and Reality*, 45.

40. Whitehead, 45.

41. Whitehead, 108.

42. Hosinski, *Stubborn Fact and Creative Advance*, 59ff.

43. Kling, "Whitehead's Metaphysics as a Cosmological Framework for Transpersonal Psychology," 192–93.

44. Hosinski, *Stubborn Fact and Creative Advance*, 84.

45. Hosinski, 74.

46. Whitehead, *Process and Reality*, 244.

47. Hosinski, *Stubborn Fact and Creative Advance*, 73.

48. Hosinski, 59.

49. Alfred North Whitehead, *Science and the Modern World* (New York: The Free Press, 1967), 69–70.

50. Leslie A. Muray, *An Introduction to the Process Understanding of Science, Society and the Self: A Philosophy for Modern Humanity*, vol. 26, Symposium Series (Lewiston, NY: Edwin Mellen Press, 1988), 6.

51. Hosinski, *Stubborn Fact and Creative Advance*, 84.

52. Hosinski, 85.

53. Mattingly, "Whitehead's Theory of Eternal Objects," x.

54. Mattingly, vi.

55. Mattingly, 171.

56. Mattingly, x, 103.

57. Mattingly, 102.

58. Bernard J. Lee, *The Becoming of the Church: A Process Theology of the Structures of Christian Experience* (New York: Paulist Press, 1974), 66.

59. Lee, 66.

60. Sarkar, *Whitehead's Four Principles from West-East Perspectives*, 29–30.

61. Edward G. Ballard, "Kant and Whitehead, and the Philosophy of Mathematics," in *Studies in Whitehead's Philosophy*, vol. 10, Tulane Studies in Philosophy (New Orleans: Tulane University, 1961), 13.

62. Kling, "Whitehead's Metaphysics as a Cosmological Framework for Transpersonal Psychology," 189–90.

63. Faber, *God as Poet of the World*, 87.

64. Ballard, "Kant and Whitehead," 13.

65. Faber, *God as Poet of the World*, 87.

66. Mattingly, "Whitehead's Theory of Eternal Objects," 100.

67. Mattingly, 100.

68. Odin, *Process Metaphysics and Hua-Yen Buddhism*, 167–68.

69. Lee, *The Becoming of the Church*, 62, 89.

70. Whitehead, *Process and Reality*, 164.

71. Lee, *The Becoming of the Church*, 89.

72. Ballard, "Kant and Whitehead," 15.

73. Mattingly, "Whitehead's Theory of Eternal Objects," 64.

74. Kraus, *The Metaphysics of Experience*, 47.

75. Whitehead, *Process and Reality*, 164.

76. Whitehead, 33, 70.

77. Whitehead, 240.

78. Hosinski, *Stubborn Fact and Creative Advance*, 86.

79. Hosinski, 87.

80. Hosinski, 87.

81. Hosinski, 89.

82. Hosinski, 89.

83. Hosinski, 100.

84. Whitehead, *Process and Reality*, 24.

85. Whitehead, 25.

86. Hosinski, *Stubborn Fact and Creative Advance*, 81, 106.
87. Hosinski, 101.
88. Hosinski, 108.
89. Hosinski, 110.
90. Hosinski, 111.
91. Hosinski, 121.
92. Pittenger, *The Lure of Divine Love*, 25.
93. Kraus, *The Metaphysics of Experience*, 18.
94. Joseph Petek, "Introduction," in *Rethinking Whitehead's Symbolism: Thought, Language, Culture*, ed. Roland Faber, Jeffrey Bell, and Joseph Petek (Edinburgh: Edinburgh University Press, 2017), 2.
95. Whitehead, *Process and Reality*, 32.
96. Hosinski, *Stubborn Fact and Creative Advance*, 159.
97. Hosinski, 174.
98. Odin, *Process Metaphysics and Hua-Yen Buddhism*, 171.
99. Griffin, "A Metaphysical Psychology to Un-Locke Our Ailing World," 240.
100. Robertson, *Jungian Archetypes*, 133.
101. Kelsey, *Encounter With God*, 71–72.
102. Hosinski, *Stubborn Fact and Creative Advance*, 228.
103. Griffin, "A Metaphysical Psychology to Un-Locke Our Ailing World," 241.
104. Whitehead, *Adventures of Ideas*, 181.
105. Pittenger, *The Lure of Divine Love*, 35.
106. Donald W. Sherburne, ed., *A Key to Whitehead's Process and Reality* (Chicago: University of Chicago Press, 1966), 852.
107. Kling, "Whitehead's Metaphysics as a Cosmological Framework for Transpersonal Psychology," 194–95.
108. Mattingly, "Whitehead's Theory of Eternal Objects," 58.
109. Mattingly, 59.
110. Faber, *God as Poet of the World*, 22.
111. Faber, 23.
112. Whitehead, *Symbolism*, 7.
113. Steven Shaviro, "Whitehead on Causality and Perception," in *Rethinking Whitehead's Symbolism: Thought, Language, Culture*, ed. Roland Faber, Jeffrey Bell, and Joseph Petek (Edinburgh: Edinburgh University Press, 2017), 14.
114. Whitehead, *Symbolism*, 21.
115. Whitehead, 50.
116. Hosinski, *Stubborn Fact and Creative Advance*, 51–52.
117. Hosinski, 66.
118. Loomer, "The Size of God," 24.
119. Whitehead, *Symbolism*, 16, 39, 43.
120. Shaviro, "Whitehead on Causality and Perception," 18.
121. Hosinski, *Stubborn Fact and Creative Advance*, 70.
122. Shaviro, "Whitehead on Causality and Perception," 19–20.
123. Griffin, "A Metaphysical Psychology to Un-Locke Our Ailing World," 241.
124. Griffin, 242.

125. Whitehead, *Religion in the Making*, 90, 102.
126. Whitehead, *Symbolism*, 6.
127. Whitehead, 18.
128. Shaviro, "Whitehead on Causality and Perception," 22.
129. Kling, "Whitehead's Metaphysics as a Cosmological Framework for Transpersonal Psychology," 195.
130. Griffin, "A Metaphysical Psychology to Un-Locke Our Ailing World," 244.
131. Hosinski, *Stubborn Fact and Creative Advance*, 174.
132. Whitehead, *Process and Reality*, 244.
133. Loomer, "The Size of God," 40.
134. Loomer, 40.
135. Loomer, 40.
136. Hosinski, *Stubborn Fact and Creative Advance*, 138–39.
137. Joseph A. Bracken, *The One in the Many: A Contemporary Reconstruction of the God-World Relationship* (Grand Rapids, MI: Wm. B. Eerdmans Publishing Company, 2001), 4.
138. Lee, *The Becoming of the Church*, 62.
139. Loomer, "The Size of God," 41.
140. C. Robert Mesle, *Process-Relational Philosophy: An Introduction to Alfred North Whitehead* (West Conshohocken, PA: Templeton Press, 2008), 3.
141. Loomer, "The Size of God," 41.
142. Lee, *The Becoming of the Church*, 62.
143. Loomer, "The Size of God," 25.
144. Pittenger, *The Lure of Divine Love*, 143.
145. Pittenger, 144.
146. Pittenger, 144.
147. Whitehead, *Process and Reality*, 6.
148. Whitehead, 246.
149. Whitehead, 6.
150. A. H. Johnson, *Whitehead's Theory of Reality* (New York: Dover Publications, 1962), 76.
151. Whitehead, *Process and Reality*, 108.
152. Hosinski, *Stubborn Fact and Creative Advance*, 138.
153. Kling, "Whitehead's Metaphysics as a Cosmological Framework for Transpersonal Psychology," 190.
154. Alfred North Whitehead, *Modes of Thought* (New York: The Free Press, 1968), 232.
155. Pittenger, *The Lure of Divine Love*, 9.
156. Pittenger, 10.
157. Loomer, "The Size of God," 29.
158. Loomer, 29.
159. Whitehead, *Adventures of Ideas*, 187–88.
160. Kraus, *The Metaphysics of Experience*, 59–60.
161. Hosinski, *Stubborn Fact and Creative Advance*, 65.
162. Hosinski, 44.

163. Mesle, *Process-Relational Philosophy*, 23.
164. Mesle, 23.
165. Hosinski, *Stubborn Fact and Creative Advance*, 51.
166. Whitehead, *Adventures of Ideas*, 189.
167. Whitehead, *Modes of Thought*, 21, 114.
168. Whitehead, *Adventures of Ideas*, 189.
169. Whitehead, *Process and Reality*, 75–76.
170. Cobb Jr. and Griffin, *Process Theology*, 115.
171. Hosinski, *Stubborn Fact and Creative Advance*, 43.
172. Bruce G. Epperly, "Process Theology and the Healing Adventure: Reflections on Spirituality and Medicine," in *Handbook of Process Theology*, ed. Donna Bowman and Jay McDaniel (St. Louis, MO: Chalice Press, 2006), 95.
173. Alan W. Watts, *The Tao of Philosophy*, audiocassette (Electronic University Publishing, 1995).
174. Faber, *God as Poet of the World*, 46–47.
175. Robertson, *Jungian Archetypes*, 230.
176. Christ, *She Who Changes*, 56.
177. Epperly, "Process Theology and the Healing Adventure," 95.
178. Mesle, *Process-Relational Philosophy*, 5.
179. Faber, *God as Poet of the World*, 24.
180. Faber, 24.
181. Cobb Jr. and Griffin, *Process Theology*, 60.
182. Hosinski, *Stubborn Fact and Creative Advance*, 176.
183. Whitehead, *Process and Reality*, 343.
184. Lee, *The Becoming of the Church*, 66.
185. Whitehead, *Process and Reality*, 344.
186. Pittenger, *The Lure of Divine Love*, 6.
187. Hosinski, *Stubborn Fact and Creative Advance*, 187–88.
188. Hosinski, 201.
189. Sarkar, *Whitehead's Four Principles from West-East Perspectives*, 71.
190. Faber, *God as Poet of the World*, 15.
191. Whitehead, *Process and Reality*, 346.
192. Sarkar, *Whitehead's Four Principles from West-East Perspectives*, 64.
193. Mattingly, "Whitehead's Theory of Eternal Objects," 153.
194. Whitehead, *Process and Reality*, 345.
195. Loomer, "The Size of God," 50.
196. Pittenger, *The Lure of Divine Love*, 14–15.
197. Cobb Jr., *God and the World*, 20.
198. Pittenger, *The Lure of Divine Love*, 15.
199. A fuller exploration of God as necessary in Whitehead's thought first appeared in Kling, "Whitehead's Metaphysics as a Cosmological Framework for Transpersonal Psychology," 186–87.
200. Whitehead, *Process and Reality*, 350.
201. Hosinski, *Stubborn Fact and Creative Advance*, 159.
202. Mattingly, "Whitehead's Theory of Eternal Objects," 99.

203. Hosinski, *Stubborn Fact and Creative Advance*, 159–60.
204. Joseph A. Bracken, *The Divine Matrix: Creativity as Link between East and West* (Maryknoll, NY: Orbis Books, 1995), passim.
205. Faber, *God as Poet of the World*, 76.
206. Johnson, *Whitehead's Theory of Reality*, 70.
207. Christ, *She Who Changes*, 93–94.
208. Sarkar, *Whitehead's Four Principles from West-East Perspectives*, 15.
209. Hosinski, *Stubborn Fact and Creative Advance*, 94–95.
210. Kraus, *The Metaphysics of Experience*, 2.
211. Kraus, 3.
212. Christ, *She Who Changes*, 45.
213. Cobb Jr. and Griffin, *Process Theology*, 59.
214. Cobb Jr. and Griffin, 59, 60.
215. Whitehead, *Process and Reality*, 102.
216. Whitehead, 249.
217. Whitehead, 184.
218. Cobb Jr. and Griffin, *Process Theology*, 59.

Chapter 4

Empirical

An Integrated, Relational Psyche

INTRODUCTION

This chapter on C. G. Jung's analytical psychology begins with goals similar to those in the previous chapter: in order for this system of thought to counter the fragmenting effects of the dominant worldview in American culture it, too, must show (1) that we have value, that we *matter*; (2) that we *belong*; and (3) that we can experience *positive change*. In addition, if it is our goal to synthesize Whitehead's theoretical and Jung's empirical resources, we must also show that Jung's psychology is to the human psyche as Whitehead's metaphysics is to the cosmos. In the following pages, I will demonstrate that Jungian thought (1) describes the depths of unconscious experience as the source of vitality, dynamism, and creativity in human life; (2) describes an integrated and relational psyche; and, (3) respects and fosters individual contributions of value.

PSYCHOLOGICAL FOUNDATIONS

We will begin by examining the foundations of Jung's psychology, focusing on the conscious and unconscious psyche, ego and Self, the relationship between mind, body, and world, how human experience includes persona, neurosis, and trauma, and the process of individuation. Whereas in the last chapter we discussed the *beginnings* of experience, here we will explore the primordial life and objective psyche at the *depths* of experience followed by an analysis of Jung's ideas regarding transpersonal reality, including the collective unconscious, archetypes and archetypal images, archetypal value and synchronicity, and finally Jung's understanding of God and the healing power of the unconscious.

CONSCIOUS AND UNCONSCIOUS

The foundations of Jung's analytical psychology begin with the human psyche, something that, in many respects, is impossible to define. Because the psyche "mediates all experience," Shelburne reminds us that there is no place from outside psychic life that would "enable us to form an ultimate judgment of what the psyche is."[1] Though we may never be able to definitively define the nature of the human psyche, we can begin to explore the ways in which it seems to function. Jung and his early teacher Sigmund Freud developed their own theories. Freud viewed the human mind as a system constantly attempting to maintain a dynamic equilibrium between opposing forces. His "structural hypothesis" described the mind as tripartite and made up of ego, id, and superego. Those three "are not immutably demarcated compartments," explains Jacob Arlow, "but operational concepts." Intrapsychic conflict reveals these different functional centers.[2] For Freud, the mind's equilibrium "was constantly being disturbed and reestablished."[3] Following his mentor's lead in this area, Jung also describes the human psyche as a "self-regulating system that maintains itself in equilibrium as the body does."[4] For both Freud and Jung, the human psyche is both conscious and unconscious.

Jung described consciousness as "intensive and concentrated," "transient" and more concerned with what is immediately present. He considered anything that came into awareness as taking on the quality of consciousness and what did not rise to consciousness, remained unconscious. In Jung's system, as in Freud's, the "organ of awareness" is referred to as the "ego," yet for Jung, there was another sphere outside the ego that he characterized as the unconscious, non-ego field. The unconscious is not concentrated, but "shades off into obscurity," is "highly extensive" and "can juxtapose the most heterogeneous elements in the most paradoxical way."[5] The ego is a "changeable" *complex* with a "fluctuating composition"; it is the "image or reflection of all the activities comprehended by it"[6] and so is not a substantial entity. Consciousness and unconsciousness are in a constant state of dynamic interplay and so they are understood as being part of the same system, though not alike.[7] In the same way that particle physicists can only view subatomic particles "through their by-products," Robertson notes that the unconscious can only be seen through its by-products as well.[8] Because Jung perceived effects that did not originate in consciousness, he was "compelled" to hypothesize their roots to be in an unconscious realm.[9]

According to Singer, Jung differentiates even further between two layers of the unconscious by identifying a *personal unconscious* and a *collective unconscious*. Moreover, the collective unconscious is impersonal, transpersonal, universal, and "detached from anything personal." He described it as universal because its contents are found "everywhere."[10] A favorite metaphor of Jung's was that "individual consciousness is only the flower and the fruit of a season, sprung from the perennial rhizome beneath the earth . . ."[11] For Jung, the collective unconscious is built up over time with layer after layer of human experience. If we were to personify it, Jung writes, it would include both sexes, all ages, birth, death, and "would possess the living sense of the rhythm of growth, flowering and decay."[12]

Jung taught that the interplay between consciousness and unconsciousness is compensatory in nature, meaning that whenever the attitude of the conscious ego goes too far in one direction (preferencing any one of the inherently opposing energies in the psyche over its counterpart), there is an "immediate" and "inevitable" opposite movement "called forth" from the unconscious to bring the system back into balance.[13] Robertson compares its functioning to that of a "complex version of a thermostat . . . cooling things down when they get too hot, heating them up when too cold."[14] This movement sparks a flow of symbolic imagery that can appear in dreams and in other nondirected, or nonconscious, thinking. When unconscious elements are energized by the psyche's unbalanced state, those contents break into consciousness and disrupt conscious intentions.[15] Such adjustments are crucial for the existence of both the human metabolism and human psyche.[16] The problem in modern times, Jung felt, was that the overemphasis on the directedness of consciousness and dismissal of the unconscious material as "incompatible" had created such an inhibition of unconscious material that the compensatory function was no longer effective. "To this extent," he wrote, "the psyche of civilized [people] is no longer a self-regulating system but could rather be compared to a machine whose speed-regulation is so insensitive that it can continue to function to the point of self-injury, while on the other hand it is subject to the arbitrary manipulations of a one-sided will."[17]

The key elements of this section reveal that Jung saw the human psyche as made up of a conscious ego and an unconscious non-ego field, with these two aspects in a constant dialectical relationship. Due to the compensatory nature of the relationship between conscious and unconscious, we can understand the unconscious as providing whatever the conscious ego needs to regain its balance. In other words, it provides whatever the individual needs to flourish. It is important to note that as with Whitehead, the most basic elements of Jung's system are in no way static entities; rather, they are fluid elements in dynamic interplay. In Jung's description of the individual consciousness as arising from the perennial rhizome of the unconscious, we are reminded of Whitehead's view that individual entities particularize the extensive continuum. Each is a rupturing, a breaking through of individuality and of uniquely expressed value.

Ego and Self

Whereas in Whitehead's thought the individual person we know ourselves to be—what we typically refer to as the *self*—is viewed as a *historic route of occasions*, we might refer to Jung's *ego* as a *historic route of images*. Jung describes the *ego* or *ego complex* as a composite of images of sensory functioning from internal and external stimuli and of the accumulated images of past processes all held together by the "powerful cohesive force" of conscious, directed thinking.[18] In addition to the compensatory role of the psyche, there is an element in the unconscious that plays an organizing or ordering role, and it is from these unconscious depths of human life that the more-fleeting consciousness emerges. Robertson uses the example of driving a car to note how the unconscious apparently organizes and makes available to consciousness the memories of previous driving experience. When we draw upon those past experiences of driving—that we are not accessing consciously in every moment—those memories must be organized and presented by some aspect of psyche that is at a "higher level" than the memories themselves. Echoing Whitehead's view that a necessary God presents relevant possibilities to each forming moment, Jung's unconscious cannot be just a static memory bank or repository, but must be an active "organizational entity which serves and even anticipates the needs of consciousness."[19]

Jung saw the psyche as "archetypal," and its "structuring or ordering principle" he called the archetypal *Self*.[20] McGehee describes this Self as an integrative "force" that holds all the "disparate, paradoxical, and often conflictual elements" of the psyche together.[21] The Self is "that factor in the psychic economy which establishes wholeness" and the "unifying center" of the person and, therefore, is "indistinguishable from the God-image, which represents the highest unifying factor."[22] It is experienced by the ego as a "spiritual event" and Kalsched notes that it has been referred to by mystics historically as the "ground of the soul," "the little castle," the "secret dwelling where God resides," and "the center of my created being which remains permanently united with God's creative act . . . the sanctuary without images."[23]

In his ideas on the Self, Jung drew from Hinduism's concept of *Atman*; the relationship between the "ineffable subject of the unconscious" and the "phenomenal subject of consciousness" creates an ego-Self axis that guides the individuation process.[24] Tacey goes so far as to summarize Jung's entire psychology as a "science of the relations between the human person (ego) and the God Within (the Self)."[25] Jung first encountered this "not-I"[26] or "objective 'knower'" in the psyche in a dream of his own wherein a "superordinate wisdom from the deep unconscious" communicated:

> I can see your wholeness . . . and in order to convince you of this, I'm going to present my image of your wholeness in universal imagery of aliveness, beauty, color, and light, all around a radiant center which has everything to do with you, and only with you. And the closer you get to this center of your own particular, individual, irreplaceable life—including your own abysmal sadness—the closer you get to me.[27]

Though the common understanding of the term "self" typically equates it with the conscious ego, Jung saw the archetypal Self as both personal or immanent *and* transcendent. It is the "paradox from which all paradox originated" and "cannot be limited by human expectations."[28]

The Self and its wisdom produce dreams; working with dreams, then, is the "paramount method in Jungian analysis."[29] In fact, it is because of the space- and time-ranging images in dreams that Jung determined the Self to stand outside of space and time. The Self is "the dreamer's deepest personality, the process of development, and the goal of the process" all at the same time.[30] It is a center that the ego "circumambulates" while also being the "superordinate factor" to which the ego "is subordinate."[31] It represents both the "centering tendency" of the psyche as well as its "final conscious unity"; it is "the teleological aim of individuation," and the "union of opposites."[32] Haule likens the Self to the life of an amoeba, a being which has no ego or "organ of command" while still having the ability to organize its own capacities for optimum life experience. He describes human wholeness as a "ceaseless homeodynamic system operating mostly out of our awareness."[33] Over time, Jung came to associate various themes and images with the Self including circular mandalas and "quadrated figures,"[34] totality, the union of opposites, "the central generative point, the world navel, the axis of the universe," the "elixir of life,"[35] a great tree or mountain, or even "the Wise Old One" or "the Queen" (or King)."[36] But the Self is not a static, once-for-all-time image; it is a God-image that changes with personal and collective needs.

Now we can see that the human psyche, as Jung understood it, is highly relational in its constant dialogue between conscious and unconscious, and between ego and Self. The Self, moreover, integrates and orders the psyche's experience, holding it all together, and is both immanent God-image within, and transcendent because it is outside of space and time. Yet, for Jung, transcendent never means disembodied or supernatural and it is, in fact, the archetypal Self that unifies mind and body.

Mind, Body, World

Jung was certainly no dualist. In *The Structure and Dynamics of the Psyche*, he wrote that he could not imagine life in the abstract sense, but only "in the form of a living body."[37] The body is not a "mere heaping together of inert matter" but is a "material system ready for life" that yet cannot live without the "living being" or "psychic factor" made up of "living processes."[38] What he called "the psyche" is made up of an "almost infinite series" of images reproduced by the brain to represent unconscious bodily states and impressions and the conscious ego is the unifying force that holds them together.[39] When Jung asserts that what is real to us is psychic, some have interpreted his stance in a Kantian sense. Such an interpretation is unwarranted because Jung was trying to counter the materialist and mechanistic views that were in vogue at the height of modernism. As a counterpoint to physicalist positions in behaviorism and the hard sciences, he thought it "almost absurd" to believe that existence is only physical; instead, he wrote, "the only form of existence of which we have immediate knowledge is psychic."[40] Moreover, his use of the term "immediate knowledge" was most likely used to indicate "conscious awareness" or "understanding,"[41] which, of course, is entirely psychic.

Jung in no way believed that the mind created the objective world. He had no doubt that an objective world was "encountered outwardly"; yet he also gave the same credence to an objective world that was "experienced inwardly." Inner and outer worlds are "nature,"[42] and, he speculated, both could be known only "as phenomena and never as the 'thing-in-itself'" because humans could not yet understand the true nature either of matter or of God.[43] In fact, Jung speculated that psyche and matter were ultimately identical[44] because he saw archetypes as participating in both. They are *material*, existing in the body "at the level of instincts" *and* they are *immaterial*, existing transpersonally as form. They have a "bodily, instinctual" pole and a spiritual pole, and both are "vitally interrelated."[45] Rowland compares Jung's "subtle body" to Judith Butler's "discursive body," noting that Jung's subtle body is not a creature of either body or mind; it is their unification rather than their bifurcation. For Jung, only symbols can serve to describe the subtle body.[46] In fact, it is the archetype of the Self that serves as the unifying point for body, soul, mind, and spirit, forming an "integrated whole" especially in the process of individuation, when unconscious contents are assimilated to the ego.[47]

In her critique of Jung's archetypal theory, Goldenberg claims that "feminine theory [should] radically depart from the Jungian archetype, from the Platonic form, from all systems of thought which posit transcendent, superhuman deities" suggesting instead that it focus on the body as the center of all human experience.[48] Yet basing all our inspiration in the solitary human body seems antithetical to the principle of interrelatedness and interconnectedness so crucial to feminist thought. Even contemporary Jungians question this stance, as does James Hillman in his forward to Theodore Roszak's text *EcoPsychology* where he asks where the "me" ends and "the other" begins. "For most of its history," writes Hillman, "psychology took for granted an intentional subject: the biographical 'me' that was the agent and sufferer of all 'doings.' For most of its history, psychology located this 'me' within human persons defined by their physical skin and their immediate behavior." Yet in recent decades, he notes, much of that thinking has either been called into question or "junked" entirely, as we can no longer be sure where to "make the cut between 'me' and 'not-me.'" Making that cut between the self and the natural world, he concludes, is "arbitrary" and we must recognize that we cannot be certain about such differentiation.[49] Stephen Aizenstat of Pacifica Graduate Institute, too, sees the human psyche as essentially rooted "in the rhythms of nature."[50] Goldenberg's charges of dualism aimed at Jung are therefore clearly misplaced. Moreover, there are still valid and valuable resources within the Jungian frame to counter the dualistic, mechanistic thinking that contributes to our fragmentation. We turn now to the psyche's response to the slings and arrows we inevitably encounter as we move through life.

Persona, Neurosis, and Trauma

As the First Noble Truth of Buddhism tells us, life is suffering. To be human, it seems, is to have problems; here again we encounter the wounding of life experience. When the inevitable problems arise, resourceful and creative humans can often find a myriad of ways to resolve them—both individually and collectively. On the other hand, mental health providers' offices are full of people with seemingly unsolvable problems while many more suffering people never even grace the thresholds of those that stand ready to help. For many, self-sabotaging behavior and difficult interpersonal relations seem to return with revolving-door regularity, often correlated with substance abuse or despair. Such distress may often fall into the clinical category of neurosis.

For Jung, personality only develops at all because of the tensions between opposing forces that "underpin" the psyche.[51] Such conflicts include those between the instinctual and the spiritual and those between our personal desires and collective expectations. Halligan notes that we must compromise in order to manage those conflicts, especially during the first half of life when one's gender identity and ego-strengths are developing. The compromises we make require "role-playing and a certain degree of falsification" and so the way we move through the world is called our *persona*.[52]

While one's persona is held in consciousness, any elements of personality that we do not accept—whether the qualities we find unappealing or the positive aspects we are not yet willing to claim—are held in the unconscious and make up what Jung called the *shadow*. In dream images, the shadow is typically personified as the same sex yet very unlike the dreamer. The shadow figure may carry characteristics that repel or attract us; either way, those characteristics are not embraced. The shadow represents what we have denied or repressed about ourselves.[53] As Robertson notes, it is in a compensatory response that the shadow is activated when one's ego consciousness has become unbalanced and is no longer manifesting the natural wholeness of the organizing Self. The shadow develops whenever the "ego has accepted a limited definition of itself, at the expense of undeveloped possibilities or denied desires, frequently those of the body."[54]

In his clinical experiences with patients, Jung observed that their dreams included images of both masculine and feminine characters, and so he concluded that the psyches of men and women contain both masculine and feminine aspects. Every culture, society, or era generally considers some behaviors more acceptable than others for each gender, and so behaviors typically associated with one's opposite sex are often relegated to the unconscious where they are personified as contra-sexual figures in the same way that unembraced characteristics of personality become a same-sex shadow figure. "This female within the male Jung called the anima," Robertson writes, while "the male within the female he termed the animus."[55] As noted in chapter 2, it is this area of Jungian psychology that has drawn the most serious criticism from feminist scholars. Yet it is important to note that at their most basic levels, Jung believed that the archetypes of anima and animus are merely predispositions to form personified images that represent the relationship between the ego and the unconscious, and are therefore empty of specific content.[56] Specific images or symbols formed are the result of personal experience and cultural conditioning. Therefore, the function precedes the personification. As one's personality develops beyond gender identity and a functioning ego, the process that Jung called individuation becomes more focused on wholeness and unification of the personality. This requires that what was held in the unconscious must be integrated within one's conscious identity. He referred to this result as the "inner marriage."[57]

Also within the unconscious human psyche are the complexes that can so negatively affect our personal lives. Even if we experienced healthy childhoods and loving parents, McGehee reminds us that having complexes is just part of every human life.[58] Complexes emerge because the psyche is naturally dissociative and tends to "divide itself up into parts" whenever it is "faced with anxiety."[59] Jung first posited the existence of psychological complexes when he observed patients who exhibited slower responses to certain words during word association exercises. For example, a patient may have responded more slowly to any words having to do with the idea of "mother," and so Jung surmised that psychic or emotional energy had become trapped in the psyche around mother.[60] The purpose of analysis, then, is to dig beneath personal memories to uncover the root of the complex. When Jung did this work with his patients, he found that the core of the mother complex was not so much personal memories of mother, but "a collective, archetypal memory of the complex relationship between child and mother," according to Robertson. He discovered that in situations that resemble those long-repeated in human history, archetypes are activated, and personal memories and images "accumulate" around those archetypes to form complexes.[61]

In other words, there is a basic idea of what *mother* is and does that then acts as the lattice structure upon which each era or culture's specific expectations of how mothers behave is hung. When our personal experience collides with those expectations, Young-Eisendrath and Hall note that we can tend to "collect" our own experiences around a "compelling affective-imaginal core" in a "loosely coherent" way that then becomes a "motivational system of emotion and image-formation that is associated with habitual thoughts, actions, feelings, and other images."[62] Our unconscious complexes can wreak havoc in our personal lives, as they are most often triggered in our significant relationships, causing something akin to a "trance state" when we are "beside ourselves" and automatically "re-experience" emotions and images that arise simply because another person's mannerisms or appearance evoke that unconscious complex.[63] At such times, we can appear to be incapable of acting consciously. McGehee describes complexes as constrictive, "chronic, low-grade, and often lifelong viewpoints we have about ourselves" that limit human wholeness and well-being.[64] Yet—and this is good news for anyone with adverse childhood experiences that have become entrenched as limiting beliefs—such complexes will "fall apart" when brought to consciousness and integrated into the personality.[65]

Jung viewed neurosis as the result of a "self-division"[66] or "inner cleavage" wherein one's conscious mind and unconscious mind are in opposition.[67] Polarized factions might be one's spiritual self against one's sensual self—one's "better angels" against one's "lesser angels"—or even just what is consciously known and accepted versus what is unconscious and denied. According to Jung, "What drives people to war with themselves is the intuition or the knowledge that they consist of two persons in opposition to one another . . . It is what Faust meant when he says: 'Two souls, alas, dwell in my breast apart.'"[68] Regardless of the cause, what differentiates mere problems from neuroses is that a neurosis is the result of an inability of the individual to solve their own intra-psychic conflicts.[69] But it may be even broader than that. Within his own analytic practice, Heisig finds that he can no longer "distinguish clearly between neurosis of self and neurosis of world" due to the culture's fragmenting forces, and that he must dramatically extend his understanding of neurosis and psychopathology.[70] It seems we may be justified, then, in calling into question the presumed originating causes of modern neuroses and again draw the lens back to see the effects of our culture and worldview upon our personal psyches. Persona, shadow, and complexes are all interwoven parts of the human psyche; and—as in Whitehead's metaphysics—so is the basic drive to bring something of value individually and creatively to the communal web of life.

Individuation and Value: One's Own Being

As we saw in our earlier discussion of the structure of the psyche, Jung considered the ego to be the center of consciousness and the Self to be the center of the complete person that integrates the unconscious with the conscious part of the psyche. One might be forgiven for describing the Self as an "enigma wrapped in a paradox," for it is maddeningly both the "state of wholeness that is the goal of individuation" while also being "the state of undifferentiated wholeness from which we come."[71] Most importantly, the Self is the "not known," the "numinous, potential, unconscious nature of every person" and knowledge of one's Self is the purpose of *individuation*.[72] According to Singer, the energy that "provides the thrust" for the process of individuation is "goal-directed" and "purposive." Being in the pull of such energy

> feels as if one were being drawn toward a center of great luminosity, yet to fly straight into it would be like a moth darting into a flame or the earth hurtling itself into the center of the sun. So one moves around the center instead, close enough to see the brightness, to feel the warmth, but maintaining the orbital tension, a dynamic relationship of a small finite being to a source of light and energy that has no limits.[73]

Individuation is the journey and the process of developing an ongoing dialogue between one's conscious and unconscious, persona and shadow, conscious gender and unconscious contra-sexual elements,[74] so as to consciously realize and integrate "all of the possibilities contained within the individual."[75] Robertson links it to finding a "harmonious balance" between the physical, emotional, mental, and spiritual aspects of human life. While modern society's drive for humans is to use rationality to keep instincts and spiritual needs in check and the Church's drive is for spiritual "perfection," both have contributed to the repression of all that is not valued into the unconscious shadow. Jung alternatively realized that wholeness or personal unity should be our "proper goal."[76] This unity cannot be made at the expense of the unconscious psyche and demands "both control and harmony."[77]

For Jung, Kalsched reminds us, wholeness is not merely an abstract idea, but specifically tied to "psycho-spiritual integration."[78] The journey to such wholeness is "a lifelong task" and an "elaborate and subtle process" in which one develops one's "recessive potentials"[79] and develops a "healthy recognition and acceptance of who one truly is, in one's essence and totality."[80] Kalsched sees this urge for human wholeness and fulfillment of potential as central to Jung who understood it as universal and an idea that pursues us as much as we pursue it. It unfolds from within us as the process of individuation.[81] To realize oneself, as Jung wrote in his *Seven Sermons to the Dead*, means to actualize the distinctiveness of one's being.[82] Though teleological, the Self is not so much a goal but the image that "governs" the process of individuation; "one does not so much 'become' [the Self] as one allows it to manifest itself."[83]

What is the value of manifesting "one's own being" in the world? For Jung—who witnessed the devastation of two world wars—conforming to "collective consciousness" and becoming what he called a "mass man" was to be the subject of "stifling" collective attitudes. Far from aligning with the status quo, Jung saw the individuation process as one that led to the ability to live according to one's own lights and purpose[84] rather than being seduced by various negative but powerful ideologies. People entranced by any "'ism" are those, according to Jung, who have "the least access to their interior selves and have strayed the furthest from their instinctual roots into the truly chaotic world of *collective* consciousness."[85] He argued that true morality rests on the *individual's* moral sense and freedom whereas "the morality of a society as a whole is in inverse ratio to its size; for the greater the aggregation of individuals, the more the individual factors are blotted out, and with them morality . . ." For the "mass man," mediocrity rules.[86]

Jung's student, Erich Neumann, developed this idea even further, noting that morality comes from the "Voice of the Self" and through acceptance of one's shadow which "involves a growth in depth into the ground of one's own being, and with the loss of the airy illusion of an ego-ideal, a new depth and rootedness and stability is born." Such a stance initiates a perspective wherein "continuous self-questioning and self-control is now required."[87] In order to be self-reflective, argue Young-Eisendrath and Hall, one must be able to differentiate oneself from one's original identity that was so strongly shaped by parental complexes. These tend, in the first half of life, to "overtake conscious subjectivity with ideas, moods, and habits" that seem to be "autonomous."[88] In other words, if one remains unconscious and unintegrated, one becomes the "puppet" of one's unconsciously held complexes and agendas. The degree to which parental complexes remain unquestioned components of one's reality is the degree to which one will be incapable of becoming a "psychological individual—one capable of self-reflection, personal responsibility, and personal meaning."[89]

Human development is a process of growth and learning; through individuation, archetypes educate the ego due to the compensatory relationship between consciousness and the "superior and better guide" of the unconscious.[90] According to Singer, the process is marked by development of the personality, it is inherently relational and cannot happen in isolation, and it requires some opposition to invalid social norms, because, as has already been noted, the more one is shaped by collective norms, the more immoral one is likely to become.[91] The process of individuation does not lead one to a solipsistic soliloquy of self-containment. Instead, it is the act of becoming "an indivisible unity, a particular, single, and unique person" that allows one to be in relationship with others. Ann and Barry Ulanov expand on Jung when they argue that real individuals are built out of "hard fact and experience," and such life experience is what gives a person the tools to build actual relationships with others and relate to them in an authentic way. "Pseudo individuals" who have not constructed their individuality and a genuine psychic core can only relate to others in a surface way because "only a sham person is there." Individuated people, on the other hand, recognize that "all people have the same kind of inner life and the same kind of urge to become unique, unified, and whole persons."[92]

Being in real relationship with others seems to be in short supply in modern America. Yet the good news—not only for those suffering from the effects of alienation, loneliness, or adverse childhood experiences but for every one of us—is that the psyche is intrinsically self-healing and uses the process of individuation to achieve greater wholeness and psychic health. "If the ego is damaged by traumatic events, or has evolved in too fragile a manner," notes Kalsched, "then the unconscious will compensate and provide positive energies." On the other hand, an ego that is overly confident "will find itself facing tremendous and perhaps horrifying opposition from below."[93] Although it can be a "difficult and perilous path"[94] where "inadequate patterns" die[95] and may feel like a "via crucis,"[96] individuation is a "teleological process" wherein the limited ego consciousness learns to "bow" to the more widely perspectival Self "to develop an ever-deeper relationship with the mythical, numinous forces of the unconscious in order to make it a journey of meaning and value."[97] This difficult but enriching process, according to Singer, increases a person's sense of self-worth even when she may be rejected by the collective, and establishes her inner values, thereby restoring her faith in herself. Even those who achieve worldly acclaim may learn through individuating that they had access to untapped riches in their own unconscious.[98]

Yet Bulkeley cautions us not to conclude that we must reject consciousness in favor of unconscious guidance at every turn. No, the "vital task" of consciousness is not to control or surrender to the unconscious but to "understand," integrate, and "actualize" its contents to broaden and balance self-awareness.[99] Haule calls the Self a "trickster sage" and notes that Neumann advised that the Self's tempting and anti-establishment Voice "must always be listened to—though not always followed" because it is "unpredictable, inexhaustible, and dangerous when taken seriously."[100] Creativity in its most raw form is not necessarily moral, and this may be as true for Whitehead as it is for Jung. Overall, though, individuation is a healthy process and goal that dissolves grandiosity, helps individuals to withdraw projections, and ultimately results in "greater consciousness of the full range of conscious and unconscious impulses, actions, and symbolic meaning."[101] From this center, notes Aizenstat, we can "witness" what is happening in the moment without being "compelled to act" and interact with the images that arise from the unconscious "more freely."[102] Even more important, realizing the unifying capacity of the Self is to manifest "the highest point on the scale of objective values" where one's symbols "can no longer be distinguished from the Imago Dei."[103] With Clement of Alexandria, Jung stresses that "he who knows himself knows God."[104]

In thinking about the relationship between what is "above" and what is "below," or between the macro and the micro, we can—in a way that may be more similetic than ontologically comparative—imagine Jung's thought described above as the macro level and Whitehead's thought as the micro level. For example, at Jung's macro level of the human being, a person in the process of individuation brings unconscious material to consciousness for consideration and integration; at Whitehead's micro level of the moment of experience, an entity in the process of concrescence uses its supplemental phases to bring unconscious propositions and propositional feelings to intellectual feelings for consideration and integration. At Whitehead's micro level, "the many become one and are increased by one,"[105] an idea that may, at first, seem oppositional to Jung's idea that the distinct individual arises from undifferentiated wholeness and then returns to wholeness. But in Whitehead, this is not a linear process with a clear and distinct beginning in either unity or differentiation; it is much more circular in nature. On Whitehead's micro level, the individual entity is constituted by its relationships with others and encounters those objective others within itself. It then decides what it will be in its own solitude, and, upon perishing as a subjective unity, is again in relationship with the rest of the world. Similarly, on Jung's macro level, the human person is formed through its relationship with the unconscious, integrates his or her own experiences within him/herself, and, as an integrated, whole person, can then enter into truly intimate relationships with others. In the next section, we will see how this encounter with the unconscious at the depths of the psyche is truly—as at Whitehead's micro level—an encounter with an objective Other.

THE DEPTHS OF EXPERIENCE: PRIMORDIAL LIFE AND OBJECTIVE PSYCHE

Evocative of Whitehead's "living immediacy" and *creativity*, Sigmund Freud and Carl Jung both described a psychological reality where the human encounters that "original strata of human life" or the "rushing river of being"[106] that flows through one in a torrent of unconscious, active, generative life. Freud called this *primary-process thinking* and Jung called it *non-directed thinking*; for both it is primordial human experience. Ann and Barry Ulanov call it "inexhaustible," and an "eternal flow of life" that rushes beneath our ratio-centric experience. This raw, primordial aspect is "eternal, unconscious, infantile life" in Freud's perspective and other forms of mental life evolve out of it. While it has the capacity to be "ruthless," it also engenders fertility when channeled productively.[107]

This level of the psyche holds great riches; it is essential to one's experience of life, vitality and creativity to be in ongoing relationship with it. For Jung, individuals flourish by being in dynamic relationship with the unconscious, through bringing unconscious material to consciousness and integrating that material over one's lifetime into a whole personality. The personal unconscious, formed by family relationships and personal experience, explains Rowland, is a "lesser aspect" of the unconscious proper, yet very real. Whereas Freudian thought fears the unconscious, Jungian thought honors it as "crucial" to human life. Jung saw the unconscious as "far superior" to the ego and as the source of human meaning, feeling and the possibility of finding value.[108] Unconscious material is brought to consciousness by working with the images that arise in dreams (and through other kinds of inner work); such images are thought to be mediated by the archetypal Self, the God-image in the psyche. The Self is understood as a pattern of wholeness in the psyche and is both the process of building the personality and its *telos*. Those images that lure us toward the wholeness of the Self-serve a purpose similar to that of the initial aims and propositions that lure Whitehead's entities toward realization of novel possibilities.

According to Ann Ulanov and Alvin Dueck, through the Self, we encounter the "living God" that "[gives us] food from the heart of reality."[109] "Affect-laden images" arise "autonomously, spontaneously" from the body's emotions that "picture" our instincts.[110] As will be explained in chapter 5 using the work of Ernest Hartmann, brain activity in what is called the default mode network (DMN) reflects such non-directed thinking. Although primordial experience or non-directed thinking may be "alarming" and show us "dark and hateful things," these "psychic depths are nature, and nature is creative life."[111] In seeing the "created world" as a "creating principle,"[112] Singer resonates with Whitehead's understanding of the very creative process at the base of actuality. This creative process is transpersonal and, when encountered, carries the kind of sacred authority that Otto describes in numinous experience. Yet rather than speculating about a transcendent God, Jung spoke of God as an image—a "living mystery"[113]—in the psyche that was yet this "'Numinosum,' this totally 'Other.'"[114]

In the previous chapter on Whitehead, we examined the "weft" of the beginnings of experience and discovered the living immediacy of the present moment and the dead factual past; we also examined the "warp" of transpersonal reality and discovered a dipolar God, mutual immanence, and novelty. In this chapter on Jung, we examined the "weft" of the depths of experience and discovered primordial life and the objective psyche; next we will examine the "warp" of transpersonal reality in order to discover the collective unconscious, the God-image in the psyche, and the archetypal imagination.

TRANSPERSONAL REALITY: COLLECTIVE UNCONSCIOUS, ARCHETYPAL IMAGINATION AND THE GOD-IMAGE

Collective Unconscious

In *Ego and Archetype*, Edward F. Edinger calls Jung's discovery of the unconscious or archetypal psyche as his most "far-reaching."[115] One key difference between Freud and Jung is that whereas Freud believed the powerful unconscious forces that often disrupted human life were merely the repressed contents of individual experience, Jung's clinical observations led him to conclude that there was a transpersonal or "pre-personal"[116] nature to the broader unconscious because he noted that very similar "myth motifs" and images emerged in disparate cultures and places across the globe. He found these "mythologems" to be "independent of tradition" and to carry a nearly "universal parallelism."[117] Jung found through his clinical research that these common images were not the result of "merely forgotten or repressed material," but arose in people for whom direct knowledge or experience of the material was unlikely, if not impossible.[118] He believed that this collective "psychic system" did not develop individually in humans but was "inherited,"[119] "common to all humanity,"[120] and was a "deeper stratum"[121] of the unconscious.

In 1959, Jung described the collective unconscious as a deep layer below the surface of the conscious psyche that was not derived from personal experience. Rather, he saw it as an inborn inheritance of a "psychic substrate" common to all humans.[122] In other words, the kinds of basic behaviors and emotions that humans typically display (laughter, shame, a sense of self) do not have to be reinvented in every individual person. It is because humans have engaged the same "vital problems," generation after generation that the "universal, collective matrix out of which we all live" manifests itself in "instinctual actions and their accompanying emotions."[123] Robertson notes that "typical situations in life" produce archetypes to match them. Such situations are "engraved" into the human make-up initially as "forms without content" that merely "represent" the "possibility of a certain type of perception and action."[124] For Jung, it was an observed fact of life that "certain ideas exist almost everywhere and at all times" that were not "made by the individual, they just happen to him"; Jung saw this not as "Platonic philosophy" but as "empirical psychology."[125] Archetypes are "remembered patterns" from generations of ancestral experience of commonly encountered situations[126] into which present-day experiences of the living individual "fall" so as to be "given shape."[127]

Kelsey describes a compelling (and frequently cited) experience Jung had with a young schizophrenic patient of a mental hospital, who had been confined there for most of his life. The man

> stopped Jung in the corridor one day and asked him to look at the sun. Jung was interested and noted his instructions, "Hold your head this way, and you will see the tube hanging down, swinging back and forth and that is the source of the wind." It was a spontaneous vision with an eerie quality. But a few years later Jung was startled into awareness. He was reading an obscure work by a learned philologist; there, in a language his patient had never known, was a translation of almost precisely the same vision, even to the words. It came from an ancient magic papyrus which had lain unedited for years in the Bibliotheque Nationale in Paris. This kind of experience was repeated several times during his practice, often connected in some unaccountable way with an associated outer event.[128]

In relating the same historical anecdote, Robertson notes the origination of the vision as from a Mithraic sun-ritual to which Jung's patient could never have been exposed. Since it was entirely unlikely that the patient discovered the sun ritual and incorporated it into his delusions, it was much more likely that the patient tapped into some kind of collective memory, drawing upon knowledge outside of his personal experience. Moreover, the patient's use of this metaphor was not random but purposeful, as he "wanted to initiate Jung into religious mysteries."[129] Support for the existence of the collective unconscious has also come through the study of language. A report from 1969 by Joseph Jaffe, M.D., notes that scientists had discovered what was described as a "symbolic machinery, common to all [people]" that had been used prior to the emergence of formal language to communicate about basic human concerns, including birth, death, love, combat, and fear.[130]

Jung saw the collective unconscious as something like "an unceasing stream" or "an ocean of images and figures" that surfaced into consciousness via dreams or "abnormal states of mind."[131] Singer likens the relationship of consciousness to the unconscious as an island that emerges "from the great sea" where the wet rim of sand is equivalent to the personal unconscious while the collective sea from which it arises is the "birthplace" of consciousness. From there the historic patterns of human life emerge "and their connections with contemporary situations are initiated."[132] Lest we imagine this collective unconscious as only a source of past possibilities, Shelburne notes that the unconscious also presents "completely new thoughts and creative ideas."[133] Singer also describes the relationship between consciousness and the unconscious as one of microcosm to macrocosm; exploring our "inner space," she argues, is more challenging than our exploration of "outer space."[134] The unconscious is "unknowable," "primary" and "the paramount reality, the unknowable 'ground'"; what we consciously know to be true "is continually undercut by the unconscious other"[135] that confronts us and "speaks with authority."[136] Again, Jung's collective unconscious evokes Whitehead's dipolar God, both in God's primordial and consequent natures; much more will be said on this in chapter 6. Now we will turn to the products of this transpersonal and collective reality and the effects it produces—the archetypes and their images.

Archetypes and Archetypal Images

While Jung believed that the personal unconscious contained mostly the "feeling-toned complexes," the collective unconscious contains the archetypes.[137] Because of his repeated observations of patients who related psychic contents with common myth motifs independent of their personal experience or history, Jung concluded that these contents did not originate in the "space-time world" or one's personal consciousness. He was compelled, then, to assume that he was "dealing with 'myth-forming' structural elements in the unconscious psyche" that revived "these mythologems, independent of all tradition."[138] Jung called these structural elements *archetypes*, meaning "a pre-existent form" or "organizing principle"[139] in the collective unconscious. He drew the term from historical references, including Philo Judaeus's usage of it in relation to the "*Imago Dei* (God-Image) in man," and from Iranaeus.[140]

As described earlier, the central organizing archetype in the psyche is the Self. Because Jung observed that the archetypal Self sometimes manifests in dreams via animal symbols, he speculated—again evoking Whitehead's dipolar entities—that archetypes possess both an "instinctive, body-based pole" as well as a "spiritual pole."[141] Kelsey claims archetypes as numinous and attractive with life-changing potential that may or may not be loaded with material from one's personal unconscious.[142] Hoss describes archetypes as "collective forces and patterns from within."[143] Young-Eisendrath and Hall argue that Jung's important contribution to the theory of human instincts is his addition of image to the general human experience of "emotional or situational patterns." Jung's archetypes indicate "a universal predisposition to construct an image, usually in an emotionally aroused state"; they serve to organize "emotion and image into universal forms" and arise in human life due to patterns of human emotion that seem to be ubiquitous.[144] Archetypes are "preverbal," "infused with emotion," and "powerfully motivating" as they organize psychological experience; moreover, their meaning exceeds that which can be articulated through language.[145]

Because they are unconscious, archetypes are not directly observable; they are only observed in their effects because they have no content that can be "represented to the mind." They only become manifest in their organization of images and ideas which is always an unconscious process, detectable only after the fact.[146] Archetypes manifest as the symbols and images that arise in dreams and spontaneous fantasies of the mind, and because they "lead us from the known to the unknown," they improve self-understanding and insight.[147] The differentiation between the archetype and its image is given shape for students in Clodagh Weldon's classes through a demonstration she typically performs in which she hides a large magnet under a sheet of paper and then shakes iron filings onto it. A student for whom the magnet's presence is unknown is subsequently asked to tap the sheet of paper so all may observe the pattern or image "that reveals the magnetic field" and illustrates the formative power of an unconscious archetype.[148] The archetypal image is both an image "in its own right" *and* a "*dynamism* which makes itself felt" in its "numinosity and fascinating power."[149]

Archetypal Value and Synchronicity

In process thought—because every forming entity is, to some degree, a subject that feels and experiences the world and its influences upon it—the cosmos is understood as *panexperiential*. In the same way that Whitehead understands human consciousness as something that naturally emerges from its roots in beings of lesser complexity, Jung understands that everything in the universe "has a psychelike quality, a capacity for responsiveness." This is the basis of his theory of synchronicity, a principle that he adds to the three universal principles of gravity, electromagnetism, and quantum uncertainty.[150] As Jung began to investigate what he called "synchronistic phenomena," writes Card, he saw that archetypes seem to mediate mental and physical events that are connected through meaning.[151] Therefore, archetypes go beyond a "neurophysical basis" alone and impact the "general dynamical patterns of all matter and energy."[152] Jung thought this possible because he posited an *unus mundus*, or "unitary existence that underlies the duality of the mind (psyche) and matter (physis)." Again evoking Whitehead's ontological theory of one reality, Jung wrote that multiplicity and unity are not two different worlds existing "side-by-side" or "mingled with one another," but that archetypes are the mediating factors of the entire *unus mundus*. "When operating in the realm of *psyche*, [archetypes] are the dynamical organizers of images and ideas; when operating in the realm of *physis*, they are the patterning principles of matter and energy" and responsible for "acausal orderedness."[153]

Jung developed his ideas on synchronicity while working with physicist Wolfgang Pauli, one of the founders of quantum theory.[154] He ultimately saw archetypes as patterns of meaning that were autonomous while existing within things and which seem to structure both psyche and matter, dissolving the subject-object split. In agreement with Tarnas, Maxwell notes that the "ultimate philosophical implication of Jungian synchronicity (as opposed to the psychological implications . . .) is that formal causality must be reinstated as a valid form of causation if our experience is to be understood in all of its multivalence."[155] An uncanny resonance between Whitehead's eternal objects and Jung's archetypes is apparent when we review two independent passages about mathematical numbers.[156]

In an essay in *Man and his Symbols*, Jung's student Marie-Louise von Franz notes that the number two illustrates that numbers, because they were not consciously invented by humans, are "spontaneous and autonomous products of the unconscious." Moreover, while numbers are abstract symbols, they also "adhere" to real objects in the space-time world. They are, according to von Franz, a "tangible connection between matter and psyche."[157] Whitehead pondered a similar question on the "status of mathematical entities" in *Science and the Modern World*, where he also uses the number two as an example of how numbers are both "involved in the real world" *and* abstractions that are "exempt from the flux of time." He concludes that such formal elements as number and shape are what lie "at the base of the real world."[158]

Also resonant with Whitehead, Haule describes Jung's universe as "not a collection of unrelated elements but ordered as an internally responsive organism, a nested hierarchy of psychoid components." Such a psychoid universe "cannot enjoy the status of 'absolute truth,' for that does not exist," writes Haule. Instead, its truth is a "mythic truth," and to accept a psychoid universe is "a mythic-metaphysical leap" that slices "the Gordian knot of the body-mind or matter-soul problem" and shows us "that soul and consciousness are not limited to Homo sapiens" but are present in some way and to some degree "all the way down," even to what has typically been seen as "dead, inert matter."[159]

Our exploration of Jung's transpersonal reality has revealed a dynamic process of psychic encounters with both an objective Other and immanent God-image at the depths of human life. This divine "Other" presents organizing forms and patterns filled with contextualized images that lure us toward unique expressions of value in a meaning- and value-soaked world to which we matter and within which we belong. Moreover, such encounters may grace us with their transformative and healing powers.

God and the Healing Power of the Unconscious

Jung saw God as an experience rather than a concept, as an immanent presence within the psyche that unified thinking and feeling, giving one a sense of participation in the divine life.[160] John P. Dourley, Roman Catholic priest, Jungian analyst and professor emeritus at Carleton University in Ottawa, Canada, has done extensive comparative work on Paul Tillich and Jung. He writes in *Psyche as Sacrament* that both Jung and Tillich understood their work as serving humankind's religious nature.[161] Jung, Dourley argues, can help Christians better appreciate their own symbols by revealing their source in the depths of the psyche. Dourley shows that both Jung and Tillich believed that humans could regain their self-understanding as an image of God if they could recover the meaning of religion through an inner divine encounter.[162] He continues,

> In the debate between modern theologies that would deny a natural continuity between the divine and the human, and those that would base their conception of [the] religious [person] upon such a continuity, Tillich and Jung clearly align themselves with the latter. To understand [humans'] relation to God in any other way is to place God as a being wholly beyond [humans] and to conceive of [God] as addressing or entering human life wholly from beyond it. Such intrusive revelations are experienced by their recipients as emanating from a source foreign to life, and tend to split rather than heal the life and consciousness they invade. Tillich and Jung seek to heal this breach by proposing a dialectical unity between [one's] sense of [self] as autonomous and God's approach to [him or her] as a power transcendent to [his or her] humanity but not discreetly separable from it.[163]

For Jung, what one encountered in religious experience was what he also called "primordial experience," and such an experience could not be differentiated from what the religious traditions called "God" or "original Mystery." Primordial experience bursts upon one's consciousness with suddenness and great power and a kind of blazing intensity. Religion, Jung believed, was a "true container" for primordial experience that balances and integrates the human's relationship to it in two ways: (1) One can be carried away by the intensity of primordial experience and fall into "the abyss" never to return; religion can provide a container within which to understand the experience through the community's tradition and texts; and, (2) It can protect a person's individuality and autonomy by giving them an "extramundane" authority and referent, to prevent humans from becoming "mass-minded."[164] Unfortunately, some expressions of religion seem as likely to demand conformity as the State that Jung so frequently targeted for critique.

On the one hand, Jung felt that his articulations could not touch the "essence" of God because of the limitations of human conception and the "feebleness and poverty of language"; on the other hand, he understood the archetypal "emotional foundation" of numinous experience to be "unassailable by reason" and as "psychic fact."[165] As Rowland notes, Jung, unlike Freud, thought religious experience to be "genuine and authentic."[166] After his own "breakthrough experience," Jung wrote, "Suddenly, I understood that God was for me at least one of the most certain and immediate experiences of life."[167] The authenticity of such experience lies in the archetype, not in its proof of religious doctrine, and while the experience may, in fact, be manifesting a transcendent god "working through the unconscious (because all reality is psychic)" it may also be the unconscious itself.[168]

Though Jung did not necessarily *equate* the collective unconscious with what Christians would call God, he saw them as "empirically indistinguishable"[169] and Jung understood experiences of the numinous to be arising from its psychic depths. As Walter Shelburne notes, while Jung did not see the collective unconscious as necessarily identical with God, he understood it as "the medium from which religious experience seems to flow." In Jung's psychology, God plays "an absolutely necessary psychological function of an irrational nature" and that function is unrelated to God as an ontological reality. The question of God's existence is unanswerable and unprovable, even while the idea of God is "present everywhere."

> The existence of God is once and for all an unanswerable question . . . We find numberless images of God, but we cannot produce the original. There is no doubt in my mind that there is an original behind our images, but it is inaccessible . . . All that I have learned has led me step by step to an unshakable conviction of the existence of God. I only believe in what I know. And that eliminates believing. Therefore I do not take [God's] existence on belief—I *know* that [God] exists.[170]

Drawing from Elaine Pagels, McGehee notes similar positions held by both modern psychotherapy and Gnostic Christianity—in contrast to orthodox Christianity—that the psyche contains its own potential for "liberation or destruction."

> Few psychiatrists would disagree with the saying attributed to Jesus in the Gospel of Thomas, "If you bring forth what is within you, what you bring forth will save you. If you do not bring forth what is within you, what you do not bring forth will destroy you."[171]

Bringing forth what is within you is the very nature of the collective unconscious working through the Self. As Rowland reminds us, the unconscious has "healing sublime powers"[172] working within us for our greater aliveness and wholeness. If every human psyche bears both liberation and destruction within itself, and if the healing power of the unconscious is also collectively available, then we are confronted again with the wounding and healing of reality in its ever-present dipolar dance.

SUMMARY

Jung's analytical psychology was developed through empirical observations of his patients as well as his own deep dives into the unconscious. For him, as for Whitehead, experience must be both the departure point and terminus of any theoretical flights. Based on his observations, then, Jung describes a psyche that is both conscious and unconscious, in which directed ego-thinking is but the "spotlight" in contrast to the non-directed thinking that is the "floodlight" through which we illumine the primordial dynamism and vitality available to us universally as embodied human beings. In Jung's system, mind, body, and world are interrelated and archetypal meaning is the lattice structure in which psyche, matter, and image all cohere. Individuals—even as opposing intrapsychic energies result in persona, neurosis, and trauma—are capable of individuating toward psychic integration and wholeness through the numinous images of the archetypal Self. Such a process results in greater aliveness and inner authority, more intimate relationships with others, and more individuality and value returned to the world. As dreams are the primary language of both the unconscious and the process of individuation, it is time now to turn to the practical resources for this project—dreams and dream-related research.

NOTES

1. Shelburne, *Mythos and Logos*, 15–16.
2. Jacob A. Arlow, *Legacy of Sigmund Freud* (New York: International Universities Press, Inc., 1956), 45.
3. Arlow, *Legacy of Sigmund Freud*, 27.

4. Jung, *Modern Man in Search of a Soul*, 17.
5. Jung, 186.
6. C. G. Jung, *The Structure and Dynamics of the Psyche*, trans. R.F.C. Hull, Corrected, vol. 8, The Collected Works of C.G. Jung, Bollingen Series (New York: Pantheon Books, 1969), 324–25.
7. Singer, *Boundaries of the Soul*, 15.
8. Robertson, *Jungian Archetypes*, 143.
9. Shelburne, *Mythos and Logos*, 27.
10. Singer, *Boundaries of the Soul*, 103.
11. Shelburne, *Mythos and Logos*, 29.
12. Jung, *Modern Man in Search of a Soul*, 186.
13. Jung, 17.
14. Robertson, *Jungian Archetypes*, 211.
15. Shelburne, *Mythos and Logos*, 27.
16. Jung, *Modern Man in Search of a Soul*, 17.
17. C. G. Jung, *The Portable Jung*, ed. Joseph Campbell (New York: Viking Press, 1971), 285–86.
18. Jung, *Psychology and Religion*, 1969, 8:323.
19. Robertson, *Jungian Archetypes*, 160.
20. Edinger, *Ego and Archetype*, 3.
21. McGehee and Thomas, *The Invisible Church*, 78.
22. Georg Nicolaus, *C.G. Jung and Nikolai Berdyaev: Individuation and the Person: A Critical Comparison* (London, New York: Routledge, 2010), 127.
23. Kalsched, *Trauma and the Soul*, 7.
24. Kalsched, 128.
25. Tacey, "The Challenge of Teaching Jung in the University," 18.
26. Singer, *Boundaries of the Soul*, 210.
27. Kalsched, *Trauma and the Soul*, 168.
28. Robertson, *Jungian Archetypes*, 205–6.
29. Fredrica R. Halligan, "Jungian Theory and Religious Experience," in *Handbook of Religious Experience*, ed. Ralph W. Hood (Birmingham, AL: Religious Education Press, 1995), 246.
30. Robertson, *Jungian Archetypes*, 206.
31. Singer, *Boundaries of the Soul*, 210.
32. Halligan, "Jungian Theory and Religious Experience," 241.
33. John Haule, "Personal Secrets, Ethical Questions," in *Teaching Jung*, ed. Kelly Bulkeley and Clodagh Weldon, AAR Teaching Religious Studies (New York: Oxford University Press, 2011), 152.
34. Halligan, "Jungian Theory and Religious Experience," 243.
35. Edinger, *Ego and Archetype*, 4.
36. Halligan, "Jungian Theory and Religious Experience," 243.
37. Jung, *Psychology and Religion*, 1969, 8:320.
38. Jung, 8:321.
39. Jung, 8:323.
40. Jung, *The Basic Writings of C. G. Jung*, 591.

41. Coward, "Taoism and Jung," 488. Coward quotes Jung as saying that "to understand metaphysically is impossible; it can only be done psychologically."
42. Robertson, *Jungian Archetypes*, 139.
43. Kelsey, *Encounter With God*, 98, 105.
44. Rowland, *Jung*, 133.
45. Rowland, 134.
46. Rowland, 135.
47. Robertson, *Jungian Archetypes*, 209.
48. Goldenberg, "Archetypal Theory and the Separation of Mind and Body," 64.
49. Stephen Aizenstat, "Jungian Psychology and the World Unconscious," in *Ecopsychology: Restoring the Earth, Healing the Mind*, ed. Theodore Roszak, Mary E. Gomes, and Allen D. Kanner (San Francisco: Sierra Club Books, 1995), xvii–xviii.
50. Aizenstat, "Jungian Psychology and the World Unconscious," xviii.
51. Rowland, *Jung*, 30.
52. Halligan, "Jungian Theory and Religious Experience," 239. The word "persona" is taken from the Latin word for stage masks used in ancient Greek theater.
53. Halligan, 239.
54. Robertson, *Jungian Archetypes*, 209.
55. Robertson, 193.
56. Robertson, 194.
57. Halligan, "Jungian Theory and Religious Experience," 240.
58. McGehee and Thomas, *The Invisible Church*, 50.
59. Kalsched, *Trauma and the Soul*, 165.
60. Robertson, *Jungian Archetypes*, 169.
61. Robertson, 169.
62. Young-Eisendrath and Hall, *Jung's Self Psychology*, 3.
63. Young-Eisendrath and Hall, 3.
64. McGehee and Thomas, *The Invisible Church*, 50.
65. McGehee and Thomas, 50.
66. C. G. Jung, *Two Essays on Analytical Psychology*, trans. R. F. C. Hull, vol. 7, The Collected Works of C.G. Jung, Bollingen Series (New York: Pantheon Books, 1953), 20.
67. Jung, *Modern Man in Search of a Soul*, 236.
68. Jung, 236–37.
69. Jung, *Two Essays on Analytical Psychology*, 7:20.
70. Heisig, "The Mystique of the Nonrational and a New Spirituality," 211.
71. Fraser N. Watts, *Theology and Psychology* (Hampshire, England: Ashgate Publishing, 2002), 120.
72. Rowland, *Jung*, 33.
73. Singer, *Boundaries of the Soul*, 134.
74. Halligan, "Jungian Theory and Religious Experience," 240.
75. Singer, *Boundaries of the Soul*, 134.
76. Robertson, *Jungian Archetypes*, 207–9.
77. Robertson, 209.
78. Kalsched, *Trauma and the Soul*, 165.

79. Lauter and Rupprecht, "Feminist Archetypal Theory," 224.
80. Halligan, "Jungian Theory and Religious Experience," 239.
81. Kalsched, *Trauma and the Soul*, 165.
82. Singer, *Boundaries of the Soul*, 385.
83. Wehr, *Jung & Feminism*, 68.
84. Singer, *Boundaries of the Soul*, 135.
85. Jung, *The Basic Writings of C. G. Jung*, 96–97.
86. Haule, "Personal Secrets, Ethical Questions," 153.
87. Haule, 153–54.
88. Young-Eisendrath and Hall, *Jung's Self Psychology*, 27.
89. Young-Eisendrath and Hall, 27.
90. Rowland, *Jung*, 30.
91. Singer, *Boundaries of the Soul*, 355–56.
92. Ulanov and Ulanov, *Religion and the Unconscious*, 37.
93. Kalsched, *Trauma and the Soul*, 30.
94. Singer, *Boundaries of the Soul*, 157.
95. Sylvia Brinton Perera, "The Descent of Inanna: Myth and Therapy," in *Feminist Archetypal Theory: Interdisciplinary Re-Visions of Jungian Thought*, ed. Estella Lauter and Carol Scheier Rupprecht (Knoxville: University of Tennessee Press, 1985), 143.
96. Kelsey, *Encounter With God*, 117.
97. Rowland, *Jung*, 31.
98. Singer, *Boundaries of the Soul*, 135.
99. Kelly Bulkeley, *An Introduction to the Psychology of Dreaming* (Westport, CT: Praeger, 1997), 35.
100. Haule, "Personal Secrets, Ethical Questions," 154.
101. Young-Eisendrath and Hall, *Jung's Self Psychology*, 27.
102. Stephen Aizenstat, *Dream Tending: Awakening to the Healing Power of Dreams* (New Orleans: Spring Journal Books, 2011), 30.
103. Wehr, *Jung & Feminism*, 69.
104. Singer, *Boundaries of the Soul*, 239.
105. Whitehead, *Process and Reality*, 21.
106. Ulanov and Ulanov, *Religion and the Unconscious*, 13, 26.
107. Ulanov and Ulanov, 26.
108. Rowland, *Jung*, 29.
109. Ulanov and Dueck, *The Living God and Our Living Psyche*, 69.
110. Ulanov and Dueck, 72.
111. Jung, *Modern Man in Search of a Soul*, 215.
112. Singer, *Boundaries of the Soul*, 378.
113. Clodagh Weldon, "God on the Couch: Teaching Jung's Answer to Job," in *Teaching Jung*, ed. Kelly Bulkeley and Clodagh Weldon, AAR Teaching Religious Studies (New York: Oxford University Press, 2011), 118.
114. Singer, *Boundaries of the Soul*, 384.
115. Edinger, *Ego and Archetype*, 3.
116. Edinger, 3.

117. Singer, *Boundaries of the Soul*, 98–100.
118. Singer, 98–100.
119. Robertson, *Jungian Archetypes*, 156.
120. Robert J. Hoss, "Evidence of Wisdom in Dreams" (Annual Conference of the International Association for the Study of Dreams, Asheville, NC, 2010).
121. Shelburne, *Mythos and Logos*, 28.
122. Jung, *The Basic Writings of C. G. Jung*, 359.
123. Wehr, *Jung & Feminism*, 50–51.
124. Robertson, *Jungian Archetypes*, 167.
125. Jung, *The Basic Writings of C. G. Jung*, 585.
126. Robertson, *Jungian Archetypes*, 167.
127. Singer, *Boundaries of the Soul*, 101.
128. Kelsey, *Encounter With God*, 113.
129. Robertson, *Jungian Archetypes*, 158–59.
130. Singer, *Boundaries of the Soul*, 121.
131. Jung, *Modern Man in Search of a Soul*, 186.
132. Singer, *Boundaries of the Soul*, 373–74.
133. Shelburne, *Mythos and Logos*, 29.
134. Singer, *Boundaries of the Soul*, 104.
135. Rowland, *Jung*, 143.
136. Haule, "Personal Secrets, Ethical Questions," 152.
137. Jung, *The Basic Writings of C. G. Jung*, 359.
138. Singer, *Boundaries of the Soul*, 100.
139. Singer, 133.
140. Singer, 126–27, 133.
141. Ann Belford Ulanov, *The Functioning Transcendent* (Wilmette, IL: Chiron Publications, 1996), 20.
142. Kelsey, *Encounter With God*, 113.
143. Hoss, "Evidence of Wisdom in Dreams."
144. Young-Eisendrath and Hall, *Jung's Self Psychology*, 1–2.
145. Young-Eisendrath and Hall, 2.
146. Jung, *The Basic Writings of C. G. Jung*, 128.
147. Singer, *Boundaries of the Soul*, 133.
148. Weldon, "God on the Couch," 119.
149. Jung, *The Basic Writings of C. G. Jung*, 103–4.
150. Haule, "Personal Secrets, Ethical Questions," 161.
151. Card, "The Archetypal View of C.G. Jung and Wolfgang Pauli," 27.
152. Card, 27.
153. Card, 28.
154. Card, 29.
155. Maxwell, "Archetype and Eternal Object," 65.
156. Whitehead, *Science and the Modern World*, 27–28.
157. Marie-Louise von Franz, "Conclusion: Science and the Unconscious," in *Man and His Symbols*, ed. C. G. Jung (Garden City, NY: Doubleday, 1969), 310.

158. This similarity has been previously noted in Sheri D. Kling, "Avoiding a Fatal Error: Extending Whitehead's Symbolism beyond Language," in *Rethinking Whitehead's Symbolism: Thought, Language, Culture*, ed. Roland Faber, Jeffrey Bell, and Joseph Petek (Edinburgh: Edinburgh University Press, 2017), 137–38.

159. Haule, "Personal Secrets, Ethical Questions," 163.

160. McGehee and Thomas, *The Invisible Church*, 113.

161. John P. Dourley, *The Psyche as Sacrament: A Comparative Study of C.G. Jung and Paul Tillich* (Toronto: Inner City Books, 1981), 7.

162. Dourley, *The Psyche as Sacrament*, 7–8.

163. Dourley, 9.

164. Ulanov and Ulanov, *Religion and the Unconscious*, 25–39.

165. C. G. Jung, *Psychology and Religion: West and East*, trans. R.F.C. Hull, Corrected, vol. 11, The Collected Works of C.G. Jung, Bollingen Series (New York: Pantheon Books, 1963), 361.

166. Rowland, *Jung*, 33.

167. McGehee and Thomas, *The Invisible Church*, 113.

168. Rowland, *Jung*, 33.

169. Odin, *Process Metaphysics and Hua-Yen Buddhism*, 165.

170. Shelburne, *Mythos and Logos*, 76–77.

171. Elaine Pagels, *The Gnostic Gospels*, Reissue (New York: Vintage, 1989), xv.

172. Rowland, *Jung*, 148.

Chapter 5

Practical

The Integrative Power of Dreams

INTRODUCTION

Practical Purposes

To this point, I have shown how Whitehead's integrated and relational cosmos and Jung's integrated and relational psyche provide resources more than adequate to the task of promoting human wholeness and flourishing. Whitehead's metaphysical framework and Jung's psychological system both point to a reality wherein individuals have value, are related to God and world, and can experience positive change. Yet even with this abundance of intellectual riches, we know that Bulkeley and Zimmerman would remind us that taking only a cognitive turn away from a dualistic and alienating worldview toward a more life-enhancing worldview is not enough. We must find a way to facilitate transformative *experiences* of the kind of nondual consciousness that reveal a world of value, relatedness, and transformation.

Value, belonging, and transformation must take center stage if our lived experience is to reflect anything other than meaninglessness, alienation, and suffering. Therefore, we must also offer practical resources that *work within* our metaphysical and psychological frameworks to facilitate such experiences. I will show in this chapter that a practice of spiritual dream work that recognizes the potential for at least some of our dreams to be healing religious or mystical encounters can foster psycho-spiritual wholeness and flourishing when interpreted as a meeting place between transpersonal reality and embodied existence. To reach that destination, we will briefly examine dreams and dreaming from a psychological view, a scientific view, a communal view, and a mystical view.

Dreams in Context

From all appearances, to be human is to dream. Bulkeley indicates that there is evidence of human fascination with dreams in even the oldest texts we have.[1] Dreams have also had a significant impact on culture, science, and technology. In *Dreaming in Church*, Presbyterian minister Geoff Nelson points to five cultural and technological breakthroughs in which dreams played a significant part, including Eastman's advances in film technology, Kekule's work on the benzene ring, Einstein's theory of relativity, Handel's *Messiah*, and Howe's invention of the sewing machine.[2]

Ironically, the very dualistic system on which this project lays much of the blame for our current state of alienation and division was inspired in Descartes by a series of three dreams he had in November of 1619 which led him, according to Kelsey, "from chaos to clarity." Yet, in Descartes's view of humans as purely rational intellect, he "excluded the source of his own inspiration," leaving us with the splitting effects of that "intellectual blunder" ever since.[3] Bulkeley underscores the blunder in his own way when he explains that neither classical dualism nor materialism can explain how physical changes in the brain can affect conscious experience or even consciousness itself. Scientists working in dream research with reductionist approaches cannot yet explain how a person's electrical, chemical, anatomical, cognitive, or personal life aspects combine to give us the multisensory experience of dreaming.[4]

Our rationally skewed culture tends to dismiss the value of dreams. This dismissal is just one indication of a more widespread "undervaluation of the human psyche" that reflects an "appalling lack of wisdom and introspection."[5] Yet we often disregard what we cannot pin down into neat categories. Such has not been true in the religious arena. Because dreams have always seemed mysterious, arriving without conscious will or intention, Bulkeley notes that there is a broad acceptance among world religions of the idea that dreams refer to religious realities.[6] Dreams have maintained a prominent position in religious traditions because they are typically seen as relating us to a powerful, sacred reality that transcends individual human life.[7] Yet the rise of "secularization"—forces of science, economics, and cultural change that have diminished religious authority in the West—has ushered in a transition from "a religious to a psychological view of dreams" where psychologists have become the new authorities on their significance.[8]

In the remainder of this chapter, we will examine dreams from several viewpoints: (1) a *psychological* view of dreams, focusing on the Jungian tradition; (2) a *scientific* view of dreams, focusing on research in the cognitive sciences; (3) a *communal* view of dreams and the rise of dream-sharing groups; and, (4) a *mystical* view of dreams that accepts at least some dreams as the meeting place between transpersonal reality and embodied existence—or dreams as religious experience. I will show that the integration of these four perspectives allows us to situate dream work as a practical resource alongside our metaphysical and psychological resources for this project because: (1) the *psychological* view connects dreams with personal *and* transpersonal meaning, value, belonging, and transformation as well as with the natural world; (2) the *scientific* view connects mental experience of dreams with the body's functioning and our perceived world, supporting the psychological view of dreams and transformation; (3) the *communal* view connects dreams and dream work with shared experience, shared meaning, belonging, and transformation; and, (4) the *mystical* view connects dreams with God or transpersonal reality, as well as with meaning, value, belonging, and transformation.

A PSYCHOLOGICAL VIEW OF DREAMS

Great advances in the study of human nature as related to dreaming have been made by the psychological sciences since the release in 1899 of Freud's seminal work *The Interpretation of Dreams* established him as a preeminent authority on the phenomenon. Ever since, psychology has explored dream phenomena, seeing them as a way to access deeper mental life.[9] In this section, I will show how psychology—especially in the Jungian tradition—connects dreams with meaning, value, and transformation, that dreams can be seen as *natural* yet *purposive* and carriers of transpersonal meaning and value, and that there are specific methods and tools that can be used to understand dreams, such as *association*, *amplification*, and *active imagination* or *animation*.

According to Bulkeley, dream researchers have been primarily interested in the cause of dreams, the function of dreams, the interpretation of dreams, and whether they carry meaning or are just "random nonsense."[10] Extensive research into dreams has shown that they are capable of revealing aspects of mental life related to personality, memory, reason, and emotion, resulting in "a revolution in how we view human nature."[11] Despite this revolution, Bulkeley is not enamored with the kind of simplistic approaches—endemic to religion *versus* science debates—that would pit "ancient religion" with its presumed stance that all dreams are of divine and external origin and purpose against "modern psychology" with its presumed "proof" that all dreams are merely brain-generated and therefore without any intent or meaning. It is that very "false antithesis" that he would like to "dissolve"[12] when he argues that most religions, in fact, view the majority of dreams as "relatively trivial and mundane" and based in ordinary experience. On the other hand, there are those dreams—what in his early work he calls "divine dreams"[13] and later "big dreams"[14]—that "come with a special clarity, energy, and vividness." Such dreams have resulted in religious conversion, spiritual insights, and sometimes revitalization movements.[15]

Though Jung invoked multiple functions of dreams, Bulkeley notes two as key: (1) serving that primary process of compensation between the conscious ego and the unconscious—Jung's "basic law of psychic behavior"; and, (2) anticipating the course of development of the dreamer's individual potential.[16] Robert J. Hoss, author of *Dream Language,* director of the Dream Science Foundation, and an officer and former president of the International Association for the Study of Dreams (IASD), describes the compensatory function in dreams as a process that recognizes the ego's misconceptions and then attempts to "bring our awareness back to reality, and warn of the dangers of our present course."[17] He relates the story of a woman who, in her waking life, anxiously and frequently tried to suppress a side of herself she considered evil. A dream vividly illustrates the compensatory function by first illuminating the viewpoint of her ego and then compensating by warning of the dangers of such a viewpoint. She "dreamed that this evil person had come alive again and [she] feared that an evil 'entity' was at work. [She] went through a ritual of exorcism to eliminate the entity, but the more [she] tried the darker the sky became. Suddenly a voice said, 'stop—you are only making it worse.'"[18]

Hoss links a dream's propensity to anticipate future possibilities to Jung's transcendent function that works to amplify our conscious awareness with unconscious content. When recognized and integrated, such unconscious material can extend consciousness to an unlimited field of experience. Such an expansion of awareness can initiate the emergence of a personality that is "more integrated . . . wider and more mature"; moreover, a new attitude may arise in which the conscious and unconscious selves are more closely integrated and collaborative.[19] Sanford describes such teleological aspects of dream functions as both pushing and leading us into a new future.[20]

Such researchers as Pagel, Beaulieu-Prevost, and Zadra conclude that dreaming is a phenomenon experienced by "the vast majority of the human population" even if those dreams are not always recalled. In fact, having a "negative attitude" toward dream recall can affect actual recall.[21] Regarding the question of whether dreams have intrinsic meaning, Bulkeley shows that dream content very often reflects those key concerns of our waking life. He argues that strong *continuities* between the dreamer's waking life and dreams can often be identified without any input from the dreamer.[22] *Discontinuities* that also arise are indicative of the wealth of possible meanings that extend beyond immediate waking life.[23] To make the point that dreams "picture" a person's emotional concerns and can therefore have multiple layers of meaning, Ernest Hartmann relates a Talmudic tale of twenty-four different dream interpreters who gave twenty-four different interpretations, all of which were claimed as true by the dreamer.[24] Any meanings associated with a dream arise from the images contained therein, and so we now turn to Jung's view of dream images.

Jung and Dream Images

Freud and Jung are both considered to be insightful and pioneering psychologists who conducted research into the nature of dreams and dreaming; yet it is Jung's work that has been more influential on contemporary dream psychology.[25] Like Freud, Jung did *not* see dreams as arising solely out of bodily sensations or the day's events but believed they can reveal the ways in which the unconscious is instructing the dreamer.[26] As opposed to Freud's perspective that dream content represented "repressed infantile wishes and drives," Jung believed that dream images originate "in the collective human psyche." Singer identifies the experience of dreaming as "the clearest proof we have that the unconscious exists."[27] Freud believed dreams to be made up solely of repressed sexual content and inherently deceptive; for this reason, he used free association to uncover the denied content and memories of past experience.[28] While seeing Freud's idea that dreams are the "royal road to the unconscious" to be highly significant, Kelsey considers his view of dreams as "scrambled code" that only reflects what has been repressed by the individual to be too simplistic.[29] Freud maintained a rationalist stance, assuming that the unconscious would communicate rationally if only one's internal censorship would not distort that communication. Jung, on the other hand, believed the unconscious to only have the capacity for symbolic and metaphorical thought processes and therefore only able to communicate via images. It is the symbolic nature of dreams rather than "purposeful distortion" that makes dreams so difficult to understand.[30]

Jung's theories emerged from his own dream life; he considered dreams to be part of nature, and therefore honestly expressing the state of the psyche without disguise or deceit.[31] Because it is hypothesized that our conscious mind is to the entire psyche as the visible tip is to the entire iceberg, the bulk of our psychic life is unknown to us; therefore, our dreams "picture" our "inner situation," writes Sanford, who compares the examination of a dream to "looking out of the window of a bathysphere at the wonders that exist under the sea."[32] The unconscious—through dreams and synchronicities, or meaningful coincidences—presents us with a picture of our inner landscape, or a point of view that "enlarges, completes, or compensates the conscious attitude."[33] Symbols from the unconscious might picture obstacles blocking our growth, fears or even objections to the direction in which we are headed and therefore show us our inner reality.[34]

Because his patients' dream images so often resembled those found in mythology, religion, and world literature and had clearly not arisen from their personal pasts, Jung considered them to be "archetypal," collectively inherited, and held by all humankind. In his later writing, he distinguished between the archetype and the archetypal image; the archetypes themselves he understood as "blueprints for images" or "inherited patterns of thought" that framed human experience and feeling.[35] For Jung, symbols do not have "fixed meanings" but reflect a deep, unconscious, human wisdom. Dream symbols can be seen as "universal" or "transcendent," but only in the sense that they transcend individual consciousness and are understood *transpersonally* within entire cultures.[36] Jung considered both archetypes and archetypal images to be a "bequest from the past,"[37] capable of expressing "something of the grand story in which we live,"[38] and connected to every individual through the collective unconscious which he understood as the evolutionary history of humankind.[39] Johnson, Kelsey, Sanford and other Jungian-influenced writers insist that dreams should not be taken literally, and advise us to look beyond the surface story to a deeper pattern or attitude.[40] Dreams take the individual into realms beyond personal life[41] yet the unconscious will provide—if one works with the dream—the explanatory associations for every symbol. The dreamer's task is to look for their own spontaneous associations with the symbols that appear in their dreams.[42]

Unraveling the mystery of dreams is not an easy task because modern humans no longer seem to think symbolically. Even so, our dreams will speak, reflecting an "objective, autonomous reality."[43] Though dreams may seem nonsensical, Johnson claims they are "completely coherent," "masterpieces" even, of symbolic communication, the "native idiom" of the unconscious.[44] Dreams may lead us toward new futures, and Hoss notes that the Self serves as an "inner wisdom" in dreams that initiates a process of transformation or rebirth following the death of the old ego belief.

> It begins when the ego abandons the existing belief system (personal myth) that no longer works, and journeys within to find a new belief system (a new myth). At some point the organizing principle (the inner "Self") begins the transformational process by first revealing the old myth (the misconceptions) and guides the dream ego, either through direct revelation or the parable of the dream story, toward a new self or new belief system (new myth). Jung indicated that in order for the transcendence to take place the dream ego must accept what is being presented by the unconscious.[45]

Crediting Clare Johnson with the characterization of dreams as "deep but not direct,"[46] Nelson asserts that

> Dreams reveal the deepest parts of us, but they do it in ways that usually start out gentle and mild. If we are willing to work with our dreams, we may find resolution to the issue in our life the dream is trying to address. If we ignore the dream, we find we have recurring dreams that give us the same message. If we persist in ignoring the recurring dreams, the images in the dreams may become more and more frightening until the dream takes on the feelings of a nightmare. Deep parts of ourselves are revealed in our dreams.[47]

For Jung, the symbol is the center on which everything turns; the dream image must therefore be held in a position of primacy and respected accordingly. Its meaning typically eludes us initially, writes Halligan, because "its very nature is to take one beyond."[48] Rowland emphatically argues that dreams should not be immediately dismissed as Oedipal fantasies as Freud would do, but should be understood as "messages from a superior 'other.'"[49] In fact, she sees dreams as spontaneous products of archetypes and as expressions of one's true self that lies in the unconscious; therefore, to interpret them from the level of ego consciousness is a violation.[50] Jung argued that we must stay close to the "manifest content" of the dream:

> If someone dreams of a lion, the correct interpretation can lie only in the direction of the lion; in other words, it will be essentially an amplification of this image. Anything else would be an inadequate and incorrect interpretation, since the image "lion" is a quite unmistakable and sufficiently positive presentation.[51]

Hillman similarly cautions against moving too quickly from the affective visual level to the interpretive level.[52] He saw dream images as less like signs and more like "living animals" with "presence, place, and body" that "show us our fate and await a response from us."[53] Nelson summarizes the respect dreams deserve when he claims they "will not always speak nicely, but they will speak honestly."[54]

Methods of Interpretation

Methods abound for decoding one's own dreams, but steps commonly include (1) approaching dreams seriously and with conscious intent; (2) writing them down upon awakening (Kelsey states that 95 percent of dreams that go unwritten or unshared are forgotten within five minutes)[55] and often phrased in present tense; (3) recording the major images (characters, settings, colors, emotions, activities, etc.) within the dream; (4) listing one's associations with each image; (5) exploring the transpersonal nature of some images and noting archetypal content; and, (6) paying attention to what rings true or "clicks" regarding a possible meaning. More specifically, Jungian-influenced writers incorporate such techniques as *association*, *amplification*, and *active imagination* or *animation*, with each tapping a deeper level of the psyche.

Association

Freud used *association* to uncover connections between the image and repressed psychic contents. Jungians use this step to elicit the *affective* link between an image and the dreamer.[56] For example, if the color "blue" appears in a dream, the dreamer might note such associations as "sky," "sea," or "Grandma's kitchen table." Another important consideration at this level of exploration is whether the dream image relates primarily to the *objective* level of meaning or the *subjective* level. Jungian writers generally understand human characters in a dream as representing intrapsychic, *subjective* aspects of the dreamer, rather than *objective* concerns, even if a dream figure is someone familiar. When we dream of other people, those dreams are more often about aspects of ourselves that are like those people, rather than about them objectively. While we may occasionally dream of others objectively, it is difficult to determine when such a dream may or may not involve projection.[57]

Though there are exceptions, Sanford agrees that most dreams are about the dreamer's life, problems, and "relationship to self and world."[58] Rather than relating objective content about the outside world, Johnson claims that dreams are most often about areas of life that are shaping our inner world or aspects of life of which we need to become conscious.[59] For Kelsey, it is imperative to remember that dream symbols can only be understood within the context of the dreamer's life and never applied as shorthand from a book.[60]

Amplification

After the dreamer (often with the help of an analyst) has explored his or her personal context and affective associations to dream images, the next step is often what Jung called *amplification*. In this step, one draws from myths, fairy tales, or religious texts and tradition[61] for the purposes of discovering possible connections to transpersonal, cultural themes that may be historical or contemporary.[62] For Kalsched, amplification is like "gathering the free associations of the entire cultural canon to a particular image—mythology, religious iconography, folk lore, literature, etc."[63] Unlike in association where one might understand a lion to symbolize infantile rage, Aizenstat notes that through amplification the image of the lion "now points to something regal, noble, fierce, or big-hearted in our nature." This method honors the image's "full stature as an archetype," and reveals how that archetype is currently active in the dreamer's life, and may provide "tremendous insight into our lives."[64]

Active Imagination and Animation

In *active imagination*, the dreamer intentionally bridges conscious and unconscious through imaginatively re-entering the dream story and taking it forward to enable it to continue its unfoldment.[65] Aizenstat's method of Dream Tending uses *animation* in a way that follows Hillman's view of the images as a "presence," inviting the dreamer to animate the image as a living reality. The dreamer is encouraged to examine this entity closely to explore how it interacts with and affects the dreamer. When we have assumed this posture toward the image, we can then ask two critical questions: "Who is visiting now?" and "What is happening here?"[66] With these questions, the dreamer moves from a position of intellectual inquiry to an affective experience of the image in its "living, embodied reality." The lion,

> rather than just referring to our childhood rage or the universal archetype of nobility now takes on a physical existence, actually present in the room, on the prowl, roaring with its fanged mouth, lashing its tail and licking its huge, furry paws. Furthermore, this is not like watching a lion in a movie, because in Hillman's animation we are able to actually interact with the lion, talk to it, ask it questions, pet its fur, hear what it has to say, and follow it through its habitat. It's a full-immersion, interactive experience.[67]

Hoss has developed his own six-question, Gestalt-based process called *image activation* to animate a dream image wherein one "becomes" the image that holds the most energy, emotion, or numinosity for the dreamer and then asks these questions of "oneself" as the image: (1) Who or what are you? (name and describe yourself as the dream image); (2) What is your purpose or function?; (3) What do you like about what you are?; (4) What do you dislike about what you are?; (5) What do you fear most?; and (6) What do you desire most?[68] After answering these six questions, the dreamer then relates the image and answers to waking life to see what new perspectives arise. Johnson offers his own unique type of animation when he suggests taking a ritual step to give the dream "immediacy and physical concreteness" to affirm its message.[69] For example, if one were to dream of a turtle, one might then acquire a turtle figurine to bring the dream and its meaning into daily life.

Ultimately, dream interpretation ultimately boils down to whether the dreamer has gained something from looking at her dream. Jung believed the only "legitimate criterion for a valid interpretation is its therapeutic value"; if the resulting interpretation is meaningful, it has succeeded.[70] In summary, we may now connect dreams with psychological compensation, the transcendent function and transformation. We can recognize that dreams are *natural* yet *purposive,* may be carriers of transpersonal meaning and value, and that there are specific methods and tools that can be used to understand them. If the interpretation of dream images allows an individual to glean meaning from his or her dreams in such a way that fosters positive change, connects one to transpersonal reality, and enhances one's ability to contribute something worthy to the greater whole, then it clearly is a practice that brings value, belonging, and transformation. What next can we learn from what cognitive researchers have to say?

A SCIENTIFIC VIEW OF DREAMS

The last two decades have witnessed a surge of interest in scientific study of the dreaming brain. Now that we have explored a psychological view of dreaming, we must gain an understanding of what research in cognitive/neuroscience reveals. In this section, I will show that we can link dreaming to body, to world, and to transformation because of what recent research has revealed about the brain and the entire body during REM and non-REM sleep, the brain regions active during dreaming, the spectrum of consciousness and the connection of the dreaming end of that spectrum to perception, and the relationships between dreaming, emotion, learning, change, and neuroplasticity.

Over the years, researchers have determined that dreams typically last between fifteen and ninety minutes, that humans typically dream from five to seven times per night, and that awakening someone during a dream may result in their temporary immobility due to areas of the brain being inactive during dreaming.[71] It also appears that an absence of dreaming activity can negatively affect mental health.[72] Yet researchers in the psychological sciences have bitterly disagreed about significant aspects of dream research, including whether dreams are merely the result of higher-level mental functions imposing order upon lower-level chaotic input or, as Jung and Hillman have insisted, "spontaneous expressions of a powerful symbolic intelligence which is different from but not inferior to waking rational thought."[73]

Another point of dissention has been whether dreams experienced outside a controlled laboratory environment are valid; Foulkes says no, but Hunt assesses laboratory-experienced dreams as "generally fairly boring." Meanwhile, Bulkeley describes a "sleep lab effect" which has a tendency to homogenize people's dreams, and notes that studies that rely on laboratory data may not accurately represent human dreaming.[74] Hunt sees such a polarized approach as unnecessary, preferring to use a more comprehensive model that classifies dreams into six types: (1) *personal-mnemonic*, related to one's personal, ordinary life; (2) *medical-somatic*, related to one's physiological processes; (3) *prophetic*, related to the future; (4) *archetypal-spiritual*, related to powerful, transcendent forces; (5) *nightmares*; and (6) *lucid dreams*, where the dreamer is aware he or she is dreaming.[75]

Theories abound. Part of the difficulty in sorting through various theories of dreaming is that there is yet no universally accepted theory of mind—no agreed upon understanding of how our minds and physical brains are related. This project does not answer that question but considers Whiteheadian *panexperientialism*, Hartshornian *pansomatism*, and Philip Clayton's arguments for *strong emergence*[76] of mind to all be compelling and exciting. While unhesitatingly rejecting both physicalism and dualism, my preference regarding mind, brain, and body is to widen the lens beyond mind to psyche, which is both mind and body, conscious and unconscious awareness, neither of which can be limited to only the brain. Along with Whitehead, Jung, and Clayton, this work (as mentioned in chapter 2) does not hold biology to be solely determinative of the individual or culture but, rather, argues that human intentionality and self-awareness emerge from an *a priori* structure. In a one-world, integrated cosmos, we must accept that humans—and every aspect of human behavior—emerge from a natural world in which creatures co-create themselves.

Human subjective experience is of vital importance: as Clayton argues, "subjective experiences *matter*, and matter to us as *persons*."[77] We know that there are "neural correlates of consciousness"[78] that show that the brain is somehow associated with our thought and conscious awareness. The implications of such findings though are not easy to pin down. As Clayton argues,

> Research into the neural correlates of consciousness—one of the most fruitful research areas in the study of consciousness today—can offer no more than its name promises. At most one will be able to establish a series of *correlations* between brain states and phenomenal experiences as reported by subjects. Such correlations are of immense empirical significance. But if the resulting explanations are given exclusively in neurological terms, they will by the nature of the case not be able to specify what are the phenomenal experiences or *qualia* that the subjects experience. Nor will the causal effects of conscious experiences, if they indeed exist, be recognizable by these means.[79]

At the same time, it has become widely accepted that the gut and vagus nerve are somehow involved in the transmission of "gut instincts" to the brain.[80] This suggests that we cannot limit human "awareness" to the brain or even to conscious thought. Human awareness is fully embodied and spans the consciousness-to-unconsciousness spectrum. Moreover, as will be discussed later, we know that activities both real and imagined can be identically reflected in the brain, suggesting that it is impossible to determine strictly by brain activity what is happening in the body or whether or not there are external, objective stimuli at play. For example, partnered sexual activity and solo sexual fantasy are indistinguishable in terms of brain activity. As well, by looking at brain activity we cannot distinguish between optically viewed and imagined tennis matches. In other words, we cannot point with any certainty to the cause or original stimulus of experience based on brain activity. It seems questionable, then, to make causal assumptions regarding the relationship between physical brain and mind, or even between mind and body. Therefore, while Benjamin Libet may conclude that "conscious experiences reliably lag behind the brain events that presumably evoke them,"[81] I am unwilling to leap to the conclusion that the same is true of *unconscious* experiences and overall *somatic awareness*. In fact, by using the term *somatic awareness*, I am telegraphing that I question limiting awareness to the brain-mind system at all.

As was noted earlier in this chapter, brainstem reductionists have yet to be able to explain how the physical aspects of brain activity during sleep "add up to the multisensory experience of a dream."[82] The reason to include brain research in this project is not to establish a particular theory of mind but to establish clearly that dreaming involves mind, brain, *and* body, and must be understood in this integrated way. Such research compels because it grounds Jung's theories of dreaming and the psyche in embodied functions. Yet it is crucial to keep in mind that neither the mental nor physical aspects of dreaming provide definitive answers as to the source of human consciousness. Recognizing these limitations to what can be discovered in this arena, let us now turn to a limited survey of how researchers in the cognitive sciences currently understand sleeping—and dreaming—brains.

The Dreaming Brain

The most recent sleep laboratory research has determined that there are four stages of non-rapid-eye-movement (NREM) sleep, and sleepers "descend" through those four stages until the first period of REM sleep is typically experienced approximately ninety minutes after sleep onset. The pattern of "regular alteration" of REM and NREM sleep stages occurs throughout the night. During REM sleep,

> Brain wave activity increases dramatically, muscle tone changes, heartbeat and respiration become irregular, and blood flow to the genitals increases (resulting

> in enlargement of the clitoris in women and erection of the penis in men) . . . Research by Dement and by Michel Jouvet, a French neurosurgeon, demonstrated that a very similar cycle of REM-NREM sleep alteration occurs in cats. Other sleep laboratory researchers soon confirmed that all mammals (with the apparent exceptions of the spiny anteater and the bottlenose dolphin . . . experience substantial amounts of REM sleep.[83]

According to Hartmann (d. 2013), who was a professor of psychiatry at Tufts University School of Medicine and a leading researcher on dreaming, the cycle of REM-NREM sleep is as basic to mammals as the pulse cycle or the respiratory cycle. He describes REM sleep as an organismic state of the entire body during which everything in the brain and body is controlled and regulated in a way that is different from the regulation that occurs in waking or in NREM" sleep.[84] Surprisingly, research has shown that REM sleep and dreaming are not *isomorphic*; dreaming depends not on REM sleep, but on "the brain reaching a certain threshold of activation in several different neural systems."[85] In fact, individuals who have incurred damage to certain cortical areas of their brains may stop dreaming completely while still experiencing REM sleep patterns, leading researchers to conclude that the cortical activity pattern is what underlies dreaming.[86] In the deepest stage of sleep, the brain's energy use is lower but in REM sleep, it steps up to a high energy, high activation mode. In this mode, brain centers focused on short-term memory and focused attention are less active, and motor pathways are shut down, while neural systems related to arousal, emotion, long-term memory, instinct, curiosity, orienting, and visual imagination are highly active.[87] Citing Solms's research, Bulkeley notes five different brain regions to be involved in dreaming, and these brain regions have also been shown to be active during particular human activities (shown in table 5.1).[88]

Table 5.1 Brain Regions Involved in Dreaming

Brain Region	*Associated Activities*
Basal forebrain pathways	Appetitive interests, seeking behaviors, curiosity, exploration, and expectation.
Medial occipito-temporal structures	Visual associations, symbolic representations, and complex imagery.
Inferior parietal region	Spatial cognition.
Frontal-limbic region	Mental selectivity, reality monitoring, and separation of dreaming from waking.
Temporal-limbic structures	Emotional arousal, instinctual behaviors, and seizure-like behavior.

Bulkeley, 2016, p. 98. Created by author.

Dreams, Emotion, Metaphor, and Learning

Though our experience may suggest otherwise, waking and sleep are not opposite states; in fact, during sleep the brain and associated neural systems engage in many essential aspects of waking consciousness.[89] Hartmann describes a brain function continuum in which dreaming is at the "right" end and focused-waking-thought is on the "left" end; such states as reverie and daydreaming fall to the "left" of dreaming but there is "no sudden break or discontinuity" between them and dreaming.[90] At that "right" end of the continuum,

> there is less serial processing, less task-orientation, less functioning by formal rules, less constraint. The system "relaxes" into a default mode, functioning by similarity (metaphor), rather than formal rules, guided by whatever emotions or emotional concerns are present.[91]

Using the example of a dreamer whose central dream image was of a tidal wave, Hartmann illustrates the use of metaphor in dreams to "picture" emotions or emotional concerns. The tidal wave image is not determined by a long thought process that finally culminates in a consciously chosen image; rather, the image more closely resembles the unconscious feeling than any verbal description one may give of one's emotions.[92] He describes human functioning in the default mode of the brain (sometimes referred to as the default mode network or DMN) as one in which our sensorial bodies perceive our surroundings and create a *sensorium* or "a picture of the surrounding world." During times of focused attention, our calculating, problem-solving, navigating functioning constrains default perception and we are less aware of our "sensorium, picture-making machine at work."[93]

It is that very "picture-making machine" that is most operative when children learn. Children do not learn by rules, but through "metaphoric similarities" that connect "seemingly unrelated subjects." For example, Hartmann explains, when a child first learns the concept of "bird," he or she does not internalize facts about bird physiology and behavior. Instead, "the child develops an image or an archetype of a bird something like a robin" and then compares that image to newly encountered creatures to determine their similarity. "Our brain functioning seems to work first or most easily by similarity or metaphor."[94] This use of metaphor to understand similarity, Hartmann argues, is especially true when we are dealing with our emotionally driven and wordless "primary experiences."[95] He links this capacity for metaphor, emotion, and images to dreaming and even memory by noting that we think in metaphor regardless of the specific type of mental processing. Our sense of self is built on emotion-guided memories, and Hartmann believes that dreams play a large part in the structuring of memory.[96] Moreover, emotions seem to play a strong influential role in our dream imagery, forming or shaping the imagery in the same way that they influence the poet's pen or the painter's brush.[97]

The emotional influence on dream imagery seems to be especially strong after traumatic experience; at such times, dreams may strikingly reflect the dreamer's emotional state and feature what Hartmann calls a *Central Image* that pictures underlying emotions. In fact, his research suggests that more powerful and intense emotions result in more intense Central Images. In one study, "blind" scorers read dream reports, noting particularly vivid and powerful images, and then identified any emotions from a list of eighteen that might be represented in those images. As expected, the Central Image Intensity (CII) was higher in dreams than in daydreams, and higher in REM awakenings versus non-REM awakenings. CII is often rated higher in strongly memorable dreams, and in early-life rather than recent dreams. It is especially high in dreams considered to be "big."[98] In another study, Hartmann found an increase in dreams with a higher CII following the 9/11 attacks in the United States; the images recorded were rated as mostly picturing fear/terror and helplessness/vulnerability. The correlation between higher CII and traumatic experience was also suggested in research involving the dreams of college students who reported having experienced physical or sexual abuse in early life. The dreams of those who experienced such abuse had a significantly higher CII score than those who had not experienced such abuse.[99] What purpose could such powerful, emotionally influenced imagery in dreams be serving?

Decades of research that has examined the relationship between sleep, memory, and learning seems to suggest that at least one of the purposes dreaming serves is that of learning and integration of new material. Bulkeley notes that because mammals experience REM sleep, whereas reptiles and birds do not, such sleep may have an evolutionary adaptive value. Some research suggests that sleep seems to help the mind process information, consolidate memories, and learn new skills; dreaming may also positively affect the way the brain grows and adapts, affecting how individuals respond to novel, complex, and/or anxiety-provoking experiences.[100] Hartmann's research leads him to conclude that rather than serving to "consolidate" memory through a "replay" of events of the day, dreaming "weaves in" and "integrates new material into existing memory, guided by emotion," changing the material as needed to weave it "into an ongoing story."[101] In his Contemporary Theory of Dreaming, Hartmann concludes by saying the following:

- Dreaming is a form of mental functioning, inseparable from other mental functioning, and not any kind of "alien intrusion" or "foreign language."
- Dreaming is "hyper-connective"; it involves new connections, and "is creation, not replay."

- The connections made in dreams are not random, but guided by the emotions of the dreamer.
- The "picture-metaphor" language of dreams is not unique to dreaming, but is consistent with the more "relaxed" form of processing in the "default mode" of brain functioning.
- Dreaming is an "adaptive" function where new material is "woven in" to existing memory systems to "help us build and rebuild a meaningful emotional memory system, which is the basis of our individual selves." Remembering dreams is not necessary for this to occur, but may increase "self-knowledge" and produce "new insights and creations."
- The "waking-to-dreaming continuum" serves an adaptive function that allows humans to both think in "direct, focused, serial fashion" and yet also "associate more broadly and loosely" as appropriate.[102]

Bulkeley concludes that dreams are related to psychological integration, emotional balance, and the capacity to overcome crises, conflicts, and traumas.[103] Similar conclusions have been drawn by Hoss, who has conducted various meta-analyses of the work of leading cognitive scientists investigating dreams.[104] He argues that their work supports the existence of an "emotionally guided, self-restoration, creative problem solving and behavioral learning function"[105] in dreaming. Dream activity is associated with the amygdala and limbic system, leading to such conclusions as that dreams process memories, the amygdala "orchestrates" dream activity, and dreams connect images with emotional memory associations. Dream images are "emotionally charged 'picture metaphor[s]'" that involve the visual association cortex, linking image to information to emotion.[106]

Alane Daugherty, professor of kinesiology and health promotion, links the amygdala, the hippocampus and the anterior cingulate to meaning making and emotional perception, and emotional or implicit memory.[107] On the other hand, Richard Kradin, a physician and researcher in psychosomatic medicine, disagrees that the brain stores memories at all. Instead, he prefers a model that differentiates between those memories that are registered in consciousness and "verbally accessible" by the hippocampus and those that are "encoded out of consciousness," not retrievable by conscious will, and "state-dependent." Such memories require "sensory and affective cues comparable to those available during their encoding in order to be retrieved."[108] We might infer Daugherty's claims about emotional and implicit memory to be referring only to those memories "encoded out of consciousness."

Hoss is interested in correlating cognitive scientists' findings to Jung's theories of dreaming and has noted significant parallels that seem to provide neurological support for Jung's approach, especially regarding his stances on dreams as unconscious expression, dream symbols as "emotionally charged pictorial language" that reveals the "unconscious meaning" of experiences, and on dreams as playing a role in both the psyche's compensatory function and its transcendent function.[109] Hoss notes that the use of positron emission tomography (PET) scans has revealed a "unique combination of active and inactive centers" that may provide the basis for the dream's ability to reflect "the unconscious meaning of a conscious experience." He explains that in REM sleep, our executive functions of rational thought, linear logic, episodic memory, and sensory and motor functioning are all inactive. At the same time, centers related to emotion, visual association, and other unconscious activities are active, presumably resulting in dream activity and imagery.[110] Hoss's findings are summarized in table 5.2.[111]

In another dream observation, Hoss describes a man who had been offered a teaching appointment in a field of study within which he had not been active for quite some time; the dreamer's conscious attitude was that "there is no way I can resurrect my old talents, they are gone forever." Hoss quotes the dreamer and notes the appearance of the five functions as listed in table 5.2 in his dream:

> I was wandering through a desert and saw an old rusty car. I looked inside and found a man who was not moving. I was going to give him up for dead [*conflict detected*], but my unknown companion urged me to wake the man [*resolution initiated, compensating cues*]. I argued that it was useless [*mediation*] but after much discussion reluctantly gave in and shook the man [*scenario tested*]. When I did, both the man and the car came to life [*compensation*] and the car transformed into a newer car [*emotional reinforcement*].[112]

Describing another dream, Hoss writes of a corporate executive whose company was laying off top executives; while the dreamer hoped he would be spared, he was afraid his career was over. Yet a dream "changed him."

> I am a passenger in a boat on a dark underground river trying to find a way out and a "position" in the windows where I can see daylight [*conflict detected*]. The tour guide appears behind me and points to an opening in front that I had not seen before [*compensation*] and says, "you can walk out that door" [*imagined resolution and cues*]. I didn't understand what he was telling me, but finally at his constant urging [*mediation*], I walked out the door [*scenario tested*]. When I did the boat emerged from an ice cave into a bright beautiful sunlit setting of calm water [*reinforced*].[113]

Shortly after dreaming the dream, the dreamer was offered a new position and happily left his company.

Table 5.2 Hoss's Findings

Jung's Theory	*Neurological Finding*	*Hoss's Conclusions*
Dreams are an "expression of the unconscious" and are "unconscious processes obtruding on consciousness."	Brain centers related to executive functions, waking consciousness, working memory, and conscious reflection are "demodulated" while brain centers that function "below the threshold of conscious awareness or preceding conscious awareness" are highly active. (Hobson, et al. 2002, 2003)	Dreams occur during brain states that are not identified with conscious processing.
Symbols are "emotionally charged picture language."	High levels of activity during REM sleep in the amygdala, limbic system, and medial and some caudal frontal regions which are involved in emotionally charged actions and decision-making.	Dreams "selectively process emotionally relevant memories"; the amygdala "orchestrates" the dream plot; imagery contains the "feeling state" of the dreamer; and "activity in these regions may account for the instinctive elements in dreams."
	Sensory input and primary visual center are inhibited, but "visual association cortex, temporal and certain pre-motor," and areas which form "sensory representations with information that originates totally from within" are "highly active." The right inferior parietal cortex is also active. (Hobson, et al., Hartmann, Seligman & Yellen, Dang-Vu et al.)	"Internally generated information (feelings, memories, concepts) are represented as associations and picture-metaphor"; "sensory and motor elements appear as fictive movements and sensations." The right inferior parietal cortex (involved in spatial organization and creation of dream imagery) "creates representations which are integrated into dream space."

Dreams play a role in the psyche's compensatory function "to restore psychological balance by producing dream material that re-establishes psychic equilibrium," and in the transcendent function to allow the individual to move from a deficient attitude to a new attitude.	"Dreams operate much like the brain learns—weaving new material into established memory—making new connections, expressed in picture-metaphors that reveal new perspectives & insights." (Hartmann, 2011) Five brain functions active during REM: 1) Conflict detection (*basal ganglion and anterior cingulate* play roles in error detection; *anterior cingulate* monitors conflict and anomalies; *caudal and lateral orbitofrontal cortex* "are involved in inspection of events that deviate from expectation"). 2) Resolution initiation and mediation ("*anterior cingulate* mediates action aimed at choosing between conflicting perceptions"; *basal ganglia* "generates paradoxical behavior metaphors" and involved in "novelty-related decision-making") 3) Imagining and testing of self-focused goal directed scenarios (*anterior cingulate* "imagines or observes an outcome and monitors the consequences"; the *medial pre-frontal cortex* is involved in "introspective self-referential behavioral [simulation] and rehearsal") Kringlebach, Vertes, Gusnard, Craig, Packard, Marley, Lieberman)	Evidence from PET studies allows researchers to hypothesize the role of certain brain centers on dream content based on the "role those centers play in the waking state" and "further research findings on those centers are suggestive that the dreaming brain has the potential capacity to operate in a manner supportive of Jung's observations"; that what Jung called the "transcendent function" is "organically possible." Reported dream content reflects the processes listed to the left and the adaptation and learning that results.

(Continued)

Table 5.2 (Continued)

Jung's Theory	*Neurological Finding*	*Hoss's Conclusions*
	4) Cues and "sense of knowing" influences the dream activity (*anterior cingulate* detects conditions under which errors are likely and cues other parts of the brain and "contains a representation of the self at each moment in time and acts as a comparator between these points in time . . . and is able to compare feelings of the past, present, and future"; *insula* "is involved in subjective feelings, perceptual decision making and sudden insight"; *basal ganglia* seeks "eventual rather than immediate reward"; *medial pre-frontal cortex* "self-monitors learning, provides a 'sense of knowing' and retrospective confidence judgment"; the *orbitofrontal cortex* "is involved in regulating planning behavior based on reward/ punishment so as to change ongoing behavior.") 5) Emotional Reinforcement and Adaptive Learning (*anterior cingulate* "observes and monitors performance and outcome to select an appropriate response based on anticipating & valuing rewards" and is involved in "focused problem-solving and adaptive response to changing conditions"; *basal ganglia* involved in "reward-based adaptive action planning and learning"; sections of the *orbitofrontal cortex* are involved in "decision making, expectation and regulating our planning behavior so as to change our ongoing behavior.") (Falkenstein, Bush, Allman, Botvinick, Posner, Carter, Flavio, Petrides, St. Clair, Yamada, Hayden, Apps, Luu et al., Partiot et al.,	

Hoss, 2012, pp. 1–7. Created by author.

It appears that our dreaming body-mind seems to be able to reveal new connections it has made in metaphorical pictures. *Even more important*, it seems that our dreaming body-mind has the capacity to resolve emotionally significant issues by

> recognizing anomalies, conflicting perceptions and threats to our inner sense of self; mediating a resolution by creating imagined outcomes in the form of dream scenarios; monitoring the outcome; selecting a scenario based on achieving the anticipated rewards; and encoding that result in memory as something learned.[114]

We must be somewhat cautious in our claims about what scientific research shows the dream may be doing regarding development and learning, because there is not yet a way to objectively prove even the occurrence of a dream let alone what centers of the brain are active during particular dream scenarios and the role they may play in the dreamer's experience. Yet Hoss describes the deductive conclusions we can make as "promising."[115]

Although Bulkeley describes the area of research that connects dreaming to learning as "contentious," he argues that it is helpful to examine dreams and learning through the lens of neuroplasticity which describes the brain as having the ability to adapt in response to new experience.[116] Research in neuroplasticity suggests that there is a correlation between the firing patterns of neurons and learning, meaning that the more we repeat a behavior, the more efficient the firing becomes between the neurons that are correlated with that behavior. Daugherty's work applies this concept to emotion claiming that the human limbic system connects the body and brain in such a way that when we perceive the world around us, especially if in a strongly threatening way, the body floods our system with chemicals that trigger the amygdala to "record" that experience for future reference through implicit memory patterns. Such patterns become the "blueprints" for interpreting future conditions.[117] Daugherty suggests that the more our experiences trigger the same emotions—the more the emotional "imprint" that is created by the neurons and glia in neural nets gets reinforced—the more that pattern gets re-activated. It then becomes even stronger and more likely to become one's automatic response.

Hartmann believes that when we favor those patterns of activation, they can begin to take on a transpersonal quality and show up as "typical dreams" and as archetypes and myths.[118] In what sounds astonishingly like Jung's theory of the psychological complex, that imprint or emotional reactivity pattern is then triggered whenever a situation that even remotely resembles the original experience is perceived. The stronger those imprinted patterns become, the more we are psychologically hijacked by an emotional reaction that may be only minimally relevant to the situation at hand. The bad news is that such reactivity perpetuates itself, and our biology changes in such a way as to make threat and anxiety even more likely to be experienced.[119] The good news is that we are inherently adaptive, and it seems that the structure of our brains can actually change with new experience. New experiences allow us to break entrenched patterns by creating new neural connections and nets, and new associations. This holds "staggering" potential for healing and transformation.[120]

The best news of all is not only that neurons and glia have the capacity to grow, change, and form new connections with new life experience,[121] but that our brains do not distinguish between real and vividly imagined experience.[122] Is this also true for what is dreamed? Stephen LeBarge, a leading researcher into lucid dreaming, has discovered that lucid dreams can produce the same physical effects on the dreamer's brain as corresponding waking life events[123] Daugherty also argues that while our neural networks can be "re-wired" with new experience, "it is not the conscious mind that does the rewiring, it is deeply felt *experience*, internal or external and *experience is an embodied phenomenon*."[124] Dreaming, then, seems to involve the interweaving of new embodied experience below the level of consciousness, guided by the "felt sense" and emotion that is associated with that experience, into existing memory systems—or implicit memory imprints; such interweaving can be related to new connections and new learning.

Dreams, Imagination, and Healing

Not only has recent research supported the positive relationship between dreaming and emotional processing as well as learning and change, studies also suggest a relationship between dreaming, imagination, and physical health and healing. Rendering physicalism moot, recent research into meditation, biofeedback, and prayer shows that the mind can influence the body. If we consider our cultural roots, it seems that Western medicine has forgotten its own history regarding the importance of dreams to physical health. In the ancient Greek healing temples of the god Asklepios, the tradition "pivots around the divine power of imagination that can transform a body out of illness into health."[125] Robert Bosnak, editor and contributor to *Imagination and Medicine* writes,

> Western medicine from its inception was aware of the great power of dreaming, not for emotional purposes as used now in some circles ever since the beginning of psychoanalysis but for the treatment of physical illness. For close to a millennium, the people who gave us the foundation of most of Western thought, including science itself as well as its practical applications during the Roman Empire, swore by this method of dream healing.[126]

We are only recently beginning to remember that dreams can affect belief and belief can affect the body. This would be no surprise to Marion Woodman, who stressed that because the psyche and soma are "virtually one," psychological factors are very important in physical healing.[127] As well, Dr. Esther M. Sternberg argues that there is a psychological component to every cure, estimating that "about one-third of the therapeutic effect of every pill comes from the placebo effect," because when we believe a medication will make us better, it does.[128] Moreover, learned associations can actually "change the body's nerve and hormone responses, which ultimately affect how immune cells work. In that sense, believing can make you sick or make you well."[129] As Bulkeley suggests, certain rituals and practices based in dreams may stimulate a natural placebo effect that can assist the body's innate capacities for healing. This may be related to the fact that, during sleep, the body's immune system is highly active and involved in health-related endogenous healing processes that may be enhanced by such rituals or dream practices.[130]

Recent studies have begun to examine how what was once dismissed as merely the placebo effect might be better respected as a positive response to enlisting the patient's imaginal resources. New research in this area has been explored at a series of "Imagination and Medicine" events held at Pacifica Graduate Institute and resulted in the publication of a book by the same name. It may be true that "big dreams" with stronger images and emotion may have the greatest impact on physical health.[131] Ernest Lawrence Rossi and Kathryn Lane Rossi have proffered a fascinating theory of the relationship between the mind, brain, mirror neurons, and our DNA, arguing that the mind uses the mirror neuron system to update the brain and encode "novel and numinous experiences of consciousness and dreaming."[132] His theory suggests that such experiences can activate mirror neurons and related gene expression, protein synthesis, and brain plasticity resulting in expanded consciousness and mind-body healing.[133] We must, along with Bulkeley and James W. Jones, challenge the physicalist worldview, especially in the medical field. Jones argues that what has been demonstrated in psychological laboratories and clinical practice regarding hypnosis, biofeedback, and meditation "demands a robust account of mental causation."[134] In fact, the question of how mental states have any effect at all upon the world is, in Clayton's opinion, the more difficult question when it comes to the "hard problem of consciousness."[135]

In this section, through a limited survey of research on the brain, dreaming, emotion, learning, and physical healing, I have shown that (1) although there is some disagreement among researchers as to the nature and function of dreaming and its relationship to the brain, dreaming is an activity of both body and mind; (2) the various brain regions active during dreams are correlated with the same kinds of functions described in Jung's psychology; (3) dreaming seems to involve emotion, trauma, learning, responsiveness, adaptation, integration, problem solving, and the body's perception of its surrounding world; and, (4) we can connect neuroplasticity, entrenched behavior patterns, and transformational experience through dreams because the brain cannot discern between actual experience and dreamed experience in terms of their potential effect. Because we can make these connections, we can link dreaming to body, to world, and to transformation.

A COMMUNAL VIEW OF DREAMS

Through a psychological view of dreams, we may connect them to personal life and meaning as well as to transpersonal vision and *value* through the role of archetypes and archetypal images. We have also gotten a glimpse through Jungian psychology how the embodied psyche is connected to nature, human history, and culture, and therefore how dreams connect to *belonging*. Dreams viewed psychologically are also related to *transformation* and positive change. By touching on the science of the dreaming brain and neuroplasticity, I have shown how a scientific view connects dreams to the emotional body-mind, to the body's perception of its internal and external world of concerns, and how dream research supports a Jungian approach to dreams and dream work thereby also linking dreams to *belonging* and *transformation*. Now we will turn to the communal view of dreams witnessed in the rise of dream sharing groups and explore how such groups reflect dreaming and dream work as shared experience, shared meaning, and shared growth and learning, and, therefore, connected to *value*, *belonging*, and *transformation*.

Historically, dreams had regularly been explored in religious or communal contexts, but with the rise of psychology came the secularization of dreams, wherein psychologists have focused primarily on dreams as an intrapsychic phenomenon.[136] This began to change in the late 1960s and early 1970s, when what Bulkeley calls an "interesting new twist" developed—the rise of dream sharing groups—that was prompted primarily by the writings of Ann Faraday, Patricia Garfield, Montague Ullman and Nan Zimmerman, Gayle Delaney, and Jeremy Taylor. These writers took dreams beyond the walls of professional psychotherapy to the general public. Bulkeley estimates that in excess of fifty thousand dream groups were formed in the United States alone between the 1960s and the 1990s with participation approximating 500,000 individuals.[137] Credit for this phenomenon belongs primarily to the work of Montague Ullman, a psychiatrist who opened the first community mental health center in New York City and the Dream Laboratory at the Maimonides Medical Center,[138] and to Jeremy Taylor, a Unitarian Universalist minister and author.[139]

The phenomenon of dream-sharing groups has garnered little scholarly attention to date, yet Bulkeley argues that scholars of religion and psychology should take an interest for three reasons: (1) Such groups of individuals often work with their dreams to gain spiritual insights; (2) the interplay of religion, psychology, and culture can shed some light on the secularization process in contemporary society; and (3) dream-sharing groups often experience a deepened sense of community and intimacy.[140] Dream groups have displayed great diversity in structure and processes; groups have been formed around particular interests, including Jungian psychology or personal needs (support groups, 12-Step groups). While some may be religious in nature, others draw on guided imagery, picture-drawing, or even dream theater to gather insights. Yet they do seem to share certain commonalities. Bulkeley offers this description of a typical dream-sharing group:

- Six to twelve people gather in a quiet, comfortable place;
- One serves as leader or facilitator;
- Each person briefly describes a personal dream;
- The group chooses one dream to discuss in detail, asking questions and offering comments and meanings;
- The discussion of a dream can take from fifteen minutes to two hours; and,
- Over time, everyone in the group will get to share their own dreams and comment on those of others.[141]

Despite their diversity, dream groups commonly share basic assumptions about the relevance of dreams to waking life, their potential for opening new insights, and their interpretability without professional expertise.[142]

Taylor established his first dream-sharing group while running a consciousness-raising seminar on racism to fulfill his civilian service requirements as a conscientious objector to the Vietnam War. As part of the discussion, he asked members to share and discuss dreams that featured people of color and was astonished to see the level of transformative energy the work released. It seemed to bring hidden ambivalences to light and allowed participants to own their own biases.[143] He later took a practice initially created by Ullman and developed it into what he called *Group Projective Dream Work*. This method assumes the posture that any interpretation made of another's dream is more a subjective function of the interpreter's own symbol system and preconceptions than objectively reflective of the meaning for the dreamer.

As Nelson describes the process, once the dream is shared, members ask clarifying questions in order to be able to find related associations in their own life. Members will then typically preface their interpretative comments with the phrase "If it were my dream . . ." or in some other way to indicate the projective nature of their comments and their own stance in relation to the dream.[144] In Ullman's thought, even "wrong" interpretations are useful because they can help the dreamer clarify the meaning of the image.[145] Taylor believes that a dreamer who pays attention will experience an "aha!" or a "tingle feeling" when something intuitively truthful is discovered,[146] even by another dreamer. Group projective dream work helps tease out the multiple levels of meaning that may be contained in a dream because each participant brings their own life experience, intelligence, and intuition to the process. According to Taylor, this kind of collective work "is most beneficial to the life of the imagination and can nurture a community of creativity."[147]

Although Sanford considers it difficult and dangerous to analyze a dream isolated from the dreamer's context and personal associations with the dream symbols,[148] a key aspect of group projective dream work is that the work can stay at a level that protects members' psychological safety because the dreamer's personal, private history and emotional concerns do not have to be revealed. There is therefore no effort on the part of laypersons to venture into deep psychological analysis. Moreover, Nelson cautions group members to not impose potentially anxiety-raising interpretations that go beyond the bounds of the dreamer's present awareness, insisting that "we follow rather than lead the dreamer"[149] to ensure everyone's psychological safety.

Would Jung have approved of dream-sharing groups? Not likely, speculates Singer, reminding us of Jung's distrust of "the collective" and any association with mass-mindedness. "But since his death," she writes, "we have learned so much about the value of working with groups, and dream work in groups has been shown to be valuable in ways Jung could not have dreamed of."[150] Clearly, Jung believed dream interpretation to be the most effective means of integrating the unconscious with consciousness. Yet he is somewhat at odds with himself when he recommends that patients not "depend permanently on outside help" while recognizing the difficulty of analyzing one's own dreams.[151] So where does that leave the many who do not have access to costly analytical resources? Tacey shares this concern, accusing Jungians of being "unimaginative about finding other methods to impart their work beyond the clinical model" leaving the "complex journey of individuation" open only to those who can pay for therapy, a reality against which his "social conscience rebels."[152]

In this project, I take the position that one of those "other methods" is dream-sharing groups, a phenomenon that offers many life-enhancing outcomes. Hartmann argues that dream images can function similarly to the way that art serves as an emotional-aesthetic bridge between the artist and the audience. The emotion of the artist guides the production of the work which then pictures that emotion; the art then stimulates similar emotion in the audience.[153] The same happens when a dream that features an emotional Central Image is shared: the one hearing the dream empathetically feels what the dreamer's image pictures. Ulanov illustrates this phenomenon when she describes a group experience where a woman matter-of-factly reported a dream that featured a powerful horse. It was not until a group member described the image as seeming "like a real fairy tale carried right into life" that the dreamer "felt she was about to swoon, as she often did if a remark really hit home."[154]

It is well documented that dream-sharing groups help people to gain new insights about their own dreams or waking life concerns. For example, a study of high school students who shared their dreams discovered "new sources of energy, creativity, and hope."[155] In her work with groups in prisons, Ehlert found that dream-sharing helps prisoners connect their early life with the crimes they had committed.[156] Bulkeley disputes those who criticize dream groups as fostering "navel-gazing" self-interest stressing that dream-sharing can provide insight into problems at both the personal and social levels.[157] Dream groups can restore people's sense of community[158] and help them remember their shared humanity with others unlike themselves.[159] Most importantly, such outcomes do more than just reinforce existing, homogenous communities. Taylor, pointing to his racism seminar, argues that dream-sharing groups, through shared vulnerability, can overcome barriers of race, age, sex, and class, improve intercultural relations, and foster personal and communal transformation. Such groups, Taylor argues, bring about collective change because they promote individual growth, creativity, and courage.[160]

What is the collective change we seek now? If, as has been argued since the beginning of this project, we seek a resolution to the alienation and disenchantment that dualism and secularism have wrought, might dream-sharing groups be helpful? Bulkeley answers affirmatively, arguing that through the renewal of authentic spiritual experience, dream sharing groups bring about a re-enchantment of the world.[161] While there are certainly many ways to engage the unconscious (Tacey lists religious and spiritual practices, the arts, romance and relationship, and other creative and nonrational avenues[162]), dream-sharing groups offer a way that is easily accessible with many positive benefits. As I have shown above, those benefits include being able to connect dreams and dream work to our shared experience and shared meaning at the intersection of the personal and the social in a way that helps us to gain new insights into human problems and better appreciate our shared humanity. Therefore, we can connect a communal view of dreams and dreamwork to *value*, *belonging*, and *transformation*.

A MYSTICAL VIEW OF DREAMS

We have seen how a psychological view, a scientific view, and a communal view of dreaming connects us to value, belonging, and transformation. But what might a *mystical* view add to this work? As noted earlier, our understanding of dreams first emerged as *religious* because there seemed to be transpersonal or extra-mundane powers involved. For millennia, religious traditions have sought revelation, spiritual guidance, and creative inspiration in the dream experience.[163] Even more, Bulkeley argues that it is not merely coincidental that dreams and religion have always been in close relationship. In fact, the cultural records of the world's religions indicate that dreaming may even have seeded religious ideas, feelings, and symbols.[164] Dreaming may be a "wellspring of religious experience."[165] But what is the *nature* of this experience and how might it connect to our baseline criteria of *value*, *belonging*, and *transformation*? I will show that at least some dreams may be viewed as mystical because they connect us to transpersonal reality, are purposive, and bring guidance and healing, thus fostering wholeness and flourishing.

Dreams and Religious Experience

Of course, there are many who would dismiss any view of dreams as religious experience. Freud saw them as merely garbled messages intent on hiding repressed desires. Meanwhile, because our dominant dualistic and mechanistic worldview immediately dismisses anything that smacks of the supernatural, many see dreams as merely random neuronal firings or promptings of last night's pizza. Yet this is the inherent problem: label some dreams *religious* and immediately the broader public assumes supernaturalist superstitions that should have been shed at the Enlightenment. When we consider other viewpoints—drawing from Jungian resources and beyond—we immediately see that this is not the only way to understand what is *religious*.

A Jungian approach to this question affords us a postmodern, trans-religious capacity to bridge the dream experience with human spirituality because of Jung's understanding of archetypal symbols and their accessibility in dreams. Halligan notes that Jung's analytical psychology locates dreams in human religious experience;[166] it is through inner psychic life that one has access to guidance or direction from that which is greater than the conscious ego. Even a neurosis or other psychological illness can be "purposive" and open the door to discovery, because it is at "the culmination of the illness" that Jung believed destructive forces were "converted into healing forces."[167] Similarly, Taylor teaches that "all dreams come in the service of health and wholeness"; they can help dreamers find "internal peace and spiritual comfort" and even aid in decision-making. Because a dream is often a "gripping, mysterious, numinous experience" that carries "spontaneous" helpful information, human beings have generally attributed them to divine origins.[168]

The question we ask now is: Can one understand the numinous encounter, transformation and healing that often come through dreams as truly an encounter with *God*? And if so, must that God be understood *supernaturally*? Jung recognized dreams as carrying a *numinous* quality and drew from Rudolf Otto's work in this area. Otto described a numinous experience as an encounter with a holy other that seems to exist outside of nature yet with whom one is "in communion." He differentiated two kinds of numinous experience: one he called *mysterium fascinans* and the other *mysterium tremendum*. In the *fascinans* experience, one is drawn toward what one perceives as an awesome reality—typically what researchers (James, Hood, Stace, Pargament) describe as an experience of unity. In a *tremendum* experience, one is somewhat repelled from what one perceives to be "awful" and "terrible"—this experience of "presence" typically serves to accentuate one's feeling of creatureliness versus that of power.[169] Rather than defining this "holy other" as supernatural, Jung believed it to be the unconscious that one encountered both within oneself and as an objective *other*.[170]

Jung's personal experience with this *other* in the unconscious led him to confidently claim that he *knew* that God exists,[171] yet he did not definitively claim that dream guidance came from God. Instead, he said that it is in such encounters that the archetypes come to life as independent and guide the personality in ways beyond the "willing and striving" of the ego; in such times the individual's "psyche has awakened to spontaneous life." Such experiences carry numinous power because the transformation that occurs cannot be linked to consciousness and so is experienced as a "revelation" that arises from deep within, yet which is not the "I" of personal consciousness. In such experiences, one accesses what Jung called the curative taproot of psychic life.[172]

In other words, experiencing this taproot of psychic life—the heart of the universe, the flow of life beneath all manifestation—is psychologically equivalent to experiencing God. True to his context, Nelson argues in Christian terms that although dreams are not God, they "usher us into the realm of spirit where God's Holy Spirit reigns supreme."[173] Ann and Barry Ulanov, on the other hand, refuse to lock the God that we encounter in our dreams into any one religious tradition or image, insisting instead that the divine in our dreams is "God in hiding," a "cloud of unknowing," a "great shadow of the Holy," and an "illuminating darkness" that draws near to us yet lies "outside our God-images."

> It is not so much that our images of God are wrong or our religious practices mistaken. They are simply too small in their finiteness. The dark side of God is a merciful one, effacing useless images, stretching, pushing us beyond even the best of what we have found in our traditions and created in our prayers.[174]

Dreams and Christian Experience

These discussions form a compelling case that a dialogue with the unconscious through one's dreams has value for individuals seeking wholeness. What value does dream work hold, specifically for the Christian? What stands in the way of the Church embracing such a practice? Jung points to post-Enlightenment scientism as responsible for a modern mindset that cannot incorporate dreams and other symbolic information. Since causality has taken on a sacred status and "there is no legitimate place in our world for invisible, arbitrary and so-called supernatural forces," we fail to give that which we perceive as being irrational or unreasonable their due.[175]

There has historically been strong interest on the part of a significant number of Episcopal priests in becoming Jungian analysts, a pathway embodied by Morton Kelsey, John Sanford, Pittman McGehee, and Bob Haden, among others. Those Jungians writing from a Christian perspective have no doubt about the value of the dream to one's spiritual life. Kelsey considers dreams "a consistent body of impressive and powerful materials" that show "evidence of contact with the numinous." Exploring the realm of dreams leads us to experience something beyond the physical level that is powerfully compelling no matter by what name it is called. Whether we use a term like "the spiritual world" or "the collective unconscious," it is an authoritative reality we encounter in our own depths.[176] Sanford does not hesitate to identify this "purposeful, numinous power," this "intelligence within [the] psyche" as God.[177]

As he began to work with his own dream content, Kelsey believed he encountered God there as "a wisdom greater than mine that spoke to me in my dreams and came to my aid."[178] Sanford believes that dreams "express the Mind of God within us,"[179] and Joyce Rockwood Hudson notes that we are not left alone in our struggle to make sense of our dreams.

> Our penetration into the meaning [of our dreams] does not depend solely on human skill and knowledge. The message of the dream comes from the realm of God, and the Holy Spirit participates in our understanding of it. It is necessary that we apply ourselves and do our part in working with our dreams, but in the end it is grace working in us that makes the difference and helps us arrive at those insights that we are ready to receive.[180]

Receiving these insights—for modern Christians—may require a shift in theology, doctrine, and world view. Christians will, once again, need to believe—*as Jesus did*—that God not only desires to communicate intimately with us, but is doing so regularly. If people of faith can adopt this view, Kelsey claims, then our spiritual practices can bring us into real relationship with God and dreams can offer us self-knowledge and revelation.[181]

In a letter to Kelsey, Jung wrote, "What are modern Christians to make of dreams, then, when we have opened our minds in this way to the possibility that they may speak to us of something beyond or different from our conscious egos?"[182] The fruits of understanding dreams, for Kelsey, are lives filled with vitality and dimension.[183] He witnessed the power of dreams to transform over and over again both as a professor at the University of Notre Dame and in his congregational ministry, and found that even his agnostic students were impressed by the mystery and depth of their dream lives and were opened to a new world of religious experience.[184]

The God Encountered in Dreams

Clearly, dream work offers great potential for positive outcomes, but is there anything about which we should be cautious? For some individuals, focusing on one's inner life can become all-consuming, such that one can risk losing proper perspective on the value of outer life. Hudson suggests that people who tend to over-emphasize their dreams need to learn that while dreams work beneath the surface of life, we must also pay attention to outer life because "life proceeds from life and no other way."[185] Those who have not done inner work might be suspicious that such work could lead one to become too self-centered. But Sanford argues that the opposite is true because in examining our dreams we move beyond a focus on egocentric desires to a stance of ego subordination to the greater whole.[186] This is a process of continual surrender to the God within us, an experience that can be humbling, difficult, and painful.[187]

For Kelsey, those who would apply Jungian methods to their own journey must, by necessity, undergo the same kind of direct confrontation with God that Jung himself underwent. Jung described this as both a "bloody struggle" and "supreme ecstasy." God became the only reality, one that is both "an annihilating fire and an indescribable grace." Modern Christianity, concludes Kelsey, has distanced itself from such encounters and does not seem to want to be reminded of them.[188] Sanford expresses a similar perspective when he says it is safer to "deal with God directly than to compel God to thrust us forcibly into the way that is set before us."[189]

Dreams, Re-enchantment, and Belonging

When he was a young boy, Stephen Aizenstat's great-grandfather used to tell him that *everything*—even the knife he used in his shoe-making business—was alive. Aizenstat, psychologist and founding president of the Pacifica Graduate Institute in Santa Barbara, California, was led by a dream as an adult to a book hidden in the attic of his great-aunt about his deceased great-grandfather that ignited a lifetime journey focusing on the importance of dreams and inner life.[190] Yet much in our modern culture rejects as superstition and fantasy anything that is not sensate and measurable.

Whereas "primal humans experienced a strong, meaningful, and continuous connection to the world around them,"[191] Aizenstat argues that modern humans have been "thrown out of our Eden, forgotten our place in the world, and been severed from the wisdom of its dreamlike consciousness."[192] Even our experience of the animal world separates non-human beings into either sources of danger or "sterilized, domesticated pets that have had the wildness systematically bred out of them."[193] The rise of modern science, he claims, has both been a tremendous boon to human civilization and radically transformed its philosophical foundation as it "nearly deified" the supremacy of the rational human mind. All other mental aspects such as intuition, dreams, emotions, and play have been "devalued and marginalized" as "childish, backward, fuzzy, naïve, and even dangerous."[194]

In today's world, skepticism abounds. On the other hand, an earthquake within one's life experience can sometimes have the power to reduce one's skepticism to rubble. Hudson encountered such an experience in the middle of her life when a series of events that were rich in both symbolic and existential meaning associated with the death of a close friend threw her into a tailspin. She writes,

> This tragedy marked the end for me of the world I had always known and that everyone around me seemed only to know—a world in which human consciousness is the highest source of knowledge and human will is the greatest purposeful power, religious statements ascribing higher knowledge and power to God notwithstanding . . . As for myself, I knew more absolutely than I had ever known anything that these events were not merely coincidental. And so I was left stranded alone on the shore of a new world, a world in which a reality greater than any human reality orchestrates mercies to accompany tragedies, a world in which spiritual gifts flow copiously from death, not simply in a vague, ethereal way, but in a real, embodied way. On that tragic and transforming day, I realized that I was standing more directly in the presence of God than I had ever thought possible, that all of us were, and that the meaning of God's presence in our lives was more all-pervasive than even the Church had ever taught me it could be.[195]

Yet when she sought help within the Church that could explain these and subsequent paradigm-shifting events, Hudson found none. It may be important to note that while church membership and attendance in the United States continues to decline, attendees of the Haden Institute Summer Dream & Spirituality Conference regularly report encountering numinous symbols that speak to them through their dreams, leading to a deeper faith and a richer life.[196]

In this section on a mystical view of dreams, I have shown how dreams can be connected to God (understood as transpersonal reality), meaning, value, belonging, and transformation because dream symbols spring from archetypal or transpersonal reality, and because dreams and dream images are numinous, purposive, and carry guidance and healing. Dreams connect us to a transpersonal reality that is encountered within as an objective other and that reality is concerned with, and interested in, our individual and communal wholeness and flourishing.

SUMMARY

In this chapter, I have shown how including psychological, scientific, communal, and mystical views allow us to connect dreaming and/or dream work to an embodied experience of value, belonging, and transformation, and therefore how a practice of dream work, especially when done in small groups, can foster human wholeness and flourishing. If we can conclude that interpreting one's dreams is a labor that *works*—that doing so allows one to gain something of value from one's dreams or make substantive and life-enhancing changes—and if there are specific tools and methods that can be employed, then there is no reason why we cannot claim the resources of dream work to be a worthy practical companion for the theoretical and empirical resources of this project. Even so, there are limitations that may be obstacles to a practice of dream work being embraced by those in the Church and even by those who identify as *spiritual but not religious*:

(1) The generally held modernist worldview rejects any traditional God-world relationship that would validate spiritual dream work;
(2) Generally held Christian theology does not support taking either biblical or contemporary dreaming seriously;
(3) Jungian psychology does not provide an explanatory metaphysical framework to understand how formal elements like archetypes and their role in dream symbol formation can influence human behavior without being supernatural and coercive or how Jung's archetypal Self can be an "image of God" in the psyche;
(4) The Christian church has not yet embraced a metaphysical theology that shows how *value*, *relationality*, and *positive transformation* are key aspects of embodied reality.

Even so, I, like Aizenstat, am "convinced that tending dreams holds great promise for the future"[197] and so the remainder of this project will prove how an interweaving of Whiteheadian and Jungian thought provides a fruitful theoretical-empirical framework within which spiritual dream work—informed and generatively advanced by such a framework—can become a transformative *relational-imaginal praxis for psycho-spiritual wholeness and flourishing*.

NOTES

1. Bulkeley, *An Introduction to the Psychology of Dreaming*, 2; Bulkeley, *Visions of the Night*, 23.
2. Geoff Nelson, *Dreaming in Church: Dream Work as a Spiritual Practice for Christians* (Eugene, OR: Wipf and Stock, 2016), 3.
3. Kelsey, *Encounter with God*, 73.
4. Kelly Bulkeley, *Big Dreams: The Science of Dreaming and the Origins of Religion* (New York: Oxford University Press, 2016), 100.
5. Jung, *The Basic Writings of C. G. Jung*, 597.
6. Bulkeley, *Visions of the Night*, 23.
7. Kelly Bulkeley, "Dream-Sharing Groups, Spirituality, and Community," *Journal of Religion and Health* 35, no. 1 (Spring 1996): 62.
8. Bulkeley, "Dream-Sharing Groups, Spirituality, and Community," 62.
9. Bulkeley, *An Introduction to the Psychology of Dreaming*, 2.
10. Bulkeley, 4–5.
11. Bulkeley, 2.
12. Bulkeley, *Visions of the Night*, 24–25.
13. Bulkeley, 25.
14. Bulkeley, *Big Dreams*.
15. Bulkeley, *Visions of the Night*, 25.
16. Bulkeley, *An Introduction to the Psychology of Dreaming*, 30–31.
17. Robert J. Hoss, "Evidence of a Cognitive Function within Dreams" (www.dreamscience.org, July 2010), 1, http://www.dreamscience.org/articles/Cognitive_Function_Dreaming-Hoss.pdf.
18. Hoss, "Evidence of a Cognitive Function within Dreams," 4.
19. Hoss, 2.
20. John A. Sanford, *Dreams: God's Forgotten Language* (San Francisco: HarperOne, 1989), 124.
21. Bulkeley, *Big Dreams*, 93.
22. Bulkeley, 113.
23. Bulkeley, 127, 140.
24. Ernest Hartmann, *The Nature and Functions of Dreaming* (New York: Oxford University Press, 2010), 57–58.
25. Bulkeley, *An Introduction to the Psychology of Dreaming*, 3.
26. Jung, *Modern Man in Search of a Soul*, 62–63.
27. Singer, *Boundaries of the Soul*, 249.
28. Aizenstat, *Dream Tending*, 15.

29. Morton T. Kelsey, *Dreams: A Way to Listen to God* (New York: Paulist Press, 1978), 31–32.

30. Morton T. Kelsey, *God, Dreams, and Revelation: A Christian Interpretation of Dreams*, Revised and Expanded (Minneapolis: Augsburg Books, 1991), 172.

31. Bulkeley, *Big Dreams*, 27.

32. Sanford, *Dreams*, 104.

33. Singer, *Boundaries of the Soul*, 133, 151, 249, 406.

34. Sanford, *Dreams*, 104.

35. Bulkeley, *An Introduction to the Psychology of Dreaming*, 33–34.

36. Bulkeley, 33.

37. Jung, *Modern Man in Search of a Soul*, 24.

38. Aizenstat, *Dream Tending*, 16.

39. Jung, *Modern Man in Search of a Soul*, 24.

40. Robert A. Johnson, *Inner Work: Using Dreams and Active Imagination for Personal Growth* (San Francisco: HarperOne, 1989), 21.

41. Kelsey, *God, Dreams, and Revelation*, 177.

42. Johnson, *Inner Work*, 52.

43. Kelsey, *Encounter with God*, 110.

44. Johnson, *Inner Work*, 20.

45. Hoss, "Evidence of Wisdom in Dreams."

46. Nelson, *Dreaming in Church*, 94. Nelson identifies Johnson as a member of the International Association for the Study of Dreams.

47. Nelson, 94.

48. Halligan, "Jungian Theory and Religious Experience," 246.

49. Rowland, *Jung*, 37.

50. Rowland, 37.

51. Halligan, "Jungian Theory and Religious Experience," 247.

52. Halligan, 246; Aizenstat, *Dream Tending*.

53. Aizenstat, *Dream Tending*, 19.

54. Nelson, *Dreaming in Church*, 82.

55. Kelsey, *Dreams*, 45–51.

56. Halligan, "Jungian Theory and Religious Experience," 246.

57. Kelsey, *Dreams*, 41.

58. Sanford, *Dreams*, 103.

59. Johnson, *Inner Work*, 95.

60. Kelsey, *God, Dreams, and Revelation*, 180.

61. Johnson, *Inner Work*, 60.

62. Aizenstat, *Dream Tending*, 17.

63. Kalsched, *Trauma and the Soul*, 65.

64. Aizenstat, *Dream Tending*, 17.

65. Bulkeley, *An Introduction to the Psychology of Dreaming*, 32.

66. Aizenstat, *Dream Tending*, 23, 33.

67. Aizenstat, 20.

68. Robert J. Hoss, "Image Activation Dreamwork," accessed December 16, 2016, http://www.dreamscience.org/articles/image_activation_dreamwork.htm.

69. Johnson, *Inner Work*, 97.
70. Bulkeley, *An Introduction to the Psychology of Dreaming*, 33.
71. Kelsey, *Dreams*, 32–33.
72. Kelsey, 32–33.
73. Bulkeley, *An Introduction to the Psychology of Dreaming*, 77.
74. Bulkeley, 64, 76.
75. Bulkeley, 76.
76. As is so well articulated in *Mind & Emergence: From Quantum to Consciousness*, Oxford University Press, 2004.
77. Philip Clayton, *Mind and Emergence: From Quantum to Consciousness* (Oxford: Oxford University Press, 2006), 108.
78. Clayton, *Mind and Emergence*, 112.
79. Clayton, 120.
80. Christopher Bergland, "How Does the Vagus Nerve Convey Gut Instincts to the Brain?" *Psychology Today*, May 23, 2014, passim, http://www.psychologytoday.com/blog/the-athletes-way/201405/how-does-the-vagus-nerve-convey-gut-instincts-the-brain.
81. Clayton, *Mind and Emergence*, 115.
82. Bulkeley, *Big Dreams*, 100.
83. *An Introduction to the Psychology of Dreaming*, 53–55.
84. Hartmann, *The Nature and Functions of Dreaming*, 3–4.
85. Bulkeley, *Big Dreams*, 96–97.
86. Hartmann, *The Nature and Functions of Dreaming*, 37.
87. Bulkeley, *Big Dreams*, 42.
88. Bulkeley, 98.
89. Bulkeley, 28.
90. Hartmann, *The Nature and Functions of Dreaming*, 33.
91. Hartmann, 5.
92. Hartmann, 51.
93. Hartmann, 66.
94. Hartmann, 58.
95. Hartmann, 52.
96. Hartmann, 53, 59.
97. Hartmann, 51.
98. Hartmann, 4–15.
99. Hartmann, 15, 17.
100. Bulkeley, *An Introduction to the Psychology of Dreaming*, 65.
101. Hartmann, *The Nature and Functions of Dreaming*, 23–24.
102. Hartmann, 5–6.
103. Bulkeley, *Visions of the Night*, 7–8.
104. Hoss's work cites such researchers as Hartmann, Hobson, Maquet, Peters, Braun, Balkin, Nofzinger, Mintun, Pace-Schott.
105. Hoss, "Evidence of a Cognitive Function within Dreams," 2.
106. Hoss, 3.
107. Alane Daugherty, *From Mindfulness to Heartfulness: A Journey of Transformation through the Science of Embodiment* (Bloomington, IN: Balboa Press, 2014), 54.

108. Richard Kradin, "Reply to Bessel van Der Kolk," in *Imagination and Medicine*, ed. Stephen Aizenstat and Robert Bosnak (New Orleans: Spring Journal Books, 2009), 192.

109. Robert J. Hoss, "Recent Neurological Studies Supportive of Jung's Theories on Dreaming" (Annual Conference of the International Association for the Study of Dreams, Berkeley, CA, 2012).

110. Hoss, "Evidence of a Cognitive Function within Dreams," 2–3.

111. Hoss, "Recent Neurological Studies Supportive of Jung's Theories on Dreaming," 1–7.

112. Hoss, 6.

113. Hoss, 6.

114. Hoss, "Evidence of a Cognitive Function within Dreams," 4.

115. Hoss, "Recent Neurological Studies Supportive of Jung's Theories on Dreaming," 7.

116. Bulkeley, *Big Dreams*, 49–50.

117. Daugherty, *From Mindfulness to Heartfulness*, 35–53.

118. Hartmann, *The Nature and Functions of Dreaming*, 71.

119. Daugherty, *From Mindfulness to Heartfulness*, 42.

120. Daugherty, 47.

121. Daugherty, 45.

122. Daugherty, 76.

123. Bulkeley, *Visions of the Night*, 44.

124. Daugherty, *From Mindfulness to Heartfulness*, 76.

125. Robert Bosnak, "The Physician Inside," in *Imagination and Medicine*, ed. Stephen Aizenstat and Robert Bosnak (New Orleans: Spring Journal Books, 2009), xv.

126. Bosnak, "The Physician Inside," xviii.

127. Marion Woodman, "Coming to a Door," in *Imagination and Medicine*, ed. Stephen Aizenstat and Robert Bosnak (New Orleans: Spring Journal Books, 2009), xi.

128. Esther M. Sternberg, "Can Believing Make You Well? A Decade Later," in *Imagination and Medicine*, ed. Stephen Aizenstat and Robert Bosnak (New Orleans: Spring Journal Books, 2009), 96.

129. Sternberg, "Can Believing Make You Well? A Decade Later," 88.

130. Bulkeley, *Big Dreams*, 243.

131. Bulkeley, 243.

132. Ernest Lawrence Rossi and Kathryn Lane Rossi, "How the Mind and Brain Co-Create Each Other Daily," in *Imagination and Medicine*, ed. Stephen Aizenstat and Robert Bosnak (New Orleans: Spring Journal Books, 2009), 135.

133. Sternberg, "How the Mind and Brain Co-Create Each Other," 136, 138.

134. Bulkeley, *Big Dreams*, 248–49.

135. Clayton, *Mind and Emergence*, 123.

136. Bulkeley, "Dream-Sharing Groups, Spirituality, and Community," 59.

137. Bulkeley, *Visions of the Night*, 31, 33–34.

138. Markku Siivola, "Montague Ullman, Biographical Note," accessed December 17, 2016, http://siivola.org/monte/biographical_note.htm.

139. Bulkeley, *An Introduction to the Psychology of Dreaming*, 90.

140. Bulkeley, *Visions of the Night*, 31.
141. Bulkeley, "Dream-Sharing Groups, Spirituality, and Community," 60.
142. Bulkeley, *Visions of the Night*, 33.
143. Bulkeley, *An Introduction to the Psychology of Dreaming*, 91.
144. Nelson, *Dreaming in Church*, 115–16.
145. Bulkeley, *An Introduction to the Psychology of Dreaming*, 90–91.
146. Bulkeley, 91–92.
147. Nelson, *Dreaming in Church*, 115.
148. Sanford, *Dreams*, 55.
149. Nelson, *Dreaming in Church*, 116.
150. Singer, *Boundaries of the Soul*, 261.
151. Jung, *The Portable Jung*, 283.
152. Tacey, "The Challenge of Teaching Jung in the University," 14–15.
153. Hartmann, *The Nature and Functions of Dreaming*, 28.
154. Ulanov, *The Functioning Transcendent*, 11.
155. Bulkeley, *Visions of the Night*, 34.
156. Bulkeley, "Dream-Sharing Groups, Spirituality, and Community," 64.
157. Bulkeley, 64.
158. Bulkeley, *Visions of the Night*, 37.
159. Bulkeley, "Dream-Sharing Groups, Spirituality, and Community," 65.
160. Bulkeley, *An Introduction to the Psychology of Dreaming*, 92.
161. Bulkeley, *Visions of the Night*, 34.
162. Tacey, "The Challenge of Teaching Jung in the University," 15.
163. Bulkeley, *Visions of the Night*, 7.
164. Bulkeley, *Big Dreams*, 3.
165. Bulkeley, 8.
166. Halligan, "Jungian Theory and Religious Experience," 238.
167. Jung, *Modern Man in Search of a Soul*, 242.
168. Jeremy Taylor, "Ambiguities of Privilege," in *Dreaming in Christianity and Islam: Culture, Conflict, and Creativity*, ed. Kelly Bulkeley, Kate Adams, and Patricia M. Davis (New Brunswick, NJ; London: Rutgers University Press, 2009), 237, 239.
169. Ralph W. Hood, "Mystical, Spiritual, and Religious Experiences," in *Handbook of the Psychology of Religion and Spirituality*, ed. Raymond F. Paloutzian and Crystal L. Park (New York: The Guilford Press, 2005), 356–57.
170. Rowland, *Jung*, 4.
171. Shelburne, *Mythos and Logos*, 76–77.
172. Jung, *Modern Man in Search of a Soul*, 242.
173. Nelson, *Dreaming in Church*, 23.
174. Ulanov and Ulanov, *Religion and the Unconscious*, 237–38.
175. Jung, *Modern Man in Search of a Soul*, 130.
176. Kelsey, *God, Dreams, and Revelation*, 195–96.
177. Sanford, *Dreams*, 13.
178. Kelsey, *Dreams*, 9, 44.
179. Sanford, *Dreams*, 173–74.

180. Joyce Rockwood Hudson, *Natural Spirituality: Recovering the Wisdom Tradition in Christianity*, 2nd ed. (Danielsville, GA: JRH Publications, 2001), 98.
181. Kelsey, *God, Dreams, and Revelation*, 195.
182. Kelsey, 196.
183. Kelsey, *Dreams*, 3.
184. Kelsey, *God, Dreams, and Revelation*, 213.
185. Hudson, *Natural Spirituality*, 95–96.
186. Sanford, *Dreams*, 63.
187. Sanford, 184.
188. Kelsey, *God, Dreams, and Revelation*, 186.
189. Sanford, *Dreams*, 14.
190. Aizenstat, *Dream Tending*, 4–6.
191. Aizenstat, 145.
192. Aizenstat, 146.
193. Aizenstat, 146.
194. Aizenstat, 146.
195. Hudson, *Natural Spirituality*, 6.
196. The author reported the findings of a qualitative study on the experiences of Christians who attend the Haden conference at the 2014 meeting of the American Academy of Religion in the mysticism program unit.
197. Aizenstat, *Dream Tending*, 8.

Chapter 6

Synthesis

INTRODUCTION

Although the foundational methodological framework for this project is what Christ and Plaskow describe as the embodied theological method, there are other methods used throughout this work. In chapter 1, an analytical method was used to describe the lived realities of modern life in the United States and develop a theory to explain the fragmentation identified as the problem. In chapter 2, high-level comparisons were drawn between Whitehead and Jung to establish their congeniality as theoretical and empirical resources. In chapters 3 to 5, a hermeneutical approach was used to explore the meaning and value of Whitehead's and Jung's systems of thought and of various views of dreaming and dream work in relation to their abilities to help individuals experience *value*, *belonging*, and positive *transformation*. In this chapter, I return to a comparative approach in which functional resonances are brought to light as especially related to the tension between the vision of transpersonal reality and the fact of the historical past.

FUNCTIONAL RESONANCES

When proposing linkages or *resonances* between Whitehead and Jung, we must keep in mind that each engaged in speculation to one degree or another about the nature of reality although from differing bases of observation or experience. While Whitehead developed his own terminology to theoretically describe the metaphysical workings of the cosmos, Jung developed his terminology to empirically describe the workings of the human psyche. It is therefore not particularly helpful to assert or dispute whether there are direct one-to-one correlations between terms or concepts from each school of thought; a more fruitful exercise is to connect the functions each thinker used his terminology to describe.

As was more fully detailed in chapter 2, the term *resonance* is used in this work in the musical sense to connote sympathetic vibration and potential harmony; here it suggests *congruence* rather than identity or equivalence. Again, *resonance is evocation.* With this tuning fork in hand, we are searching for ways in which an aspect of Whiteheadian thought evokes a sympathetic harmony or movement in Jungian thought and vice versa. Approaching Whitehead and Jung functionally in this section does not dismiss the importance of theory or metaphysics; in fact, it gives Whiteheadians and Jungians the freedom to consider each other as potential dance partners while remaining true to their own theoretical frames. On this dance floor, the best partners always remain distinctly *other* and alluringly exotic while still being willing to make the functional moves required for the dance to be graceful, beautiful, and successful.

Within Whitehead's metaphysical and Jung's psychological frameworks we find:

- Primacy of experience, and of the body, feeling, aesthetics, and value
- An understanding of God as both immanent primordial experience and transcendent vision and value where what is transcendent is transpersonal but not supernatural
- Formal causes that are not deterministic in a co-creative environment of real freedom
- An orientation toward positive change, creative advance, and a zest for life
- An appreciation of the undeniable power of the past balanced by the lure of the possible
- The restoration of meaning, value, and purpose to the world without nullifying multiplicity and diversity

In this project, I am not attempting to remake Whitehead into a Jungian nor Jung into a Whiteheadian. Neither am I attempting to translate Jung or Whitehead entirely "into the presuppositions and conclusions" of the other;[1] that would be a disservice to both and there is not necessarily a *direct correlation* of the two theories. However, in the cause of constructing transformative relational-imaginal theory and praxis for psycho-spiritual wholeness that foster healing religious experience, there are *suggestive echoes* and *correspondences* between the two thinkers that can be fruitfully applied to our understanding of the dreaming body-mind and what it reveals. For example, both systems understand the following:

- God and one's past world can be encountered as *other* at the beginnings or depths of experience;
- The subject is constituted by encounter with such objective *others*—the stubborn facts of the past, the collective unconscious—that must be integrated into the individual subject's experience;
- Unconscious experience is valuable and precedes conscious experience;
- The individual's purpose is to attain distinctive value, intensity of experience, zest for life, and integration of multiplicity and contrasting forces;
- Value is communicated through aesthetic patterns or images that are dynamic and laden with emotion;
- Such emotion-laden value is persuasive, and proposes possibilities that may be novel and creative;
- Novel possibilities for wholeness and value attainment are given through the presence of God in the world and in the individual;
- God's presence in the individual is not coercive and possibilities offered are not determinative; the individual entity is free to choose its response, resulting in the potential for evil, wounding, and alienation; and,
- Greater value and wholeness can be attained through an individual stance of respect for, alignment with, and actualization of God's creative possibilities.

In chapter 1, I identified three requirements that a successful synthesis of theoretical, empirical, and practical resources must meet to address the fragmentation and alienation that is the reality of modern life. Such a synthesis must show: (1) that individual humans *matter*, and can experience *value* and meaning; (2) that we *belong*, that we are inherently and intimately *related* to God and the world; and, (3) that we are not defined by our wounds, but can experience *transformation* or positive change. This chapter will demonstrate how a synthesis of Whiteheadian and Jungian thought offers a transpersonal reality that is one of formalism with freedom. In the subsequent constructive chapter, this synthesis and the addition of dream-related practical resources results in the ability to construct: (1) a *relational-imaginal theory of dreaming*; and (2) a theory of *a relational-imaginal God-Self in the human being,* understood as the historic route of initial aims.

TRANSPERSONAL REALITY AND HISTORICAL PRESSURE

Probably the key area in which Whitehead and Jung show a remarkable degree of resonance is in the way in which they describe the functions of transpersonal reality and the pressure and power of the past. In this section, I will advance Odin's suggestion of functional resonances between Whitehead's dipolar God and Jung's collective unconscious, and their reliance on formalism with forms as transcendent in the sense of being transpersonal without being considered ideal. I will also further Maxwell's comparison of eternal objects and archetypes by showing how functional resonances between their systems are only possible when archetypes and eternal objects are distinguished from archetypal images and propositions and propositional feelings, the latter trio of which are definitively related to history and contextual relevance.

Dipolar God and Collective Unconscious

Whitehead describes the nature of God as *dipolar* with a primordial nature and a consequent nature. God's *primordial* nature is "infinite," "free," "conceptual," "eternal," and "unconscious"; this aspect of God is impersonal and its focus is on intensity of experience rather than on order and preservation.[2] In similar fashion, Jung asserts that the collectively unconscious aspect of psychic reality is morally and aesthetically neutral.[3] In connecting Whitehead's primordial God with Hillman's understanding of the collective unconscious, Slusser argues that there is comparability between Whitehead's primordial nature of God and Hillman's claim that an archetypal divine imagination permeates human imagination and life.[4]

Whitehead decried Christian theology's removal of God from the world as the Absolute or Unmoved Mover. Thus, whereas God's primordial nature is unmoved for particular outcomes, focusing only on depth of satisfaction, God's *consequent* "tenderness" is very moved by particulars and directed toward individual occasions as they arise.[5] God as consequent is "temporal," "determined," "actual," "physical" and "conscious."[6] Like Whitehead, Jung believed that a God unaffected by the world is a God of no consequence whatsoever. For Jung, the theological desire for an "Absolute" God leads to a God that is detached from the world, cut off from human experience, and therefore unreal. A "psychological" God, on the other hand, is real indeed.[7]

Is Jung's collective unconscious God? According to Steve Odin, Jung did not reify the collective unconscious but believed it to be a dynamic archetypal imagination that created images that flowed phenomenologically through the human psyche and manifested as myth, dreams, fantasies and visions.[8] Following Odin's lead, we can connect the collective unconscious' function of ancestral memory with Whitehead's consequent God.[9] Jung found evidence in his study of his patients' imagery for the collective unconscious possessing "a kind of absolute knowledge" that both held memory of the past and knowledge of the future through information that arises in dreams and fantasy.[10] There is no clean break between the personal unconscious and the collective unconscious; rather, there is a fluidity between the two. At its widest, the collective unconscious encompasses contents held by the human race at all levels of organization: family, social group, tribe, and nation.[11]

It is also possible to connect the way that Whitehead's dipolar God perceives the actual world of every occasion and orders eternal objects or possibilities based on their relevance to that actual world to the functional role that the Self—one of the archetypes of the collective unconscious—plays in the compensatory nature of the psyche. Here we might say that the Self prehends the individual's actual world and conscious attitude, recognizes what is lacking, and then presents forms that activate our image-making function to represent unconscious material. Ulanov calls the unconscious an "extraordinary source of knowledge" that matches unconscious response with conscious need. When an analyst accompanies an analysand in witnessing that process, she describes it as "moving" and "impressive."

> The discovery that so astonishes both persons is that the unconscious does present things specifically addressed to—we could even say custom made for—this particular analysand. Whether through symptom, symbol, or dream, the analysand feels summoned—some force or power or someone is communicating. "Look!" it says.[12]

Similarly, Whitehead understood the flourishing of higher-grade organisms to occur through alignment with God's initial aim and through the integrative activities leading to consciousness in intellectual feelings and thereby to rational thought. Moreover, Whitehead believed one could experience religious intuitions where one feels the consequent nature of God along with God's love for the world.[13]

Formalism in Whitehead and Jung

In his comparative essay on eternal objects and archetypes,[14] Maxwell suggests that while, on the surface, Whitehead's focus on cosmos and Jung's focus on the psyche may seem unrelated, at the deepest levels, their work suggests a convergence, especially as related to formal causation.[15] In Whitehead's cosmology, the term applied to the idea of formal causes is *eternal objects*, an idea that is functionally resonant with Jung's archetypes, yet it must be noted that Whitehead regarded his entire system as "eternal formal causes of everything that occurs."[16] The formalism embraced by both men is teleological: Whitehead's subjective aim is a final cause and his creative process includes both the givenness of the past and the possibility that comes with initial and subjective aims.[17] Similarly, Jung's archetypes seem to possess a kind of foreknowledge of envisioned possibilities[18] and press for the actualization of their potentialities while not being determinative regarding specific forms.[19]

Maxwell wisely does not argue for a direct correlation between archetypes and eternal objects; he points to Hillman's differentiation between Whitehead's eternal objects and their relationship to simple qualities versus archetypes' more complex clusters or agglomerations of qualities.[20] Yet Hosinski indicates that eternal objects can be conceptually realized by God in "relationships of diversity and pattern"[21] that may be combined. We must also keep in mind that Jung primarily discussed archetypes as related to human behavior and did not consider them a basic metaphysical category to describe the way in which everything that is actualized exhibits qualities. On the other hand, he understood archetypes at their most basic as related to differentiation and the primary counting numbers, and also saw them as infusing all of life with patterns of value and meaning that become evident in experiences of synchronicity. For Jung, archetypes are pre-existent forms that exist in the collective unconscious to serve as organizing principles[22] that help shape the contents of consciousness through the regulation, modification, and motivation of those contents.[23] Archetypes serve as ready-made templates for possibilities of emotional response.[24] He connected them with human instincts because humans are biological beings that must "act in a specifically human way and fulfill [the human] pattern of behavior."[25] Jung insisted that instincts are not amorphous but bear within themselves patterns of particular situations that then initiate the instinctual response. For example, the instinct of a leaf-cutting ant carries within it "ant, tree, leaf, cutting, transport, and the little ant garden of fungi. If any of these conditions is lacking, the instinct does not function, because it cannot exist without its total pattern, without its image." The image within the instinct is *a priori* to the activity and inborn; the pattern makes the activity possible.[26]

Such is also true of humans who must have a "psychic phenomenology" that is uniquely human, for, as Jung argues, "No biologist would ever dream of assuming that each individual acquires its general mode of behavior afresh each time."[27] On the other hand, archetypes and instincts are opposites with an incredibly close correspondence that connects those instincts to meaning and supports psychic energy.[28] Whitehead similarly writes of human "habits of behavior" and "habits of interpretation" that first incarnate in human history from "penumbral" stirrings,[29] suggesting a resonance with Jung. Noting that Hillman compares archetypes to a god because they are "personified modes of potential meaning, applicable, like metaphor, on many levels of experience," Maxwell prefers to see them as both personal and impersonal forces from the "transtemporal domain" that yet manifest temporally and specifically.[30]

Transcendent Forms

While describing anything as transcendent, abstract, or universal seems to fly in the faces of both feminism and a project that claims an embodied theological methodology, such terms are metaphorically appropriate for the functions of eternal objects and archetypes. Eternal objects transcend the entities they form, because they can recur elsewhere and exist as abstract possibilities even when not actualized.[31] Because eternal objects exist "in potency everywhere"[32] and are repeatable in successive actual entities while not being exhausted, they are considered "universals."[33] They are universally available and "realiz*able* at *any time*"[34] *without being normative* for every time or every circumstance. Critical for feminism and embodiment, eternal objects, notes Faber, are not an ultimate reality—in their abstract and transcendent state they are "neither active nor concrete," and "are real solely in events and event nexuses." They do not represent the "essence" of events, argues Faber, "they instead *make it possible* for events to become what their 'essence' is."[35] Neither, notes Odin, is the archetypal realm Platonically "ideal" or more real than physical reality. The archetypal imagination, like the primordial nature of Whitehead's God, is real in the deepest sense, but is yet "actually deficient or devoid of physical feeling."[36] In response to his critics who existentially questioned Jung's archetypes, he wrote "Certainly they do not exist, any more than a botanical system exists in nature! But will anyone deny the existence of natural plant-families on that account?" Like functional repetition in nature, the figures of the unconscious exist *a priori* as forms or as biological norms of psychic activity.[37]

The argument that Whitehead would not equate eternal objects with archetypes *ontologically* is stressed by Keller and Cobb, who believe that Whitehead's eternal objects are "historical, contingent, and capable of transformation" while Jung and Hillman "often treat [archetypes] as eternal and necessary."[38] Yet Singer disagrees, noting that to use a word like "necessary" is to make a value judgment that scientists like Jung are typically not willing to make. Instead, she prefers to talk about the archetypes as a way to understand the images we use to assign meaning to and organize our life experience.[39] Additionally, in a personal conversation, Jungian analyst Jerry R. Wright noted that Jung would not necessarily have considered archetypes eternal, because though their *forms* remained the same, their *contents* (the living symbols they present to the psyche) change over time. Kelsey understands Jung as seeing Plato's Ideas as the philosophical version of his psychically concrete archetypes.[40] For Griffin, another point of difference revolves around whether archetypes can be socially constructed or are always essentially of divine origin.[41] If we examine this more closely, we find that both eternal objects and archetypes, in and of themselves, are *ahistorical* while the images and propositions they produce are *historical* and *contextual.*

For Mattingly, eternal objects cannot be described separate from specific actualities but can only be described in terms of their potential related to an actual entity.[42] Similarly, Shelburne describes archetypes as having "the ontological status of a hypothetical construct" and, like an electron, archetypes can only be detected through the effects they produce. Those effects are the images and the behavior.[43] Because he recorded the images that arose in his patients' dreams and fantasies, Jung's early work equates the images with the archetypes, conflating those terms. But his later writing reflects an evolution of the concept and a differentiation between the unknowable archetypes and the personal or cultural images that arose.[44] The unconscious—*because it is unconscious*—is "beyond examination," so Jung "could only infer its structure from the unconscious material that emerged into consciousness."[45] As *unconscious*, archetypes cannot be directly perceived *by* human consciousness, but only indirectly perceived through their effect *on* consciousness.[46] Like the mathematical model some assume is behind objective reality, archetypes are neither visible nor representable.[47]

Historicity, Relevance, and Novel Aims

While eternal objects and archetypes in and of themselves are abstract, transcendent, and universal, Jung recognized that once the image arises, it has already differed from its archetype.[48] Robertson gives the example that all complex animals seem to have a mother archetype that leads them to hold certain instinctive expectations for how a mother should behave. He recalls that zoologist Konrad Lorenz found that the lived experience of an orphaned baby goose could stretch its expectations to accommodate the maternal imprint it formed to "the very un-gooselike Lorenz."[49] Once an archetype has made itself manifest in one's personal images, it takes on characteristics of the individual consciousness that perceives it, becoming more idiosyncratic.[50]

In other words, only archetypes are universal and ahistorical; the *images* that arise from them are contextual and temporal. While some images remain personal, others may, in fact, become "collective" or "common to entire people or epochs."[51]

Eternal objects are "forms of definiteness" that make each actual entity one thing versus another; they flavor every datum with individuality.[52] Every drop of experience involves eternal objects, and they are responsible for introducing anything new into concrete reality.[53] As Mattingly argues, eternal objects *must*, in fact, exist outside of history, otherwise there could be no possibility of genuine novelty.[54] Jung recognized this in terms of human behavior as well, and so proposed two ways in which the archetypes come into existence. On the one hand, notes Robertson, there is no explanation for the psyche's creativity if archetypes do not exist as possibilities prior to conscious actualization. When the psyche generates the perfect expression for as-yet-unknown facts, we must recognize that as novelty. On the other hand, Jung recognized that those problems that have engaged humanity over the aeons have become invested with a significant amount of psychic or emotional energy and naturally then "leave a trail in the [human] psyche."[55] Odin, too, understands archetypes as both preformed patterns that help the mind organize its contents and as "psychically inherited vestiges or ancestral memories transmitted since antiquity."[56] In a resonant way, Whitehead understands eternal objects as capable of being prehended both directly from God as a—possibly novel—initial aim *and* via their actualization in past, objective fact and superjective actual entities. Functionally, then, we can consider archetypes, like eternal objects, to be both *atemporal,* and *universal* abstractions as well as having *temporal* and embodied inheritances.

Yet eternal objects do not float into the world from nowhere of their own accord; no, they are envisaged for particular occasions based on their relevance within the ongoing historical process to that forming entity. "Each eternal object," wrote Whitehead, "has a definite, effective relevance to each concrescent process." Without such ordered relevance, novelty would be meaningless and reality would exhibit a disjunction of eternal objects that we do not see.[57] Who is doing the envisaging and what determines relevance? For Whitehead, the answer is God, yet this is not a God that exists only outside of time, unrelated to the world; this is a God who is an actual entity "which can provide for the actual effectiveness of the pure potentials without destroying their status as pure potentialities and with it their capacity to explain genuine novelty in the world."[58]

This point is crucial: we can only explain true novelty in the world if possibilities exist as pure potentials before they are actualized for the first time. As Lee argues, without eternal objects, nothing truly new could appear in the world—the world could only draw upon what is already actual.[59] Ontologically, it is not clear if Jung envisioned archetypes as capable of introducing novelty. While he wrote that "there is not a single important idea or view that does not possess historical antecedents,"[60] he also states that ideas can "spontaneously create themselves quite independently of migration or tradition."[61] Regardless, on the level of function, we know that Jung stressed the creativity of the compensatory psyche and its capacity to generate possibilities—via the transcendent function operating through the archetypal Self, or God-image in the psyche—that are novel in the life of an individual. At the deepest level, the entire collective unconscious—or archetypal imagination—is an atemporal envisagement of the forms that gives rise to archetypal symbols and primordial images.[62] Frey-Rohn reminds us that Jung thought the archetypes to be "not only the focal point of ancient pathways but also the center from which new creative endeavors emanated."[63]

Because God provides each entity with its initial subjective aim, it is God who orders the progress of the temporal world.[64] In process thought, every actual entity makes a decision that "constitutes its own definiteness" in relation to some kind of aim or purpose, otherwise we would see random chaos rather than order and meaning. If the end was determined strictly by the past, then there would be no actual freedom or true novelty. Rather, the end actually comes from the future as a lure or possibility, and it is God who orders possibilities into relevant lures for every occasion.[65] It is this lure—without coercion—that constitutes there even being decision, resulting in more order, novelty, and direction in life than could be possible if all were determined by the past or by chance.[66] As was discussed in chapter 3, the purposeful end or aim that comes as a lure from the future is called the *initial aim* or *initial subjective aim.*

As Cobb notes, it is the initial aim that "makes possible the commencement of process, and which therefore makes reality possible."[67] Whitehead describes the aim as a hybrid physical feeling—meaning that it is a physical prehension or ingression of God's conceptual feeling.[68] It is both the entity's *living immediacy* and its initial standard for experiencing and determining value.[69] For Lee, the initial aim is "God's purpose at work," and it is through this aim that value, intensity, harmony, and beauty enter the world, "which is to say that creative *advance* is the overall characteristic of process."[70] As it would be impossible for forming entities to survey the entire realm of possibilities for their actualization, God is therefore the actual entity who possesses the agency to order that developing subject's potentials for actualization.[71]

The immanence of eternal objects in the world is "systematically interrelated" but not "logical"; their relationships cannot be explained *by* history but, in fact, are explanatory *of* history.[72] The fact that there is such a thing *as history*—that things are "reasonably together" as an "inter-locked community of events"—is due to the fact that the universe's creative advance demands that there be "patterns of assemblage" that are aesthetic in nature.[73] As Ballard reminds us, the present character of the world depends causally on its past character, and prior occasions limit possibilities available to the present moment.[74] The creative advance can only introduce *relevant* novelty whereby intensity is "heightened" by the presence of the limitation that order ensures when combined with the "harmonic contrasts" that can be introduced without being dismissed as "incompatibles."[75] Therefore, "novelty and relevance are intertwined."[76] As already demonstrated, a similar ordering role is performed by the collective unconscious and archetypal Self. These movements of the process of becoming—including the concrescence of actual entities, the dynamic relationship between the one and the many, between God and the world, and the appearance of novel forms all depend upon the *ultimate* that Whitehead called *creativity*.[77] We might connect Whiteheadian creativity with what Jungians refer to as the primordial mystery or flow of life.

In this section, I have described resonances between Whitehead's dipolar God and Jung's collective unconscious: they are both unconscious and conscious, eternal and temporal, and morally neutral while still holding a vision for the world. Whitehead's consequent God and Jung's collective unconscious are intimately connected to the suffering of the world and retain the world's history; at the same time, Whitehead's primordial God and Jung's collective unconscious are the source of imagination, vision, and novelty. In both systems, there is a limited teleological nature to existence. Forms are transcendent, transpersonal, and abstract yet they spur contextual and emotionally compelling numinous images that can be experienced as powerfully persuasive even though they are not wholly normative or determinative. While examining resonances in this comparative way is interesting, what value is gained from it? I will next show that the generative vision realized in synthesizing these systems is that of a *relational-imaginal reality of form and freedom*.

GENERATIVE SYNTHESIS: A RELATIONAL-IMAGINAL REALITY OF FORM AND FREEDOM

The relationship between Whitehead's eternal objects and Jung's archetypes was a point of contention between John Cobb, Catherine Keller, and Stanley Hopper in *The Archetypal Process*. Seeing archetypes as "numinous," "dynamic," and "telic" leads Keller to conclude that they are not identical to Whitehead's "pure, formal" eternal objects. On the other hand, she, too, ties archetypes to *propositions* and *objective lures for feeling*, noting that in this role they may supply content to the formal aim in a way that is causally efficacious regarding the initial aim.[78] Cobb argues that, as typical patterns of behavior, archetypes do not possess the neutrality regarding ingression of Whitehead's eternal objects. He therefore places archetypes squarely in the realm of the past world's causal efficacy, noting the ability of behavioral repetition to be a causative force in the present.[79] Helpfully, Hopper acknowledges the differing perspectives, but notes that Whitehead's terms are, at the end of the day, still metaphors that require "an imaginative leap." Rather than remaining siloed as Whiteheadians or Jungians, Hopper urges us to seek common ground.[80]

Kenneth Pargament, a leading researcher in spirituality and psychotherapy relates the story of the immunologist he met at a meeting who, when the conversation turned to religion and spirituality, asked "Isn't religion just a bunch of hormones?" The question, Pargament reflects, reveals "two biases in the medical and social sciences": one that views "human behavior as largely reactive" to primarily physical forces and one that views religion/spirituality as something reducible to more "real" processes. Yet, he argues, people are "goal-directed" beings who are "guided as much by interest as they are by instinct."[81] Instincts determine and subsume freedom; goals lure and elevate freedom. Which makes up the bulk of our experience?

Because eternal objects and archetypes are both atemporal *and* historically realized, they are powerful and persuasive but not necessarily coercively determinative. For Jung, the image "is determined as to its content only when it has become conscious and is therefore filled out with the material of conscious experience"[82] of the individual. Archetypes are only an *a priori* predisposition to form images.[83] Because neither eternal objects nor archetypes are *actual* they have no agency for their own actualization. As Ballard notes, they are dependent upon and conditioned by the historical past, if not as determinates than certainly as influences.[84]

For Whitehead, God as primordial is "the unlimited conceptual realization of the absolute wealth of potentiality" and is "not *before* all creation, but *with* all creation."[85] Even in the case of eternal objects that are offered in God's initial aim for an occasion or by the archetypal imagination, Lee notes that such an envisagement is not pre-ordained in a determinative way. God may envision the structure of possibilities but "each becoming is a free act, as a result of which the texture of reality is modified."[86] Similarly, Ulanov reminds us that while formal archetypes are "ready-made" they are only "activated by concrete life situations."[87] In fact, it is God's very physical prehension in God's consequent nature of the actual world from which a subject may emerge that joins with God's imagined possibilities for that actual world in that moment to form the objective lure for feeling for the becoming subject.

Physically, the facts of the world along with God's consequent nature are prehended or *felt* by the concrescing occasion and in this sense, it can be said that past entities exert efficient causation upon the subject.[88] On the other hand, eternal objects as *envisaged potential*—forms with subjective form or feeling from God's primordial nature—engender novelty by entering into, and being positively prehended by, an actual entity through its mental pole. This *given* initial subjective aim—prehended by the subject—is what calls the subject into being in the first place[89] but from that point on, the subject determines the form of its own actualization and, to that degree, is "'finally caused' by itself."[90] Overall, we must say that in God's many subjective unifications, creations of actualities are "free" but they arise out of "decided situations."[91] As Odin notes, momentary events are "sandwiched-in, as it were, between the primordial and consequent natures of the dipolar God. God initiates each occasion by providing its basic organizational pattern and then everlastingly remembers it as [God's] own past . . ."[92]

Archetypes are not superhuman deities or extraterrestrials, but do they have *sovereign power* over us, as Jung seems to suggest? If they are "sovereign" in the traditional sense, writes Wehr, "the images would seem an unchangeable part of the divinely ordained order of things, frustratingly unchallengeable."[93] Yet, she reminds us, at the level of experience, Jung only says that they *feel* sovereign.[94] Jung observed that the archetypal image carries compelling power and numinous fascination, and Liliane Frey-Rohn describes the relationship between the archetype and the conscious psyche as reciprocal in nature. The image "needed to be formed by the conscious ego just as much as, conversely, consciousness required an evocative idea . . ."[95] While images emerge from the psyche, the individual may feel their source to be outside his own psyche due to the combination of illumination and strangeness.[96] Archetypes are *not* coercive or oppressive because they do not determine the archetypal image to which we respond (or not). Jung made this clear when he wrote,

> Again and again I encounter the mistaken notion that an archetype is determined in regard to its content . . . It is necessary to point out once more that archetypes are not determined as to their content, but only as regards to their form, and then only to a very limited degree. A primordial image is determined as to its content only when it has become conscious and is therefore filled out with the material of conscious experience.[97]

The powerful images we encounter are our own, and therefore, according to Wehr "do not demand worship," though a "worshipful attitude" may be helpful.[98] Rather than promoting archetypes as deterministic gods, Jung rarely spoke of God as a being outside of embodied life, to the point where Martin Buber accused Jung of having a religion of "psychic immanence."[99] Shelburne agrees that Jung draws a distinction between God as experienced as an image or archetype in the psyche and God as a transcendent entity to which that image corresponds.[100]

A synthesis of Whitehead and Jung generates an appreciation of the freedom of actual entities to choose but within a context that demands a certain amount of order and stability with the past. Situating Jung's archetypes within a process metaphysic stretches them "toward their least essentialist, most historical significance" where they become "capable of much more evolution . . ."[101] Like archetypal images, what Whitehead called *propositions* can only be targeted to particular subjects of the actual world within which such a proposition is relevant[102]; they are culturally influenced, and demand a certain amount of conformity to retain stability. Therefore, novel possibilities that go against the status quo will find difficult footing initially. At the same time, false propositions—those that do not conform with the current actual world—are "the instrument of the world's creative advance."[103]

It is key to keep in mind that the goal in Whitehead's system is contrast with harmony not outright anarchy and chaos. As Mattingly notes, emerging entities may not actualize *any* form of novelty, but only those that will preserve a general stability with the past.[104] As well, the qualities and character of the past world are perpetuated in the present through eternal objects that are "re-enacted" in newly forming subjects.[105] Therefore, *normativity* is real, but it lies in the "persuasive power of the empirical and the historical" not in some independent ideal.[106] Even in such cases, the forming subject may express the subjective forms of the past in newly interpreted ways.[107] While entities are a combination of efficient and final causes—both *objective data* and *subjective aim*—living entities are permitted *original responses to given data* and retain respons-*ability* to novel forms.[108] It is this ability which, in fact, differentiates a living from a non-living entity: while non-living entities may only be able to absorb the given environment and adjust slightly for satisfaction, the aim of a living entity is "to create new material, to change the course of its environment."[109]

As noted at the start of this section, Hopper suggests that *common ground* may be reached between Whiteheadians and Jungians. Here I have shown not only that a common ground between these areas exists but that there is a generative synthesis achieved in functionally comparing the formal roles of eternal objects and archetypes, the numinous power of propositions, propositional feelings, and archetypal images, and the relationship of these to the historic pressure of the received past and the lure of novel possibilities. Such a primordial *and* consequent, formal *and* historic, teleological *and* aesthetic-emotional view allows us to embrace formalism *with freedom*.

SUMMARY

In this chapter, through a functional comparison of Whitehead and Jung and their thought on transpersonal reality and historical pressure, I have shown how we may realize a generative vision of a *relational-imaginal reality of form and freedom*. Why is this important? It is important because if there are no possibilities for *transformative change* offered us by a transpersonal reality to which we *matter* and in which we *belong*, then there is no value whatsoever in this current project and we have fewer resources with which to heal our fragmentation. Even within a project that is so fiercely grounded in *lived experience* and the embodied theological method, it is still necessary to explain *how* and *why* such experience is possible. Without such an explanatory framework, individual experiences of belonging, value, and transformation are reduced to merely individual, subjective, and random experiences that may or may not grace our paths. Value, belonging, and the possibility of transformative change *must be woven into the very fabric of existence and understood as such* if there is to be any hope, joy, wholeness, or flourishing to human life.

Part Two of this work—*Integration*—has presented theoretical resources that are both metaphysical and empirical, and practical resources that give us a toolkit of methods for interpreting our experience through dream work. In chapter 3, I established Whitehead's philosophy of organism as a metaphysics that describes an integrated, relational cosmos. In chapter 4, I established Jung's analytical psychology as an empirical system that describes an integrated, relational psyche. Chapter 5 established dreaming and dream work as having integrative power, and chapter 6 synthesized our theoretical resources into one relational-imaginal reality of formalism with freedom thereby giving our practical resources a strong foundation upon which to stand. Now we can understand our individual experiences of *value*, *belonging*, and *transformation* not just as random and elusive but as reflective of *the very nature of reality for every living human being*. It is in this knowledge that we can stand with hope and confidently face a future wherein we may realize wholeness and common flourishing. Having laid this foundation, I can now construct key elements unique to this project: (1) a *relational-imaginal theory of dreaming*; (2) a theory of a *relational-imaginal God-Self* in the human being; and (3) a transformative *relational-imaginal praxis for psycho-spiritual wholeness and flourishing*.

NOTES

1. Rowland, *Jung*, 109.
2. Whitehead, *Process and Reality*, 343.
3. Jung, *Modern Man in Search of a Soul*, 17.
4. Slusser, "Jung and Whitehead on Self and Divine," 88.
5. Whitehead, *Process and Reality*, 343.
6. Hosinski, *Stubborn Fact and Creative Advance*, 201.
7. Shelburne, *Mythos and Logos*, 77.
8. Odin, *Process Metaphysics and Hua-Yen Buddhism*, 171.
9. Odin, 168.
10. Odin, 164.
11. Singer, *Boundaries of the Soul*, 104.
12. Ulanov, *The Functioning Transcendent*, 6–8.
13. Hosinski, *Stubborn Fact and Creative Advance*, 201–2.
14. Maxwell, "Archetype and Eternal Object," 51–52.

15. An earlier version of this idea was presented in Kling, "Avoiding a Fatal Error," 135.
16. Maxwell, "Archetype and Eternal Object," 57.
17. Sarkar, *Whitehead's Four Principles from West-East Perspectives*, 26, 29–30.
18. Frey-Rohn, *From Freud to Jung*, 97.
19. Maxwell, "Archetype and Eternal Object," 58.
20. Maxwell, 59.
21. Hosinski, *Stubborn Fact and Creative Advance*, 167.
22. Singer, *Boundaries of the Soul*, 127.
23. Jung, *The Basic Writings of C. G. Jung*, 95.
24. Ulanov, *The Functioning Transcendent*, 98.
25. Jung, *The Basic Writings of C. G. Jung*, 90.
26. Jung, 90.
27. Jung, 122.
28. Jung, 97.
29. Whitehead, *Adventures of Ideas*, 249–50.
30. Maxwell, "Archetype and Eternal Object," 60.
31. Mattingly, "Whitehead's Theory of Eternal Objects," 100, 138.
32. Whitehead, *Process and Reality*, 40.
33. Mattingly, "Whitehead's Theory of Eternal Objects," 101.
34. Faber, *God as Poet of the World*, 86.
35. Faber, 86–87.
36. Odin, *Process Metaphysics and Hua-Yen Buddhism*, 175.
37. Singer, *Boundaries of the Soul*, 100.
38. Griffin, "Introduction, Archetypal Psychology and Process Philosophy," 75.
39. Singer, *Boundaries of the Soul*, 129.
40. Kelsey, *Encounter With God*, 110.
41. Griffin, "Introduction, Archetypal Psychology and Process Philosophy," 59.
42. Mattingly, "Whitehead's Theory of Eternal Objects," 132.
43. Robertson, *Jungian Archetypes*, 168.
44. Robertson, 165–66.
45. Robertson, 165.
46. Shelburne, *Mythos and Logos*, 37.
47. Jung, *The Basic Writings of C. G. Jung*, 106.
48. Jung, 106.
49. Robertson, *Jungian Archetypes*, 166.
50. Jung, *The Basic Writings of C. G. Jung*, 361.
51. Card, "The Archetypal View of C.G. Jung and Wolfgang Pauli," 22.
52. Whitehead, *Process and Reality*, 154.
53. Lee, *The Becoming of the Church*, 66.
54. Mattingly, "Whitehead's Theory of Eternal Objects," 99.
55. Robertson, *Jungian Archetypes*, 148–49.
56. Odin, *Process Metaphysics and Hua-Yen Buddhism*, 162.
57. Whitehead, *Process and Reality*, 40.

58. Mattingly, "Whitehead's Theory of Eternal Objects," 99.
59. Lee, *The Becoming of the Church*, 66.
60. Jung, *The Basic Writings of C. G. Jung*, 396.
61. Jung, 585.
62. Odin, *Process Metaphysics and Hua-Yen Buddhism*, 172.
63. Frey-Rohn, *From Freud to Jung*, 95.
64. Mattingly, "Whitehead's Theory of Eternal Objects," 137.
65. Cobb Jr., "Spiritual Discernment in a Whiteheadian Perspective," 358.
66. Cobb Jr., 359.
67. Cobb Jr., 359.
68. Sherburne, *A Key to Whitehead's Process and Reality*, 49.
69. Hosinski, *Stubborn Fact and Creative Advance*, 173.
70. Lee, *The Becoming of the Church*, 94–95.
71. Mattingly, "Whitehead's Theory of Eternal Objects," 103.
72. Mattingly, 155.
73. Lee, *The Becoming of the Church*, 62.
74. Ballard, "Kant and Whitehead," 14.
75. Lee, *The Becoming of the Church*, 62; Odin, *Process Metaphysics and Hua-Yen Buddhism*, 166.
76. Mattingly, "Whitehead's Theory of Eternal Objects," 141.
77. Hosinski, *Stubborn Fact and Creative Advance*, 213–14.
78. Keller, "Psychocosmetics and the Underworld Connection," 144–45.
79. Cobb Jr., "Eternal Objects and Archetypes," 126.
80. Hopper, "Language as Metaphorical," 129.
81. Pargament, *Spiritually Integrated Psychotherapy*, 76.
82. Card, "The Archetypal View of C.G. Jung and Wolfgang Pauli," 25.
83. Wehr, *Jung & Feminism*, 51–52.
84. Ballard, "Kant and Whitehead," 13.
85. Whitehead, *Process and Reality*, 343.
86. Lee, *The Becoming of the Church*, 89.
87. Ulanov, *The Functioning Transcendent*, 98.
88. Mattingly, "Whitehead's Theory of Eternal Objects," 85.
89. Mattingly, 153.
90. Mattingly, 85.
91. Whitehead, *Process and Reality*, 530.
92. Odin, *Process Metaphysics and Hua-Yen Buddhism*, 168.
93. Wehr, *Jung & Feminism*, 93.
94. Wehr, 93.
95. Frey-Rohn, *From Freud to Jung*, 96.
96. Frey-Rohn, 97.
97. Card, "The Archetypal View of C.G. Jung and Wolfgang Pauli," 25.
98. Wehr, *Jung & Feminism*, 95.
99. Wehr, 95.
100. Shelburne, *Mythos and Logos*, 2, 76.
101. Keller, "Psychocosmetics and the Underworld Connection," 144.

102. Hosinski, *Stubborn Fact and Creative Advance*, 107.
103. Hosinski, 108.
104. Mattingly, "Whitehead's Theory of Eternal Objects," 136.
105. Ballard, "Kant and Whitehead," 16.
106. Dean, "Introduction," 6.
107. Mattingly, "Whitehead's Theory of Eternal Objects," 92.
108. Mattingly, 91.
109. Mattingly, 92.

Part Three

TRANSFORMATION

Chapter 7

Construction

INTRODUCTION

This work has analyzed the Fragmentation of human life, especially within the context of contemporary life in the United States, and it has proposed an Integration of the theoretical, empirical, and practical resources of Whitehead, Jung, and dream work. I then developed a generative synthesis of Whitehead and Jung so as to describe a *relational-imaginal reality of form and freedom.* Now in this journey, we have arrived at Transformation, the destination toward which we pointed this ship in hope and anticipation as soon as we left the port of our Introduction. In this place, I can finally construct the pieces that are unique to this project and which offer, I strongly believe, a way out of the lonely and painful wilderness in which we Americans now find ourselves.

This constructive chapter again draws from what I see as functional resonances between Whitehead and Jung. First, I will use the concepts of causal efficacy, the collective unconscious, proposition and propositional feeling, image, emotion, symbol, and perception to build *a relational-imaginal theory of dreaming* that relates God and World through perception and dreaming. Next, I will use Whitehead's and Jung's views on teleology and God as immanent to construct a theory of a *relational-imaginal God-Self in the human being* that incorporates novelty and creativity, unity and differentiation, and promises the possibility of positive change.

GOD AND WORLD: PERCEPTION AND DREAMING

In chapter 5, we explored psychological, scientific, communal, and mystical approaches to the phenomenon of dreaming. Yet none of these limited perspectives can provide an integrated theory of dreaming that explains how dreams can be understood as embodied while still somehow capable of being guiding and healing encounters with a transpersonal reality. In constructing what I am calling here a *relational-imaginal theory of dreaming,* we can interweave the theoretical and empirical resources of Whitehead and Jung to show how dreaming can be understood as a natural function of a perceiving body-mind that (1) receives the entire actual world and God in the mode of causal efficacy with vector feeling-tone and (2) combines that emotionally laden material with archetypal images generated via propositional feelings (a hybrid of the physical prehension of the world with the conceptual prehension of eternal objects or archetypes and initial aims). These relational, emotional, and imaginal elements are then transmitted to the brain where its capacities for exploration, association and metaphor, cognition, simulation, and adaptation can be enlisted to advance learning, and emotional memory integration. Moreover, without attempting to definitively prove the physical pathways and processes involved, I will also suggest a potential role of the vagus nerve in transmitting the body's perception of the world's feeling-toned information received through causal efficacy to the brain stem where those emotions and "gut instincts" then become part of the brain's default mode network activation pattern and involved in dreaming processes.

It is primarily because we can link Whitehead's perception in the mode of causal efficacy with Jung's collective unconscious—synthesizing Jung's *depth* with Whitehead's *pastness*[1]—that we can posit such a relational-imaginal theory of dreaming. To get there, we will examine claims that link causal efficacy and the collective unconscious, functionally compare Whitehead's propositions and propositional feelings with archetypal images and their shared emotional content, and examine how Whitehead's views of symbol and perception open up his framework to include dream images.[2]

Causal Efficacy and the Collective Unconscious

Whereas post-Enlightenment moderns see themselves as masters of the world with free rein to objectify and overuse all within it as "resources," for the millennia before this attitude emerged, humans experienced the cosmos as alive and pervaded by meaning and spiritual or archetypal forces.[3] With the Enlightenment came bifurcation, yet, Keller notes, "Only a self forged in the image of an impenetrable inner hardness, mistaken for integrity, could separate itself from the matrix of all life."[4] Moreover, this Enlightenment legacy continues to fail in its doctrinal refusal to accept nonsensory perception as real. As was discussed in chapter 3, one of the groundbreaking claims in Whitehead's philosophy is his demonstration that there must be another mode of perception besides the sensory perception that he called *presentational immediacy*. Unless there is some real relationship—*internal relations*—between knower and known how can we claim to truly *know* anything at all? His doctrine of prehensions shows how internal relations between knower and known are truly possible in an event-based metaphysics. This is particularly important regarding knowledge and memory, for as Whitehead asserts, either there is something in the present moment that conveys knowledge of the past and the future or memory and induction make no sense. If the past is not somehow retained in the present, then memory is just fantasy. Moreover, if the future is not "prefigured in the past and present," then any "predictive statements are entirely arbitrary." Unless the past and the future are somehow embodied in the present moment, then all that can be said of anything is where it is located.[5]

As Sarkar reminds us, the *sensa* we perceive *carry no information* for their own interpretation. The interpretations of that which we perceive are drawn from the non-sensuous perception with which sense perception is "fused and without which it can never be." This background of nonsensory perception is what Whitehead called "pastness," and it reflects the relationships between events.[6] It is in large part made up of our perception of both the bodily states and presiding ego occasions of our immediate past. In fact, according to Whitehead, the memory of our immediate past gives us the most compelling evidence of nonsensory perception.[7] Our bodies are embedded in the natural world[8] and what is perceived through causal efficacy is "vague, haunting, and unmanageable," "the dark fringes of the present," and described by Whitehead as a "heavy, primitive experience." Keller claims Whitehead's theory is nothing short of an "epistemological revolution" that makes the case that human conscious experience rests on, and is presupposed by, a foundation of experience of which we are mostly unconscious.[9]

Jungian thought, too, understands that human experience goes beyond sense experience[10] and that "sense perceptions are first processed somewhere inside us."[11] Jung explains this as a process wherein sensory activities such as seeing or hearing create images that are then consciously perceived in relation to the ego; in fact, he defines the ego itself "as an image or reflection of all the activities comprehended by it."[12] The images that arise from the body contain meaning or purpose and "picture" the vital activities of the living person.[13] We experience subjectively the unconscious aspects of experience but those aspects are perceived as entering the psyche from outside of itself.[14] Jung considered the collective unconscious to be "suprapersonal" and "open to the sense of historical continuity."[15] Therefore, he argues, what we perceive of ourselves and the world are unconscious elements that "flow from remote, obscure [unconscious] sources."[16]

Whereas Freud based human thought entirely in language and linked dream images to sexual repression, Jung was a "theorist of the image" for whom "the unconscious image was primary"[17] and intrinsically part of what he called the "subtle body." Jung theorized the existence of a subtle body because our body appears in dreams and has therefore been psychically imaged while still tied to personal identity. This is not an isolated body: as Rowland details, it is both social and at least somewhat socially constructed.[18] Whitehead, too, did not consider the body an isolated or closed system but described it as that part of nature with which humans had the most intimacy. Person and body mutually co-exist, and the world is understood through that immanent intimacy.[19] When we prehend or *absorb*[20] God and the world through causal efficacy, we are *feeling* or grasping them objectively along with their *subjective form* or *affective tone*.[21] Because Whiteheadians use the word *feeling* to indicate both sense and emotion, Lee believes the psychic model to be "operative.[22]

For Whitehead, we remember, the subject *emerges* as a response to its predecessors and to God, and so is said to be constituted by its relationships.[23] Similarly, Jung saw the unconscious as an objective reality that produces compensating viewpoints and possibilities by exerting pressure on our subjective consciousness.[24] Whereas Freud saw the unconscious as being built up by an individual's repression, Jung recognized that there was more coming from the unconscious than merely conscious elements that have been repressed.[25] As Argyle reminds us, materials that arise from the unconscious may carry a level of intelligence, authority, and emotional force that make those materials appear to be coming from outside of us.[26] The unconscious "speaks to us as a Word of God . . . confronts us spontaneously," comes to us from "elsewhere," and "places obligations upon us."[27] The encounter with primordial mystery or God, writes the Ulanovs, is a foundational experience that creates and re-creates us, binding us to that mystery.[28] Rowland argues that this *other* in the unconscious is crucial because experiencing an immanent divine feminine is essential for countering the damaging effects of "masculine monotheism" and its "patriarchal, atheistic, planet-exploiting attitudes."[29] Keller seems to agree when she argues that we are changed internally by—and have *internal relations* with—the *others* that flow into our experience and are immanent within us.[30]

As with Whitehead's perception in the mode of causal efficacy, in Jung's system, what is unconscious is primordial, and the collective unconscious operates in the background of consciousness without being determinative.[31] Both Cobb and Hopper note the correlation between Jung's depth and Whitehead's actual past world, with Cobb referring to that correlation as potentially enriching for both traditions.[32] Griffin, too, connects Whitehead's nonsensuous perception of the past (*causal efficacy*) with Jung's collective unconscious.[33] Keller both locates Whitehead's notion of soul within causal efficacy, connecting soul to world through the unconscious, and points to

Jung's dissolution of the soul-world boundary in his placing of the human psyche within nature as one and the same world. For Keller, that mutual world is the "causal underworld where psyche and matter conspire in the dark—in the place before consciousness" where there is "interconnexity."[34]

There is a compelling linkage between Hillman's view of dream work as "feeding soul each night with new material" and Keller's view of causal efficacy as the soul-making "underworld of actuality." Describing causal efficacy as the past that "energetically" decomposes to form the ground of the present, Keller links that directly to dreams as "an instance of such a rhythm of decomposing and recomposing" wherein the mode of presentational immediacy is subordinated to causal efficacy.[35] We may imagine Jung welcoming Whitehead's ideas on causal efficacy, for, as Craig Chalquist writes, "Jung destroyed our solipsism. Something unknown, the extra-human, approaches us through symbols, through psyche. We turn inward and find the world awaiting our most genuine and heartfelt response."[36]

Proposition, Image, and Emotion

What is perceived through causal efficacy—our inner and outer actual worlds—is "heavy with emotion,"[37] "emotionally charged,"[38] and is described by Griffin as "the transference of value" and "transitions of emotion."[39] Similarly, Kelsey writes that what arises from the unconscious in the form of images during non-directed or intuitive thinking conveys "emotional meaning."[40] While what is perceived via the senses is barren, what is prehended or inherited through causal efficacy carries "vector feeling-tone" that displays "evidence of its origin."[41] *Subjectively*, aesthetics are about feeling while *objectively*, aesthetics are "essentially a patterning or ordering which harmonizes contrasts."[42] Feeling tone unites subjectivity with objectivity in a "pattern of contrasts"[43] and the combination of pattern, contrast, image, and emotion form the aesthetic experience at the "foundations of the world" that are the result of the "immanence of God."[44] For Jung, this immanence of God is evident in his "radical personification" of the psyche. As Heisig notes, Jung imagined our mental events and the psyche's complexes as persons that populate our dreams and myths. The symbols and rites that arise are not primitive "*Urdummheit*" (primeval stupidity) but projections of deep feeling. Rather than being the outcome of allegorical creativity on behalf of gifted individuals within a culture, such symbols and rites are "the work of a habitual, instinctual, ineluctable demand of the psyche" to image all aspects of life in order to give it meaning and vitality through personification.[45] Perceptions through causal efficacy *move* us, and this is even more evident when we examine Whitehead's theory of propositions—the hybrid feelings that arise in the latter phases of concrescence for more complex entities.

In Whitehead's philosophy, God is "the lure for feeling, the eternal urge of desire."[46] This urge is an aim at *contrast*[47] and this can be seen as resonant with the way in which the unconscious psyche seeks to compensate an out-of-balance ego attitude through contrasting archetypal imagery. Relevance is important here as it is the means through which entities achieve internal contrast.[48] Similarly, Young-Eisendrath and Hall note that it is the emotion-heavy image that is the organizer and base unit of the psyche. For Jung, it is the power of emotion that evokes "meaningful constellations or symbolic representations at all stages of development."[49] Like the relationship between archetypal images and archetypes, propositions blend what is potential in eternal objects with the actual entity's present situation and introduce a feeling-centered proposition. Each possibility is then relevant to actual current conditions and therefore packs an emotional punch.[50] A propositional feeling is the subjective form of the proposition, as well as the entity's subjective, evaluative, and *felt* response to it.

Jung understood the archetypes as pressing "for their own resolution"[51] and as "complexes of experience that come upon us like fate"[52] with a fascinating dynamism[53] and force.[54] Kraus hints at the same urgency when she insists that we should not understand eternal objects as "inert forms waiting to be appropriated"; rather, they are dynamic and "have the unrest of the Platonic Eros."[55] Robertson also links archetypes to feeling, not just as emotion but as *valuation*, noting that archetypes are connected to the world through feeling; they are evaluative not based on "what" something is but in "how it fits into things."[56] Such valuation is an *aesthetic* valuation. Similarly, Hosinski writes that a proposition's primary function in the becoming of an occasion is to attract us through value and persuade us to act.[57] For Odin, the pattern of eternal objects received as the immanence of God in every occasion is an "aesthetic value-pattern"; in Whitehead's system, then, aesthetic experience is primary.[58]

In noting that archetypal images or symbols evoke feeling or *numinosity*, we may relate this functionally to what Whitehead calls subjective form.[59] Subjective form carries emotion, value, and purpose.[60] When subjects prehend eternal objects conceptually, the *how* of that prehension—the subjective form—is an aesthetic reaction to the worth or value of the object. Eternal objects are first felt as being possessed by the other entity from which they are being prehended, then "felt as possible for me"; finally, the subject internalizes its own desire for personal satisfaction in forming that subjective experience.[61] When a feeling has the "datum" of an eternal object, it is known as a "conceptual feeling" and it is then a determinant of the character of the concrescing entity.[62] Whitehead considers feeling to be essential in his system; propositions function as relevant lures for feeling that move each subject toward the actualization of its subjective aim at satisfaction, its very purpose for becoming.[63]

We might similarly say that the datum of the archetype or eternal object is perceived first as an image or proposition that carries emotion or subjective form and is therefore persuasive or numinous. Like hybrid propositions that join the conceptual with feeling, archetypal images carry "living intensity," notes Walter Shelburne, and are both feeling and thought. The ability to evoke emotion is what is meant by *numinosity*, and the *numen* is the energy of the archetype[64] that is sometimes felt with a "mystical aura."[65] Archetypes are also dipolar, according to Ulanov, in that they have both an "instinctive body-based pole as well as a spiritual one."[66]

Mattingly likens the conceptual prehension of eternal objects to "imagination"[67]; functioning in the mental pole, it could be said that just as the eternal object determines and mediates the datum, the archetype determines and mediates the image. At this stage, what is being described is still objective and unconscious, and is therefore in a state of "transcendent decision," or is purely conceptual. This datum or image—whose relevance could also be described as an appropriateness for one's personal unconscious and complexes—then "provokes the origination" of prehension, or the entry into one's personal psyche, where it becomes an "immanent decision."[68] As an immanent decision, there is subjective form, affective tone, and the encounter with one's "feeling-toned complexes."[69] At this stage, the activity is now an "impure prehension" of an objective datum, image, or symbol that the concrescing actuality appropriates for itself.[70] Functioning in the physical pole, archetypal images may be prehended in various types of past occasions, including, we may presume, the dream images generated as signals by the "complex amplifier" of the human body,[71] from historical occasions in the actual world (the "massive presence of the past"[72]), and from God's consequent nature. Archetypal images continue to come into play during the integration phase of concrescence as propositional feelings that may be raised to conscious decision. The importance of this will be covered in chapter 8.

Symbol and Perception

Having established connections between causal efficacy and the collective unconscious, and functionally compared Whitehead's propositions and propositional feelings with Jung's archetypal images and their shared emotional content, I can now move us closer to a *relational-imaginal theory of dreaming* by connecting Whitehead's and Jung's ideas on symbol and perception. Both men had great respect for the power of symbol. Whitehead believed symbolism to be essential to more complex forms of life, even while he regarded symbols as somewhat suspect due to their vague, uncontrollable, and overwhelming tendency.[73] Humans, especially, need symbols to communicate and he argued that, in fact, human "expression" is "symbolism."[74]

We have already explored in great depth the centrality of symbol to Jung's view of the psyche.

Prior to writing his seminal work *Process and Reality*, Whitehead discussed key ideas on perception and language in *Symbolism: Its Meaning and Effect.* In a text by multiple authors exploring that book, I argue[75] that we can connect dreams and dream images to Whitehead's system and see them as vitalizing interaction with God for several reasons which I will only summarize here. Firstly, Whitehead's inclusion of the imaginal realms of art, music, poetry, and religious ritual—as well as their emotional components—opens the way for us to include the imaginal and emotional elements of dreams in our discussion of his thought[76] and to connect such symbols with Jung's archetypal images. Secondly, Whitehead's insistence that perception cannot be limited to sense perception invites us to include the nonsensuous perception of dream images as well.[77]

Thirdly, Whitehead's differentiation between two modes of perception illucidates that we can perceive and understand sense data only because we have already directly and internally prehended the external source of that data through causal efficacy. He used the term *symbolic reference* to describe the process by which data perceived through presentational immediacy is unified with data perceived through causal efficacy. Whitehead writes that "the human mind is functioning symbolically when some components of its experience elicit consciousness, beliefs, emotions, and usages, respecting other components of its experience. The former set of components are the 'symbols,' and the latter set constitute the 'meaning' of the symbols."[78] The interplay between the two modes of perception is possible because there is common ground between the "species of symbols" and the "species of meanings" that allows for such unification and integration.[79] The relationship between the two is one of evocation.

Fourthly, dream symbols, like symbols of language, are a kind of symbolic truth that links appearance and reality. There may be nothing in a particular dream that is directly related on the surface to a dreamer's reality, but with dream interpretation, a deep meaning that links the two may become apparent. Whitehead notes that symbolic appearance can be linked to a particular reality because the "percipient" or perceiving occasion is "peculiarly conditioned" for that meaning in its arising.[80] In this way, we may understand a dreamer with a particular history and inner psychic life to be uniquely conditioned to perceive particular dream images. The unique character of symbols and the concept of mutual immanence between God and world are key. Symbols, in Jung's system, are a way of representing archetypally the material that is unconscious. Jung believed that a symbol participates in that to which it points and joins the known with the unknown in a participatory relationship.[81] Whitehead describes God as being immanent in every occasion in its initial subjective aim, in the eternal objects prehended through the world, and also in God's superjective consequent nature; thereby, we can understand that when we perceive our world through causal efficacy, we are also perceiving God.

Though we might say that archetypal dream images are initially perceived through the mode of causal efficacy from the body, in a practice of dream work, they are recorded and analyzed, and therefore are then re-perceived through the mode of presentational immediacy. Such dream images brought to conscious awareness are then raised from unconscious propositional feelings to conscious intellectual feelings, where they participate in symbolic reference. Whitehead understood symbols to be "creative" in that they "elicit the intuition" for their own interpretation in the same way that a tuning fork elicits a response from a piano string because each are tuned to the same note.[82] Such symbols and images are the linchpin between Whitehead's modes of perception (causal efficacy and presentational immediacy) because they are both present in the psyche and participate in that toward which they point. Clearly, both Whitehead and Jung connect the "spheres of matter and psyche" through the objective function of the primordial realm of eternal objects and archetypes, as well as in the consequent realm of past fact, propositions, and numinous, historically conditioned imaginal symbols.

We can therefore directly place dreams and dream work squarely within a Whiteheadian frame for several reasons, including (1) since Whitehead included imaginal expression in his understanding of symbolism, and was open to including non-sensory perception, we can connect Whitehead's symbolism and that of Jung; (2) that functional resonances exist between Whiteheadian and Jungian schools of thought in multiple areas, including the existence of a transpersonal realm of formal causation, a dipolar God or collective unconscious, that feeling and value are integral to human experience, and that raising unconscious material to consciousness is essential for human flourishing; and (3) that an integration of Whiteheadian and Jungian thought—especially when combined with a spiritual practice of dream work—can positively influence human society's intensity of experience and our overall aliveness, vitality, and zest for life.

Construction: A Relational-Imaginal Theory of Dreaming

Holding to Whitehead's *one world* philosophy, this project rejects the possibility that dreams and dream content are somehow delivered into a sleeping person through supernatural agents—what Hobson dismisses as "secret, coded messages" that "require elaborate interpretations by special authorities."[83] But is it essential to understand the divine nature of dreams as *supernatural*? Not for Jung. Though he identified many different archetypes within the psyche—the shadow, anima, animus, etc.—for Jung, the archetypal Self is the God-image of wholeness in the psyche; it has the power to unify the personality and integrate its opposites. It does this through the process of individuation, a process that is reliant on one's dialogue between the conscious and unconscious mind through the common language of symbol and image. These "image-symbols of the unconscious," Johnson writes, reach human consciousness through dreams and imagination, both of which are capable of transforming what is unrepresentable within the unconscious into images that are knowable.[84] As noted earlier, Jung did not share Freud's belief that dreams were inherently deceptive, but saw them as natural, guileless, and expressive.[85] According to Singer, the unconscious uses dreams and other means to widen our perspective by showing us our current situation and either offering possible better futures or warning of potential disasters.[86]

Researchers in the psychological and cognitive sciences like Hobson and Hartmann seem content to restrict dreaming (and in Hartmann's case all related *default mode* activity like reverie, fantasy, and daydreaming) to a mental function generated solely by brain activity.[87] On the other hand, in our discussions of the body and the dreaming brain, we must keep in mind that to equate brain with mind is to make an unwarranted leap. Richard Kradin, a medical internist and Jungian analyst, notes that Western medicine is both Aristotelian in its reliance on what is empirical and sensate and Newtonian in that it "approaches the body through a lens of linear determinism with reductionistic goals."[88] He faults medicine for failing to appreciate that human physiology, especially the nervous system, is neither simple nor linear, and encourages us to look to "non-linear or deterministically chaotic systems" that are "exquisitely sensitive to initial conditions" instead. He continues,

> Few scientists would disagree that mind depends on the activities of the nervous system. But as an emergent phenomenon, it cannot be reduced to the materiality of the nervous system . . . mind is not brain; the two are qualitatively different, just as water does not share properties with the constituent elements of hydrogen and oxygen . . . neuroscience, as currently configured, can teach us little concerning the phenomenology of mind.[89]

Prior to Freud, scientists saw dreams as simply somatic[90] but Freud and Jung agreed that dreaming was more than sleep-time bodily sensations or the day's meal, although such mundane activities do provide the building blocks of the psyche's work. For Jung, dreams picture the dreamer's unconscious psyche.[91] He felt strongly that academic psychology's typical dismissal of everyday experiences and their bias toward somaticizing dreams was "insufferable."[92] Yet it is absolutely true that psychic processes depend on the body's nervous system by which unconscious contents are made conscious through "representation" via images, and these images reflect brain processing.[93] While Hobson claims that the brain *creates* any meaning associated with dreams out of value-free data and "random neural activities of the brain,"[94] Hillman refuses to root either dream or sensory images solely in some kind of solipsistic "basic feeling."[95] By incorporating Whitehead's notion of causal efficacy, we can understand the "basic feeling" as a *prehension* of the world and God and not just as a product of the dreamer's internal systems. We certainly can avoid seeing that feeling as something generated solely by the brain.

Emotion

Between the years of 1913–1917, after having split with Freud, Jung conducted a deep dive into his own unconscious and what impressed him most was its powerful images. During this difficult time of inner conflict, Jung realized that he felt calmer whenever he turned his strong emotions into images.[96] Could it be that dreams are the body-mind's way of processing the aesthetic-emotional information being received through perceptive experiences and turning that data into images so that the information can be raised to consciousness and used by the dreaming individual in her planning and decision-making?

The strong emotions present in dreams indicate the involvement of the subneocortical limbic brain regions common to all mammals. Bulkeley seems to accept the theory that the brain generates human emotions, in "both waking and dreaming experience."[97] Yet is there definitive proof that the brain *generates* any emotion at all? Here we benefit from the work of Daugherty who refuses to equate brain with mind and describes the difference between *reductionist* and *reflective* views of the brain. While the reductionist view assumes that any brain activity associated with experience means that the brain is *generating* the experience, the reflective view only goes so far as to assert that the experience is *reflected* in the brain.

> The mind thinks, the brain reflects that thought. The brain may reflect the soul, but it is not the soul itself. There are some scientists that will have you believe if you have an experience of God, and it is reflected in your brain, it is really only a malfunction of your brain. Therefore they "reduce" the experience to the workings of the brain itself. However, a good counter-example is the experience of sex. If I have a sex spot in my brain that is activated during sexual activity, it does not mean I am not having a sexual event. It merely means it is reflecting a sexual thought or experience I may be engaged in at the moment.[98]

Similarly, Jeffrey Kripal, a professor of philosophy and religious thought at Rice University, suggests that "your brain might be a radio." He argues that dominant "flatland models" that "shrink" human nature ignore clues over centuries of thought that suggest that in times of apparent precognitive or religious experience,

> the human brain may function as a super-evolved neurological radio or television and, in rare but revealing moments [often those associated with strong emotion and demonstrated in precognitive dreams] when the channel suddenly "switches," as an imperfect receiver of some transhuman signal that simply does not play by the rules as we know them.[99]

Studies in lucid dreaming performed by Keith Hearne and Stephen LaBerge show that there can be self-awareness in sleep, when regions of the brain normally associated with consciousness are not active. Does this prove that awareness or consciousness cannot be limited to the brain? Bulkeley writes that the sleeping brain can produce "hyper-realistic visions, deeply creative insights, and extraordinary states of awareness,"[100] but again, can we be sure that those experiences are being *generated* by the brain alone or is the brain *reflecting* what is happening in the entire body-mind organism? Clearly, Daugherty supports the latter view when she writes that being alive is a "completely embodied phenomenon" and that all human experience, even religious or mystical, is "registered in, and facilitated through our human bodies."[101]

As was already discussed in chapter 5, dreams clearly reflect emotional experience. Hartmann describes dreaming as pictured metaphors "guided by emotion" and argues that human memory uses "emotionally based similarity."[102] As well, the correlation that Kripal makes between precognitive dreams and strong emotion is corroborated by Bulkeley who points to prophetic dreaming as interweaving what he terms our "autonomous visionary capacity" with important and emotionally charged situations that have not yet become clear and for which we seek greater perceptive and predictive abilities.[103] There is nothing magical or supernatural about this because the same brain that thinks about the future during waking life continues to engage such processes during sleep when its creative and associative capacities are less restrained.[104] If Whitehead is correct that we may perceive "the creativity of the world [as] the throbbing emotion of the past hurling itself into a new transcendent fact,"[105] then we can expand our theories of dreaming from a merely solipsistic translation of internal states into a relational process that reflects information perceived through causal efficacy that is laced with aesthetic value—*feeling the world*—and is internally constitutive of our own objective *and* subjective experience.

The Vagus Nerve: Body-Mind-World Communication

By interweaving Whitehead's views of causal efficacy as felt mostly through the "withness of the body" and of body as our means of knowledge of the world[106] with Jung's views of psyche-body-world, we are now able to see humans as fully embodied beings within one world that integrates body and mind, psyche and matter. Moreover, we can know that our dreams too must be rooted in our bodies as systems that are inclusive of mind and internally related to all that we experience and perceive. In an event-based and integrated reality, body and brain are not separate, body and world are not separate, and none are completely closed systems. Is the dreaming body-mind *creating* meaning out of random signals, as Hobson suggests, or is it collecting and interpreting perceptual data that is both physical and conceptual and processing that information in a way that can be used for its own flourishing? If the latter is true, and we assume that such perception by the body-mind of world (and God) is possible, then what might be the actual means through which that occurs? Jungian analyst Marion Woodman believes that the connecting element between psyche and soma is the feeling tone of the *image*.

> The feeling-tone in the body, where the belly resonates with the resonating heart and liver, all of this is producing chemistry that is picked up by the brain. Science is now working on this grand computer, the brain, transforming feeling into image. The image gives us an understanding of what's happening in the body and some insight into the anguish in the brain and the psyche. I see psyche and soma as one. The metaphorical symbol is the connector. It requires resonating space in which to unfold.[107]

I propose that aesthetic and value-rich information perceived as feeling tone and image by the body-mind, and percepta prehended by the body, are conveyed from the viscera as emotion-heavy "gut feelings" to the brain stem via the vagus nerve's afferent fibers and its associated neurotransmitters. Once they reach the brain, the feeling-tone and emotion-heavy data activate archetypal images in the form of propositional feelings. Those images may then be processed via the dreaming brain's default mode activation pattern and its associated functions (as described in chapter 5) to facilitate adaptive learning and memory-emotion integration. Recent research has documented roles of the vagus nerve that were previously unknown that, while I have neither the space nor the expertise to conclusively prove, may support this theory. A brief description follows.

As the largest of the twelve peripheral nerves that exit the brain stem directly (rather than via the spinal cord), the *vagus* nerve (from the Latin meaning "wandering") meanders from the brain through the neck and thoracic cavity all the way to the abdomen.[108] According to Liu, et al., the vagus nerve terminates in the brain stem where it connects "directly and indirectly with brain structures including the . . . amygdala, hypothalamus, insula, thalamus, orbitofrontal cortex, and other limbic regions responsible for mood and anxiety regulation."[109] It is part of what is now called the *gut-brain axis* and although it allows for both "top-down (CNS [central nervous system] to viscera) and bottom-up (viscera to CNS)" or "bidirectional" information flow,[110] 80 percent of its fibers are *afferent* (bottom-up), meaning it is predominantly devoted to communicating visceral information to the brain. It is believed that the vagus nerve "plays an important role in body/brain interactions,"[111] notes Mersbergen. Moreover,

> The cell bodies of this nerve are housed in four large areas in the brain stem, creating a hub where nerves from different parts of the body communicate with each other. The proximity of nerve cell bodies in this area allow various parts of the body to communicate complicated information with each other, allowing for sophisticated processing of information.[112]

Using both neuronal routes and endocrine neurotransmitters, the body sends *gut instincts* or *gut feelings*—identified as *somatic signals*—to the brain that "influence decision making and behavioral responses without explicit awareness of the provoking cues" meaning that they are below the level of conscious awareness.[113] The vagus complex has been described as the "substrate for body-mind connections"[114] and a "mind-body feedback loop."[115] Bergland writes that "Visceral feelings and gut instincts are literally *emotional intuitions* [emphasis mine] transferred up to your brain via the vagus nerve."[116] Via its afferent fibers, the vagus nerve is also understood to be "the mechanism by which peripheral epinephrine activates the release of brain norepinephrine during memory consolidation."[117] Adelson explains that

> emotional events affect the body to influence how well the brain encodes information about exciting or meaningful events. First, emotionally arousing events stimulate the nervous system to release epinephrine . . . [which then] activates the ascending fibers of the vagus nerve, which in turn stimulate the brain neurons in an area of the brainstem known as the nucleus of the solitary tract (NTS) . . . NTS neurons release norepinephrine into brain structures that process memory, such as the amygdala and hippocampus . . . epinephrine regulates memory consolidation, acting via the vagus nerve.[118]

More and more is being discovered that reveals the vagus complex and its associated neurotransmitters to be involved in numerous aspects of health, including consciousness and self-referential processing,[119] cognition,[120] processing of emotionally arousing events and memory storage,[121] stress reduction, emotional regulation and heart rate variability,[122] social interaction (polyvagal theory),[123] reduction of inflammation, and is related to such serious conditions as anxiety, depression, diabetes and obesity.[124] In an article linking the vagus nerve directly with emotion, heart rate variability (HRV), environment, and health, Thayer and Lane write that

> Emotions represent a distillation of an individual's perception of personally relevant environmental interactions, including not only challenges and threats but also the ability to respond to them. Viewed as such, emotions reflect the status of one's ongoing adjustment to constantly changing environmental demands. When the affective system works properly, it promotes flexible adaptation to shifting environmental demands . . . The relationship between HRV and emotional regulation will have important implications for those that study the link between emotional states and dispositions such as depression, anxiety, anger, and hostility, alexithymia, and physical health.[125]

Interestingly, As Mersbergen concludes, the vagus nerve is "a truly amazing nerve, the superhighway of life responsible for keeping us alive and thriving in an ever-changing environment . . . an indispensable link in communication between brain and body."[126]

Another significant piece of this communication system is the limbic part of our brain, located in the region to which the vagus nerve transmits its impulses. Stephen W. Porges, a researcher in the field of psychiatry, has coined the term *neuroception* as a capacity of the human body to evaluate information received through sensory input but processed at a level below conscious awareness for utilization by the limbic system to detect safety and risk. He writes that

> Because of the phylogenetic heritage of mammals, neuroception can operate without cognitive awareness via relatively primitive mechanisms that are dependent on subcortical structures (e.g., limbic). As a product of evolution, new neural systems evolved in mammals that involved cortical regulation of subcortical structures and, in many instances, co-opted the defense functions of the primitive structures to support other functions including those related to reproductive behavior and pair bonding.[127]

Daugherty associates the limbic system with the *felt sense* we experience throughout our day as well as with "learning, motivation, memory and emotion." Such felt sense occurs at a level she calls "subconscious" or "implicit" and it is there that our bodies are "more honestly" aware than our conscious minds about the nature of our experience.[128] Here we may recall that Hartmann linked the limbic system, and primarily its amygdala, with the connections that are made in dreaming "guided by emotion."[129]

In *From Mindfulness to Heartfulness*, Daugherty describes a theory of how trauma and other emotionally charged events and our limbic systems work together to create entrenched "imprints" of emotional "programming" that become habitual and reactive. Noting that we cannot simultaneously be in both a fear and calm state, inner conditions of stress and reactivity keep us from engaging heartfully with others and the world around us.[130] When we perceive ourselves as under threat, the limbic system "hijacks" our bodies, overloading us energetically, physiologically, and biochemically, causing our brain and neurons to fire in patterns that—if repeated often enough—are theorized to become imprinted as "neural nets." The more we repeat certain thoughts, experiences, or "interpretations of events," the more that neuronal firing and glial cell activity form long-term connections that create entrenched behavior patterns.[131] As a result, we become less capable of responding to the actual events of our world consciously, and can become "consumed" by routine patterns of unconscious response.[132]

The good news from the perspective of research in neuroplasticity and learning is that such imprinted neural net patterns can change with new experience. Yet it is not conscious or reasoned thought that can make the change, but only deeply felt *embodied experience*. "When we create a deeply felt alternative experience through heartful awareness," writes Daugherty, "we begin to re-code our subconscious."[133] Kalsched notes a similar phenomenon between therapist and patient during the "right brain to right brain communication" that occurs when symbolic material is being explored. Echoing Daugherty's description of imprinted unhealthy life operating patterns, he describes "anti-wholeness defenses" that may be reparable due to the brain's plasticity, but agrees that such repair is only possible through "immersion in the particularity of experience," especially the "implicit experience in dreams and other imaginal products" that colors the "'potential space' that emerges 'between' the psychoanalytic partners."[134]

Through introducing recent discoveries about vagus nerve function and the human limbic system, we can connect this aspect of our neuroanatomy to: (1) bodily perception of environment, transmission of emotionally rich gut feelings to the brain and its areas associated with dreaming; (2) Hartmann's theories regarding the emotional basis of image, emotional processing, memory consolidation, and learning; and (3) the potential for change through deeply felt healing experience. Certainly, the brain is involved in the processing of emotion, and/or is reflective of the presence of emotion in the body, but the involvement of the gut and vagus nerve show that emotion is not housed within or generated solely by the brain. Daugherty would agree, noting that "The brain and the body work together in an awesome and staggering system that facilitates and defines human life."[135]

Implications

If proven, the implications of this relational-imaginal theory of dreaming could be far-reaching. Within this frame, we can see ourselves as intimately related to God and world and capable of receiving information that we can use to adapt to our ever-changing environments. Moreover, all of this can be experienced within our own immediate and most intimate embodied lives. Loomer reminds us of the basic empirical principle that knowledge is gained through physical experience, that through physical feelings we encounter life's "elemental forces," and that the very "heights and depths of life," all our joys and struggles, are "known first through our bodily feelings."[136] We must never discount our embodiment, because it is the instrument through which we experience all of life and a tool for our enlightenment.[137]

We may struggle with the alienating effects of dualism and loneliness and we may suffer from the consequences of adverse childhood experience, but, always, "fresh ideas" are "blowing in from the world, the ecological psyche," writes Hillman. Our human soul is both "afflicted" by this world and "commencing to turn with fresh interest" to it, because, "in this world soul the human soul has always had its home."[138] Recognizing with Jung, Whitehead, and Hillman that we are "utterly one with the world,"[139] part of the "cosmos displaying its self-enjoyment," and linked to it through feeling, aesthetics, image, and dream, we can then adopt an "aesthetic anthropology" where we understand ourselves as *homo aestheticus*—a "sense-enjoying, image-making creature . . . animals in an ecological field that affords imagistic intelligibility."[140] Dreams may then become our most intimate companions, but only, as Lauter and Rupprecht remind us, if we value and befriend them, and record and interpret their symbols.[141]

TELEOLOGY AND AN IMMANENT GOD

If Mary Oliver is correct that "the soul exists and is built entirely out of attentiveness,"[142] then in order to construct a theory that describes a *relational-imaginal God-Self* in the human being, we must turn our attentiveness to comparative territory once again to see if Whitehead and Jung are capable of making the functional movements necessary for this dance to succeed. Therefore, this section examines the ways Whitehead and Jung speak of vision, purpose, and the presence of God in the world. In Whiteheadian terms, we will explore initial aims, novelty, and creative transformation. In Jungian terms, we will explore the Archetypal Self, its relationship to the ego, and the role of the transcendent function to engender novelty in human experience. This comparison leads us immediately into a discussion of differentiation and unity.

Initial Aims and Creative Transformation

God in the World

The process of concrescence begins with a subject objectifying it's given past. But there would be no subject at all that can prehend its world and begin its selective process of objectification without God's evocation of that subject. God *as consequent* both prehends the actual world within which a subject will emerge and *is part of* that actual world. Because God desires for that subject to achieve intense satisfaction, God *as primordial* provides the lure, the initial subjective aim, that calls that subject into being. From that point forward, the emergent subject claims the aim for itself and makes its own decisions as to how it will form and what it will become.[143] In Whitehead's poetic prose, God's "tenderness is directed towards each actual occasion, as it arises" and God seeks the "evocation of intensities."[144] God is present in every event as both its transpersonal and its unconscious dimensions[145] and is, therefore, the principle of concretion. God is the actual entity, the "ground of all order," that "[conditions] an originality in the temporal world" and which begins every entity's "self-causation."[146] In fact, the fullness of God's physical feeling is a result of the objectification of the world in God and God shares the actual world of every new entity.[147] Whitehead describes God's relationship to the world as one of "mutual immanence," claiming that the world is immanent in God, and God is immanent in the world.[148]

Initial Aims, Novelty, and Creative Transformation

As shown in the previous chapter, if the end was determined strictly by the past, then there would be no actual freedom; instead, the end comes from the future as a lure or possibility, and it is God who orders those possibilities based on relevance to the actual world.[149] It is this lure—without coercion—that constitutes there even being decision, and we see more order, direction, and novelty than could be possible if all were determined by the past or by chance. The initial aim, according to Lee, reflects God's desire for entities to attain value, intensity, harmony, and beauty. This is the creative advance that is reflected in the process of becoming.[150]

It is through the initial aim that novelty enters the world, and so God is also understood as the "organ of novelty, aiming at intensification."[151] This aim, or "innermost lure to live with satisfaction," Jay McDaniel describes as the "divine breathing"[152] within us, while Cobb and Griffin understand the initial aim as the very "principle of creative transformation."[153] Yet this principle is not generic for the entire world, but is unique to the forming moment. It occurs when an entity accepts and incorporates God's initial aims as the best possible response to a situation, even though, for the human person as a society of occasions, that transformation may require us to give up ways of being to which we have become attached or habituated. Whitehead links even these "discordant feelings" to the ultimate aim of Beauty, because that which is discordant and imperfect can move us from what is outworn to something more fresh.[154] For Cobb, one's conflicts—such as tension in a young person between conservative "moral rigor" and "carefree spontaneity"—can result in a "larger perspective" that includes and appreciates both sides, thereby enriching and intensifying experience.[155] In Cobb's view, creative transformation is "contextual and particular, challenging, noncoercive" and universally available whether acknowledged or not.[156] It is produced by the "creative love of God" and is involved in all "human creative love"; it moves us to a wider future.[157]

One's individual actions—one's contribution of value—are key in Whitehead's philosophy of organism. Whitehead's cosmos is *relational*—meaning that there are real individuals who experience the whole from their unique perspective and rupture the extensive continuum with a thrust and a thirst for becoming; yet those individuals are always in relation to the larger unity. In this cosmos, individuals arise subjectively distinct from the whole, and then perish to once again return objectively to the whole, where they are harmonized and integrated by God into a unity. In this cosmos, the ongoing dance between oneness and multiplicity is the beautiful yet painful reality.

The Archetypal Self, the Ego-Self Relationship, and the Transcendent Function

God in the Self

Jung writes that while all religious statements point to something ineffable and ultimately inaccessible to us, they become visible forms or images only after being "filtered through the medium of human consciousness."[158] Within the human psyche is a psychological God-image,[159] and though Jung's teaching on the unconscious does not require an external God,[160] he strongly believed that the image in the psyche "corresponds" to "an original behind our images"—what he sometimes called "the Unspeakable itself."[161] For Jung, the human ego is the ground of *subjective* identity and the archetypal Self is the ground of *objective* identity. The self is the "supreme psychic authority" and "inner empirical deity."[162]

We meet this *Unspeakable* or *Other* especially in numinous experience, and though Jung did not fully equate this "archetypal presence" with God or Spirit, Ulanov writes that it acts in us with God- or Spirit-like characteristics. Encountering the Self may either move us to submit to its authority or to fight it "tooth and nail."[163] It is both our pathway to wholeness and the principle that structures or unifies the contents of the unconscious.[164] Singer describes it as a kind of connection point that belongs neither to the ego nor to the unconscious, yet it participates in and provides access to both.[165] Edinger notes that the symbols of the Self all point to a central source or "fountain of our being which is most simply described as God. Indeed, the richest sources for the phenomenological study of the Self are the innumerable representations that [humans have] made of the deity."[166]

In a way that suggests friendliness to Whiteheadian thought, Robertson describes the Self as "both process and goal," a point that Wehr supports when she notes that our psychic lives are both rooted in and striving toward the Self.[167] Both the collective unconscious and the Self have a fluid quality. Jung sees these as the source of religious experience[168] and, in describing how much our images of God have changed throughout history, he speculates that God may be validly perceived as much as a flowing current of vital energy as unmoved and unchanging.[169] For him, God is a living spirit with a tendency to outgrow historical images or forms and to be "eternally renewed" like ever-changing "leaves and blossoms on the stem of the eternal tree."[170] Echoing Whitehead's view that God desires that each occasion live out its own intensity, Hoss writes that Jung's Self "[has] no deliberate plan outside of an urge towards self-realization."[171]

Transcendent Function: Novelty and Transformation

Both Ulanov and Robertson link the archetypal Self to the human need for transcendence,[172] with Ulanov insisting that resolving internal conflict requires marrying its transcendence with its action in the present.[173] One of the ways the Self lives in our present moments is through what Jung called the *transcendent function*, the source of novelty and creative flourishing in the human psyche. As discussed in chapter 4, the conscious and unconscious psyche have a compensatory relationship such that when one's conscious ego attitude leans too far in one direction, the unconscious presents material to balance or complement the conscious perspective. When conflicting conscious and unconscious contents are held together, the psychological transcendent function arises.[174]

Often the disagreement is between our spiritual desires and our more instinctual desires, but the psyche seeks to address its conflicts and does so by offering us both sides of the argument.[175] The resulting tension may be painful enough to even create "violent disunion with oneself."[176] Yet to avoid this tension by sublimating one desire in favor of the other does not generally resolve the problem; in fact, it often results in some kind of neurotic or physical symptom.[177] When an individual is willing to hold opposing perspectives without repressing either one, Jung explains, the fully conscious "confrontation of the two positions generates a tension charged with energy and creates a living, third thing" that leads us to a new, more integrated situation. The transcendent function conjoins what were previously inert positions.[178] The "third thing" is not merely an unsatisfying compromise but is actually "something new."[179] Hoss illustrates the new awareness available through this function with a particular dream from a woman experiencing difficulties in her marriage. In this recurring dream, she is running away from her husband with whom she is angry. One night, she turns to face him in the dream and her husband's face becomes her father's face. The dreamer awoke with fresh insight into connections between the problems in her marriage and issues with her father.[180]

Like Whitehead's God who infuses novelty as the initial aim of an occasion's becoming, in any moment, the human psyche and it's Self are not locked in repetitive movement but are continuously capable of creative novelty. The novel third transcends the opposites at war in us, freeing us from torment and functioning like grace.[181] When we cooperate with this flow of grace, we are capable of being in relationship with an intimate presence that is still an *Other*. Within such relationship, we are able to participate in a sacred "symbolic life" and blossom accordingly. As this sacred Other becomes more visible in our lives, our ego "enlarges" and becomes more "provident," always on the lookout for this Other that responds to our notice by "eliciting our cooperation" even more.[182]

Individual Differentiation from Unconscious Unity

As noted earlier, Whitehead describes a cosmos constantly moving between unity and multiplicity, where individuals arise subjectively but perish again into objective reality. Yet it is the value that individuals contribute to the whole that brings intensity and zest to the cosmos. There is a similar tension in Jung's psychology between unity and differentiation and it is similarly related to value and enjoyment.

Birth of the Modern Self

It is easy for contemporary humans to assume that our ideas about human identity and its place in the world have been true for all humans throughout history or, conversely, to dismiss prehistorical ways of being in the world as superstitious or magical thinking. We might be tempted to assume that the triumphant vanquishing of any trace of animist participation mystique by Enlightenment rationalism signals the final truths of human progress and technological prowess. Alternatively, we may grasp nostalgically for earlier, simpler times when the world was enchanted, goddess-based matriarchal societies lived peaceably together, "noble savages" exhibited romantic relations with a kinship creation, and all was right with the world. Yet, it is such either-or, dualistic thinking that continues to ricochet us between poles, serving only to drive us farther and farther apart. On the other hand, if we are willing to acknowledge both the gains and the losses of our subject-object orientation—and hold these in tension—we may witness the birth of new possibilities that transcend both poles. To do so, we must first understand how what we now know as the modern self came into being.

Richard Tarnas, cultural historian and professor of philosophy and depth psychology at the California Institute of Integral Studies dates the emergence of the modern self to the era between Pico della Mirandola's "Renaissance manifesto for the human self" (1486) and René Descartes's *cogito ergo sum* (1637).[183] The human being that announced itself in that period was

> [d]ynamic, creative, multidimensional, protean, unfinished, self-defining and self-creating, infinitely aspiring, set apart from the whole, overseeing the rest of the world with unique sovereignty, centrally poised in the last moments of the old cosmology to bring forth and enter into the new.[184]

If we call the previous cosmology "primal consciousness," then the primal human experienced the world as "permeated with meaning," or "ensouled." According to Tarnas, such a world possessed its own interiority, creativity, and responsive intelligence.[185] "Primal experience," he writes,

> takes place, as it were, within a world soul, an anima mundi, a living matrix of embodied meaning. The human psyche is embedded within a world psyche in which it complexly participates and by which it is continuously defined. The workings of that anima mundi, in all its flux and diversity, are articulated through a language that is mythic and numinous. Because the world is understood as speaking a symbolic language, direct communication of meaning and purpose from world to human can occur . . . this participation mystique involves a complex sense of direct participation not only of human beings in the world but also of human beings in the divine powers, through ritual, and of divine powers in the world, by virtue of their immanent and transformative presence. The participation is multidirectional and multidimensional, pervasive and encompassing.[186]

The experience of the modern mind is much different. Whereas primal humans felt themselves as part of the world, modern humans experience themselves as distinct and separate in an impersonal and unconscious world.

> Whatever beauty and value that human beings may perceive in the universe, that universe is in itself mere matter in motion, mechanistic and purposeless, ruled

> by chance and necessity. It is altogether indifferent to human consciousness and values. The world outside the human being lacks conscious intelligence, it lacks interiority, and it lacks intrinsic meaning and purpose. For these are human realities, and the modern mind believes that to project what is human onto the non-human is a basic epistemological fallacy. The world is devoid of any meaning that does not derive ultimately from human consciousness . . . For the modern mind, the only source of meaning in the universe is human consciousness.[187]

Yet, as next we will see, placing all meaning in the lap of individual human consciousness is a dangerous development.

The Ego-Self Axis

The developmental journey that must be undertaken in order to establish the healthiest relationship between ego and archetypal Self is a key aspect of Jungian thought. Edinger, recognized by colleagues as "the most influential Jungian analyst in the United States from the 1950s until his death,"[188] describes the development of human identity as a process of differentiation of the individual conscious ego from an unconscious state of wholeness during which the ego completely identifies with the Self. In the infant, this is a natural state of inflation when the "small" ego has claimed for itself qualities that belong to the larger Self. The end result is that the infant experiences itself as a god in a state of ego inflation or "original sin."[189] Although our original unconscious wholeness, represented by the mythical Garden of Eden, certainly represents that oceanic and desirable oneness between humans, God, and nature, when viewed from within space-time reality, it is actually an arrogant, irresponsible, and crude state. The difficulty is achieving union with nature and God without becoming inflated.[190] If the individual conscious ego does not separate from the Self (identification with the divine), an individual can experience self-centered delusions and thereafter live a life that is only "provisional," marked by a refusal "to commit oneself to the moment."[191] In order to live a whole and authentic life, one must move from unconscious wholeness to being a *real fragment* with an actual, particular life, complete with limitations. This is the only way to actualize value.[192] Accepting one's limitations brings an appreciation of time as precious as well as greater creativity, productivity, and relatedness. Here, as with Whitehead, we see that what is actualized is particular and short-lived.

Much of feminist theology equates ego with masculine power or pride and then distances most women's typically relational and self-denying psyche from the male-privileged "heroic ego." Yet Edinger notes that an overabundance of humility or guilt is equally inflationary, just in the negative direction. Such a stance is inflationary because it does not live within natural, human limits.[193] Rather than seeing the Garden as the place for humanity's fall into sin, Edinger sees it as pointing to the birth of human ego consciousness with its new awareness of the opposites. In this understanding, eating of the tree of the knowledge of good and evil initiates the movement out of unconscious oneness with the Self—described as a mindless or animal state—into a distinct and conscious life; the human ego has been born.[194]

The ego is born and undifferentiated consciousness[195] dies; consciousness is won, but the Self is lost; non-distinction is left behind, alienation is the tragic gain. The state of alienation, marked by expulsion from the Garden, is a necessary and desirable step but disconnection from the Self or source is not desirable because the Self is what provides the essentials of human psychic health. Disconnection from the Self can leave the psyche in a state of emptiness, despair, or even self-harm.[196] Yet Edinger argues that both ego inflation and alienation are necessary for ego development and awareness of the Self[197] even if the conscious ego may initially be antagonistic to the unconscious.[198]

The key word is "initially." Such a state of antagonism and alienation from the unconscious must not be permanent. It is necessary to develop what Edinger calls the ego-Self axis, a relationship in which the ego is subordinated to the Self but is constantly in relation to it and nourished by it. Ego-Self separation is seen as a task of the first half of one's life by analytical psychologists while ego-Self reunion is a task of the second half. Yet these halves are not as clearly differentiated as this description might indicate. Edinger describes it as a "circular" process during which ego-Self union and ego-Self separation occur repeatedly in cyclic fashion.[199] Such a process brings a dependable ego-Self axis into consciousness.[200] At the individual level, then, the move is from a state of ego identification with the Self while at the collective level, the move is from a state where individual identity is subsumed in the group[201] to a state where the individual identity is unique, creative, and autonomous. As Fraser N. Watts notes, "the journey of the ego back into relationship with the Self parallels the journey of humanity back into relationship with God."[202] The idea of this relationship between ego and divine Self has resonances in Whitehead's thought, where God and world, permanence and fluency, *require* each other[203] but they are not collapsed monistically into an undifferentiated unity. Carol Christ notes that for process thinkers, although individuals *exist in* God/dess, those individuals are *distinct from* God/dess and therefore capable of entering into real relationship with God/dess.[204]

The Ego and Terror Management

In modern society, the problem is not necessarily the myth of the hero's journey, as Keller and many feminists have claimed, but the fact that within

Western society's power-driven culture, the story-pattern is not lived out in complete form; it can also be dualistically and essentially associated only with men.[205] Philosophically, Keller equates the archetypal hero with the atomistic, self-enclosed subject who is unaffected by his relationships, and who continuously seeks liberation from his human bonds. This hero's worst anxieties are aroused by intimacy and emotion.[206] Yet, is the archetypal pattern of the hero's journey the culprit or is the real problem rather that we are typically unwilling to face the necessary abyss in the cycle and remain there until the new relationship with the Self is forged? As opposed to this necessary deepening, we modern humans tend to claw our way back in a psychological regression to the ascended heights of success—or the descended lows of self-negation—and remain stuck in an inflated ego position, always the hero, yet never reconnected to our divine source of Life. The reunion with Self always requires the death of the conscious ego attitude, a move which the modern self cannot tolerate. Wehr reminds us that the ego who thinks it is "master in its house" cannot stand to be shown that its feelings of supremacy are illusory, as happens during the process of individuation.[207]

If this current atomistically heroic and individualistic worldview exacerbates our alienation and suffering, why do we cling to it so tightly? Michael Kearney, Medical Director of the Palliative Care Service at Santa Barbara Cottage Hospital, points us toward Terror Management Theory (TMT), a theory developed by Solomon, Greenberg, and Pyszczynski with roots in the work of Ernest Becker's *The Denial of Death*.[208] Originally formulated to articulate why social and cultural minorities are persecuted, the theory is based on the understanding that humans cannot tolerate their awareness of death and therefore repress it. Meanwhile, humans construct culture so as to have "symbolic immortality" and protection from "terror annihilation," but that culture must then be protected at all costs. Any threat to the dominant culture, therefore, can spark a swift and powerful reactivity on the part of members marked by attempts to first, distance themselves from the threat, second, to "disarm" the threat through "assimilation," and finally, if those attempts do not succeed, to "eliminate the threat."[209]

Kearney argues that the West's intense focus on "rationalism, materialism, and literal thinking" have subjugated into the "minority culture" anything having to do with "body, depth, complexity, intuition, and direct experience."[210] Keller may recognize this same dynamic at work in a Christian tradition that preferences a *creatio ex nihilo* while denigrating the kind of tehomic theology that embraces a chaoidic matrix of creativity with which God and world are both entangled.[211] Aizenstat speaks of our addiction to rationalism and dualism quite starkly when he notes that staying in one mode of consciousness exclusively is pathological.[212]

The Christian New Testament's reference in the Gospel of John to the idea that "I must decrease and He must increase," McGehee and Thomas argue, is talking about the process of individuation wherein one integrates one's shadow and moves into right relationship with the Self. This is generally a second-half-of-life task, when the authority of the Self emerges and speaks the truths that defy security and collective identity. They consider individuation to be "kingdom of God" work, in that it challenges us to release our territorial dismissal of others as inferior, projections that violate the transpersonal aspect of human consciousness.[213] Through individuating, humans learn to live for the Self, and thereby become persons that possess inner authority and autonomy. While existing cultural or institutional power structures may be suspicious of autonomy because they fear anarchy, McGehee and Thomas note that autonomy generally brings greater responsibility.[214]

According to Ulanov, an ego in proper relation to the Self is both "dethroned and pivotal." Dethroned, because it is no longer the center of identity; pivotal, because it is now "tough enough and alert enough" to be a devoted servant of the Self. From this orientation of service, we look for the Self's presence and work, we are more capable of making informed and creative judgments, and we know our human limits and interdependence. We can now live larger, more fully and freely, more capable of welcoming what is new. This becomes an inner mirroring process because the Self is an Other at our center that uncovers us, re-collects our parts, and connects us to the Transcendent. The transformation that results "is so momentous" that Ulanov likens it to the resurrection.[215] Marjorie Suchocki, too, sees the lure from God in the initial aim as a resurrection customized for each occasion as it forms.[216] This new relationship with Self changes our basic identity from one that is static to one that is spiritually fluid. When we realize this Self at our core, we "identify with the flowing stream (or any other metaphor of process which presents itself)" and we then become more centered and more capable of "self-realization in the highest sense."[217]

Construction: A Relational-Imaginal God-Self

Both Whitehead and Jung were concerned with the flourishing of all; as was shown above, such flourishing is inherently tied to guidance given by transpersonal reality for novelty and transformation. We have already examined teleology and an immanent God in Whitehead and Jung, and the role of purposive vision offered to individuals for their own flourishing. Having done this groundwork, I can now construct a theory of *a relational-imaginal God-Self* in the human being.

Whitehead believed that God seeks intensity of experience for all entities and, therefore, societies should seek such enjoyment as well. In a relational cosmos, societies of occasions are in an interdependent relationship with their environments, and in changing environments, societies that are less complex will be more stable but will lack intensity. Conversely, societies that are more complex with greater intensity of experience will be less stable and at greater risk.[218] Ideally, a society would achieve a balance between novel responsiveness to change and stable endurance. But how can this be achieved?[219]

Whitehead argued that such an achievement rested on "enhancement of the mental pole, which is a factor in intensity of experience,"[220] and that there are two ways to accomplish it.[221] In Whiteheadian language, the first is through "blocking out unwelcome detail" in a nexus (or society of occasions) and the second is by receiving "the novel elements of the environment into explicit feelings with such subjective forms as conciliate them with the complex experiences proper to members of the structured society."[222] In other words, one may enhance one's mental pole through what Whitehead elsewhere calls *transmutation*—or the way in which we eliminate the preponderance of detail from our perception of persons or situations (societies of occasions or nexuses) by distilling the predominant characteristics to perceive a unified whole.[223] The second way is by improving one's ability to discern the initial aims presented by God that offer novel ideas appropriate to oneself, and then integrating and aligning with those initial aims during one's process of concretion. The member, and the society, that achieves this will then enjoy more intensity of experience and more stability as well. In Jungian thought, proper relationship between ego and Self allows for the greater operability of the transcendent function, bringing both new ways of experiencing life and a new identity that is in service to the divine purposes. What new possibilities emerge when we bring together Whiteheadian ideas on initial aims and creative transformation with Jungian perspectives on the Self, the ego-Self axis, and the transcendent function?

In Whitehead's system each momentary occasion is lured by its initial aim at satisfaction, but those aims are given for momentary occasions, not for whole persons. Therefore, if those aims disappear as every momentary subjective unity perishes into objectivity, how would it be possible for a *person*—a society of many, many occasions all popping at once—to ever discern what God's aims might be within the course of one's *life*? Everything a whole person experiences is in the aggregate, yet it is unclear in Whitehead's thought if initial aims are ever aggregated in such a way that a living human being may act on them. On the other hand, within the Jungian frame, we may understand the Self as a pattern or archetypal complex that is both organizing and teleological; in a sense, the Self—as an archetypal pattern—serves as a "lattice" structure around which its contents for wholeness are collected. Generatively synthesizing these two schools of thought allows us to construct a theory of a *relational-imaginal God-Self* that addresses limitations in both systems to enhance the flourishing of individuals.

To achieve this, we must first interweave process views of personal unity, memory, and Keller's sense of "soul" as related to causal efficacy and the flow of the world's experience. In a Whiteheadian view of personal unity, there is no substantial self that endures through time. Personality or selfhood is not fixed, self-contained, or self-sufficient, but is inherently relational. My *self* is processive and ever-changing; it is a strand of unity, a historic route of occasions, and the flow of the body's experience. Such unity, according to Les Muray, is tied to memory in that "my past selves are constitutive of my present momentary self."[224] Another piece of the frame can be drawn from Keller's use of Jung's collective unconscious and Whitehead's causal efficacy in her theorizing about *soul*. She defines *soul* as a combination of one's personal route of experiences and the world's subjective experience in causal efficacy for that processive self. Because causal efficacy is an "internalization of the relevant world" and a liminal transition from one subject to another it offers a place to locate the soul. Soul connects one's past with both the past of the entire world and one's future, and world and soul "perish" and "melt" into each other.[225] For Keller, *self* is the subject's given moments of experience while *soul* is "only a special temporal arrangement of such subjects." Soul is also within the world as the primordial nature of God or "indwelling Eros," internally present in every occasion as its initial aim.[226]

We can now view the God-Self as a relational process, but what about this theory makes that God-Self *imaginal*? Here we draw from Slusser who suggests that—at least for humans—the initial subjective aim is "an imaginal process." Echoing the way Jung understands archetypal patterns as the basis of all matter and energy, current views in quantum physics describe the base of things as "organic, dancing patterns of energy." Slusser sees no reason not to make the leap from "pattern to image" wherein consciousness may be perception of patterns as images. Whitehead and Jung imbue such aims or images with intentionality and connect them to the divine. In both systems, the aim or image may be refused, ignored, or modified.[227]

What is being theorized here is that we can understand initial aims as also following a "historic route" and as aggregated for each individual through memory. Both our understanding of initial aims and of personal unity within a Whiteheadian frame are enriched by incorporating an archetypal understanding because we can now understand the unifying piece as a *complex*, *lattice*, or *framework* around which the images of one's life experience or initial aims are collected. We also gain by applying Whiteheadian thought to Jung's concept of the archetypal Self because we can now ontologically describe its fluid quality while still retaining its unity and power. A *relational-imaginal God-Self* then is the historic route of one's initial aims, collected as images around a unifying center that exists as a connecting point where the transpersonal energies of God flow into personal life with the capacity to structure and order our experience of novel aims in such a way as to spur creative transformation through the transcendent function. This presence of God in the individual evokes our intensities, harmonizes our contrasts, and, when we live in proper relationship to it, we can more fully actualize God's aims for greater flourishing.

SUMMARY

In this chapter, I have shown how the theoretical and empirical systems of Whitehead and Jung can be generatively synthesized to enhance our understanding of body-mind-world experience in both human dreaming and in human transformation toward novel expressions. Moreover, I have shown how this synthesis reveals that such human experience is deeply related to God and to God's activity within both the wider world and individuals. Yet such knowledge and understanding is impotent unless it can be intentionally and regularly accessed in ordinary human lives and thereby *experienced* as *lived reality*. Now we must incorporate *practice*.

NOTES

1. A similarity first suggested by Catherine Keller, Stanley Hopper, and John Cobb in *The Archetypal Process*.
2. As mentioned in the Introduction, some of the ideas developed here appeared in earlier form in my essay "Avoiding a Fatal Error: Extending Whitehead's Symbolism beyond Language" in *Rethinking Whitehead's Symbolism: Thought, Language, Culture*, published in 2017 by Edinburgh University Press.
3. Tarnas, *Cosmos and Psyche*, 19.
4. Catherine E. Keller, *The Face of the Deep: A Theology of Becoming* (London, New York: Routledge, 2003), 94.
5. Kraus, *The Metaphysics of Experience*, 17.
6. Sarkar, *Whitehead's Four Principles from West-East Perspectives*, 5.
7. Hosinski, *Stubborn Fact and Creative Advance*, 52.
8. Hosinski, 52.
9. Keller, "Psychocosmetics and the Underworld Connection," 138–39.
10. Kelsey, *Encounter with God*, 41.
11. Robertson, *Jungian Archetypes*, 153.
12. Jung, *Psychology and Religion*, 1969, 8:325.
13. Jung, 8:326.
14. Kelsey, *Encounter with God*, 104.

15. Jung, *Modern Man in Search of a Soul*, 67.
16. Jung, *Psychology and Religion*, 1969, 8:327.
17. Rowland, *Jung*, 7.
18. Rowland, 135.
19. Hosinski, *Stubborn Fact and Creative Advance*, 43; Whitehead, *Process and Reality*, 119.
20. Ballard, "Kant and Whitehead," 15.
21. Whitehead, *Adventures of Ideas*, 176–77.
22. Lee, *The Becoming of the Church*, 69.
23. Mattingly, "Whitehead's Theory of Eternal Objects," 72.
24. Ulanov, *The Functioning Transcendent*, 97.
25. Robertson, *Jungian Archetypes*, 143.
26. Argyle, *Psychology and Religion*, 105.
27. Slusser, "Jung and Whitehead on Self and Divine," 87.
28. Ulanov and Ulanov, *Religion and the Unconscious*, 15.
29. Rowland, *Jung*, 65–66.
30. Catherine E. Keller, "Self and God: Separation, Sexism, and Self," in *Creating Women's Theology: A Movement Engaging Process Thought*, ed. Monica A. Coleman, Nancy R. Howell, and Helene Tallon Russell (Eugene, OR: Pickwick Publications, 2011), 92.
31. Ulanov, *The Functioning Transcendent*, 97.
32. Cobb Jr., "Eternal Objects and Archetypes," 127.
33. Griffin, "Introduction, Archetypal Psychology and Process Philosophy," 14.
34. Keller, "Psychocosmetics and the Underworld Connection," 144–46.
35. Keller, 139–40.
36. Chalquist, "Who Was Carl Jung and Why Should We Study Him and His Work?"
37. Alan Brinkley B., "Whitehead on Symbolic Reference," in *Studies in Whitehead's Philosophy*, vol. 10, Tulane Studies in Philosophy (New Orleans: Tulane University, 1961), 44.
38. Kraus, *The Metaphysics of Experience*, 75.
39. Griffin, "A Metaphysical Psychology to Un-Locke Our Ailing World," 241–42.
40. Kelsey, *Encounter with God*, 110.
41. Mattingly, "Whitehead's Theory of Eternal Objects," 112.
42. Pittenger, *The Lure of Divine Love*, 28.
43. Pittenger, 4.
44. Hopper, "Once More," 111.
45. Heisig, "The Mystique of the Nonrational and a New Spirituality," 192–93.
46. Whitehead, *Process and Reality*, 344.
47. Mattingly, "Whitehead's Theory of Eternal Objects," 97.
48. Mattingly, 142.
49. Young-Eisendrath and Hall, *Jung's Self Psychology*, 2.
50. Hosinski, *Stubborn Fact and Creative Advance*, 106–7.
51. Jung, *The Basic Writings of C. G. Jung*, 193.

52. Jung, 391.
53. Jung, 103–4.
54. Frey-Rohn, *From Freud to Jung*, 97.
55. Kraus, *The Metaphysics of Experience*, 47.
56. Personal phone conversation with Robin Robertson held in the Fall of 2015.
57. Hosinski, *Stubborn Fact and Creative Advance*, 102.
58. Odin, *Process Metaphysics and Hua-Yen Buddhism*, 167.
59. This argument was first introduced in Kling, "Avoiding a Fatal Error," 137.
60. Whitehead, *Process and Reality*, 33, 70.
61. Hosinski, *Stubborn Fact and Creative Advance*, 86–87.
62. Whitehead, *Process and Reality*, 240.
63. Whitehead, 250.
64. Shelburne, *Mythos and Logos*, 43–44.
65. Jung, *The Basic Writings of C. G. Jung*, 96.
66. Ulanov, *The Functioning Transcendent*, 20.
67. Mattingly, "Whitehead's Theory of Eternal Objects," 94.
68. Whitehead, *Process and Reality*, 164.
69. Whitehead, *Adventures of Ideas*, 76–77.
70. Whitehead, *Process and Reality*, 164.
71. Whitehead, 182.
72. Sherburne, *A Key to Whitehead's Process and Reality*, 173.
73. Whitehead, *Symbolism*, 60.
74. Whitehead, 61–62.
75. Kling, "Avoiding a Fatal Error."
76. Whitehead, *Adventures of Ideas*, 249.
77. Whitehead, 180.
78. Whitehead, *Symbolism*, 7–8.
79. Whitehead, *Process and Reality*, 181.
80. Whitehead, *Adventures of Ideas*, 248.
81. Shelburne, *Mythos and Logos*, 43.
82. Whitehead, *Religion in the Making*, 117–18.
83. Bulkeley, *An Introduction to the Psychology of Dreaming*, 58.
84. Johnson, *Inner Work*, 20.
85. Bulkeley, *An Introduction to the Psychology of Dreaming*, 30.
86. Singer, *Boundaries of the Soul*, 151.
87. Bulkeley, *An Introduction to the Psychology of Dreaming*, 58; Hartmann, *The Nature and Functions of Dreaming*, 31, 62.
88. Kradin, "Reply to Bessel van Der Kolk," 189–90.
89. Kradin, 190–91.
90. Sigmund Freud, *The Basic Writings of Sigmund Freud*, trans. A. A. Brill (New York: Modern Library, 1995), 185.
91. Singer, *Boundaries of the Soul*, 244, 246.
92. Jung, *Psychology and Religion*, 1969, 8:529.
93. Jung, 8:322.
94. Bulkeley, *An Introduction to the Psychology of Dreaming*, 58–61.

95. Griffin, "A Metaphysical Psychology to Un-Locke Our Ailing World," 244.

96. Robertson, *Jungian Archetypes*, 147.

97. Bulkeley, *Big Dreams*, 202.

98. Daugherty, *From Mindfulness to Heartfulness*, 43.

99. Jeffrey J. Kripal, "Visions of the Impossible," *The Chronicle of Higher Education*, March 31, 2014, http://www.chronicle.com/article/Embrace-the-Unexplained/145557/.

100. Bulkeley, *Big Dreams*, 271.

101. Daugherty, *From Mindfulness to Heartfulness*, 73.

102. Hartmann, *The Nature and Functions of Dreaming*, 53.

103. Bulkeley, *Big Dreams*, 232.

104. Bulkeley, 237.

105. Whitehead, *Adventures of Ideas*, 177; Hopper, "Language as Metaphorical," 131.

106. Brinkley, "Whitehead on Symbolic Reference," 43.

107. Woodman, "Coming to a Door," xii.

108. Miriam van Mersbergen, "Viva La Vagus!," *Choral Journal* 55, no. 3 (October 2014): 68.

109. Jun Liu et al., "Transcutaneous Vagus Nerve Stimulation Modulates Amygdala Functional Connectivity in Patients with Depression," *Journal of Affective Disorders* 205 (November 15, 2016): 322, https://doi.org/10.1016/j.jad.2016.08.003.

110. Melanie Klarer et al., "Gut Vagal Afferents Differentially Modulate Innate Anxiety and Learned Fear," *The Journal of Neuroscience: The Official Journal of the Society for Neuroscience* 34, no. 21 (May 21, 2014): 7067, https://doi.org/10.1523/JNEUROSCI.0252-14.2014.

111. Mersbergen, "Viva La Vagus!," 70.

112. Mersbergen, 68.

113. Klarer et al., "Gut Vagal Afferents Differentially Modulate Innate Anxiety and Learned Fear," 7067.

114. Lisa E. Goehler, "Vagal Complexity: Substrate for Body-Mind Connections?" *Bratislavske Lekarske Listy* 107, no. 8 (2006): 275.

115. Bergland, "How Does the Vagus Nerve Convey Gut Instincts to the Brain?"

116. Bergland.

117. Rachel Adelson, "Stimulating the Vagus Nerve: Memories Are Made of This," American Psychological Association, April 2004, http://www.apa.org/monitor/apr04/vagus.aspx.

118. Adelson, "Stimulating the Vagus Nerve."

119. Jiliang Fang et al., "Transcutaneous Vagus Nerve Stimulation Modulates Default Mode Network in Major Depressive Disorder," *Biological Psychiatry* 79, no. 4 (February 15, 2016): 266, https://doi.org/10.1016/j.biopsych.2015.03.025.

120. Goehler, "Vagal Complexity," 275.

121. Adelson, "Stimulating the Vagus Nerve."

122. Julian F. Thayer and Richard D. Lane, "Claude Bernard and the Heart–Brain Connection: Further Elaboration of a Model of Neurovisceral Integration," *Neuroscience & Biobehavioral Reviews*, The Inevitable Link between Heart and Behavior: New

Insights from Biomedical Research and Implications for Clinical Practice, 33, no. 2 (February 2009): 82, https://doi.org/10.1016/j.neubiorev.2008.08.004.

123. Mersbergen, "Viva La Vagus!," 72.

124. Mersbergen, 72.

125. Thayer and Lane, "Claude Bernard and the Heart–Brain Connection," 85.

126. Mersbergen, "Viva La Vagus!," 73.

127. Stephen W. Porges, "Social Engagement and Attachment," *Annals of the New York Academy of Sciences* 1008, no. 1 (December 1, 2003): 31–47, https://doi.org/10.1196/annals.1301.004.

128. Daugherty, *From Mindfulness to Heartfulness*, 49.

129. Hartmann, *The Nature and Functions of Dreaming*, 65.

130. Daugherty, *From Mindfulness to Heartfulness*, 39.

131. Daugherty, 40–41.

132. Daugherty, 46.

133. Daugherty, 50.

134. Kalsched, *Trauma and the Soul*, 179.

135. Daugherty, *From Mindfulness to Heartfulness*, 44.

136. Loomer, "The Size of God," 24.

137. Daugherty, *From Mindfulness to Heartfulness*, 73.

138. James Hillman, "Forward," in *Ecopsychology: Restoring the Earth, Healing the Mind*, ed. Theodore Roszak, Mary E. Gomes, and Allen D. Kanner (San Francisco: Sierra Club Books, 1995), xxiii.

139. Jung, *The Basic Writings of C. G. Jung*, 382.

140. Hillman, "Back to Beyond," 226–27.

141. Lauter and Rupprecht, "Feminist Archetypal Theory," 233.

142. Parker J. Palmer, "The Gift of Presence, The Perils of Advice," *On Being* (blog), April 27, 2016, http://www.onbeing.org/blog/parker-palmer-the-gift-of-presence-the-perils-of-advice/8628.

143. Mattingly, "Whitehead's Theory of Eternal Objects," 146.

144. Whitehead, *Process and Reality*, 161; Mattingly, "Whitehead's Theory of Eternal Objects," 147.

145. Odin, *Process Metaphysics and Hua-Yen Buddhism*, 159.

146. Whitehead, *Process and Reality*, 108, 244.

147. Whitehead, 345.

148. Whitehead, 348.

149. Lee, *The Becoming of the Church*, 94.

150. Lee, 94–95.

151. Whitehead, *Process and Reality*, 67.

152. Donna Bowman and Jay McDaniel, eds., *Handbook of Process Theology*, annotated edition (St. Louis, MO: Chalice Press, 2006), 238.

153. Cobb Jr. and Griffin, *Process Theology*, 104.

154. Whitehead, *Adventures of Ideas*, 257.

155. Cobb Jr. and Griffin, *Process Theology*, 99–100.

156. Monica A. Coleman, "An Exchange of Gifts: Process and Womanist Theologies," in *Handbook of Process Theology* (St. Louis, MO: Chalice Press, 2006), 162–64.

157. Cobb Jr. and Griffin, *Process Theology*, 100.
158. Jung, *Psychology and Religion*, 1963, 11:360.
159. Shelburne, *Mythos and Logos*, 77.
160. Rowland, *Jung*, 33.
161. Jung, *Psychology and Religion*, 1963, 11:360.
162. Edinger, *Ego and Archetype*, 3.
163. Ulanov, *The Functioning Transcendent*, 10.
164. Edinger, *Ego and Archetype*, 3.
165. Singer, *Boundaries of the Soul*, 274.
166. Edinger, *Ego and Archetype*, 4.
167. Wehr, *Jung & Feminism*, 68.
168. Shelburne, *Mythos and Logos*, 77.
169. Jung, *Psychology and Religion*, 1963, 11:361.
170. Jung, *Modern Man in Search of a Soul*, 244.
171. Hoss, "Evidence of Wisdom in Dreams."
172. Robertson, *Jungian Archetypes*, 212.
173. Ulanov, *The Functioning Transcendent*, xi, 15.
174. Jung, *The Portable Jung*, 273–74.
175. Ulanov, *The Functioning Transcendent*, ix.
176. Robertson, *Jungian Archetypes*, 150.
177. Robertson, 150–51.
178. Jung, *The Portable Jung*, 298.
179. Robertson, *Jungian Archetypes*, 259.
180. Hoss, "Evidence of a Cognitive Function within Dreams," 4.
181. Ulanov, *The Functioning Transcendent*, x.
182. Ulanov, ix.
183. Tarnas, *Cosmos and Psyche*, 3.
184. Tarnas, 4.
185. Tarnas, 16.
186. Tarnas, 17.
187. Tarnas, 17.
188. Ford Burkhart, "Edward F. Edinger, 75, Analyst and Writer on Jung's Concepts," *The New York Times*, August 2, 1998, http://www.nytimes.com/1998/08/02/us/edward-f-edinger-75-analyst-and-writer-on-jung-s-concepts.html.
189. Edinger, *Ego and Archetype*, 61.
190. Edinger, 11.
191. Edinger, 13–14.
192. Edinger, 14.
193. Edinger, 15.
194. Edinger, 18.
195. Watts, *Theology and Psychology*, 121.
196. Edinger, *Ego and Archetype*, 43.
197. Edinger, 48.
198. Edinger, 20.
199. Edinger, 5.

200. Edinger, 21. Unbeknownst to me until this very writing, Edinger notes that the initiation of "a whole new attitude and orientation" is commonly imaged in dreams as "being bitten by a snake," and such "transition" dreams are recognized to be "of considerable importance."

201. McGehee and Thomas, *The Invisible Church*, 110.

202. Watts, *Theology and Psychology*, 121.

203. Hosinski, *Stubborn Fact and Creative Advance*, 199.

204. Christ, *She Who Changes*, 46.

205. This is beginning to change, as women have begun to claim the cycle for themselves, sometimes using the hero epics but often using such myths as the descent of Inanna or of Persephone as feminine developmental patterns.

206. Keller, "Self and God," 86.

207. Wehr, *Jung & Feminism*, 100.

208. Michael Kearney, "Healing the Soul in a Culture of Fear," in *Imagination and Medicine*, ed. Stephen Aizenstat and Robert Bosnak (New Orleans: Spring Journal Books, 2009), 38.

209. Kearney, "Healing the Soul in a Culture of Fear," 38.

210. Kearney, 38.

211. Keller, *The Face of the Deep*.

212. Aizenstat, *Dream Tending*, 148.

213. McGehee and Thomas, *The Invisible Church*, 79.

214. McGehee and Thomas, 105.

215. Ulanov, *The Functioning Transcendent*, 21–27.

216. Bowman and McDaniel, *Handbook of Process Theology*, 186.

217. Singer, *Boundaries of the Soul*, 420.

218. Whitehead, *Process and Reality*, 101.

219. See Kling, "Avoiding a Fatal Error," 133–34.

220. Whitehead, *Process and Reality*, 101.

221. An earlier version of this idea was presented in Kling, "Avoiding a Fatal Error," 134.

222. Whitehead, *Process and Reality*, 101–2.

223. Hosinski, *Stubborn Fact and Creative Advance*, 143–44.

224. Muray, *An Introduction to the Process Understanding of Science, Society and the Self*, 26:20.

225. Keller, "Psychocosmetics and the Underworld Connection," 141–42.

226. Keller, 142.

227. Slusser, "Jung and Whitehead on Self and Divine," 88.

Chapter 8

Transformation

INTRODUCTION

In the previous chapter, a *relational-imaginal theory of dreaming* was constructed as well as theory of a *relational-imaginal God-Self in the human being*. All well and good, and yet stopping there in the quest to facilitate psycho-spiritual wholeness and flourishing would be premature. We must go deeper, to the level of *praxis*. In this final chapter, I will show how the suffering that inevitably comes within an embodied life that is always in the process of becoming can be healed through religious experience or mystical encounter with the sacred. We will also explore the meaning of the terms wholeness and flourishing in process and Jungian thought, and touch on the validity of approaching dream work as a *spiritual* practice. Then, using the results of a qualitative exploratory study, we will gain a glimpse into the lived experience of Christian dream workers—especially in the context of those who attend the Haden Institute Summer Dream and Spirituality Conference in North Carolina—so as to evaluate the claim that dreams can be viewed as healing encounters with religious reality and foster human wholeness and flourishing.[1]

A TRANSFORMATIVE RELATIONAL-IMAGINAL PRAXIS FOR PSYCHO-SPIRITUAL WHOLENESS AND FLOURISHING

At this point in our journey it is apropos to revisit the conversation between Anderson and his parishioner. As his congregant noted,

> [I]t was easy to agree to the omnipotence of God—that [God] could do everything—but what was of more immediate concern was whether God could do

> anything in particular. If it is important to know and believe that God is omnipresent—that [God] is everywhere present—one could readily assent, but what one really longed for was to discover God present in the small space of one's personal life.[2]

If we are to meet God in the small spaces of our personal lives, God must be available to us in a real way, *within the context of our embodied lives*. Such a view is not theologically unprecedented, as has already been noted in Tillich's theology, even if it is less widely appreciated. Whereas classical Christian theism often describes a God who is Absolute or the Unmoved Mover, Whitehead conceived of the relationship between God and the world as one of "process and possibility in mutual relationship"[3] where each is a datum received by the other, and where each influences—and *is influenced by*—the other. In Whitehead's philosophy of organism, the infinite and finite, the eternal and temporal, are inextricably joined. Hopper claims Charles Olson as a "process poet" and quotes him as musing that "no event is not penetrated, in intersection or collision with, an eternal event."[4] For Sarkar it is not simply that God and world are mutually immanent, but that these two realities are so bound up with each other that they "cannot be torn apart" because every occasion both embodies God and is embodied in God.[5] In Whitehead's philosophy, "The world lives by its incarnation of God in itself."[6] To fully grasp this radical truth, individuals must be able to *meet* that God within embodied life, and experience the kind of *healing encounters* that can transform our alienation, loneliness, and suffering into wholeness and flourishing. Such encounter has always been understood in the field of spirituality to require praxis.

The need to go beyond theory is not new to most process thinkers, although process thought has often been guilty of remaining an intellectually focused endeavor. In his essay on "A Metaphysical Psychology to Un-Locke an Ailing World," Griffin makes this point especially clear when he suggests that those engaged in metaphysics should see this work as therapeutic for the world. He compels us, even more explicitly than Whitehead, to counter the "deadening images" of modernity with more "enlivening" images that open us to the "mutual sacredness and bondedness" of all life.[7] Noting that we must ground theory in practice, Griffin reminds us of Whitehead's stance that practice is the "final *test* of all theory."[8] As decidedly *empirical*, Faber insists that process theology must not be content with "an ethical praxis of creative transformation," but should view such praxis as "a spiritual encounter with God" so we might understand God's uniquely intimate relationship with the world.[9]

Suffering and the Power of Healing Encounters

In chapter 3, I touched on the perpetual perishing, flux, and creativity at the heart of reality that results in both the suffering and the joy we experience.

In this section, I will show that religious experiences—mystical encounters with sacred reality—can be powerful forces for healing in a world that is inherently tragic. Keller vividly describes our incarnational reality as one that continues to bleed despite classical theology's discomfort with the carnage that inevitably accompanies incarnation.

> There is no deity who causes the suffering or rescues us from it; no divine life-saver. To incarnate intentionally the Wisdom may in fact heighten the risk of crucifixion; but the aim, the lure, is for new creation. This Sophia accepts no "blood payment"; her justice and her mercy do not organize themselves within the economies of sacrifice. Yet her creativity is not squeamish. Every death is within its capacity. Its births come spattered with blood. Its lives feed on each other. The religions of the book, however, while steeped in the blood of manly slaughter, have been queasy about the blood of life, the life of bodies. Having almost erased *tehom* from its book, our tradition has helped to rub out the living bodies. We receive back the flesh of faceless surfaces.[10]

In a somewhat similar way, the Ulanovs question our tendency to see the world only in oppositions between good and evil and transpersonal reality as ultimately only good. Whereas Whitehead typically separates *God* from *creativity* and Keller talks about a primordial chaotic *tehom* that is always part of our reality, the Ulanovs mix it up a little bit more by using Winnicott's work in object relations. In this theory, the infant moves from relating to its mother image as self to "killing the mother" through its spontaneous expression, resulting in a relationship to the mother of "object usage" where the mother becomes objectively real yet still present for her child. The same movement can occur in our relations to God when we "kill" our psychological God-image[11] only to find that an objectively encountered God exists outside of our projection. Often then, as we witness evil continuing to flourish, our "fantasies of a good and loving world where we will all be well and happy" collapse and take with them our projected image of God as solely good. Those whose faith dies at this stage might not have noticed that God remains. For those that do, they see God's otherness in even more stark relief, they see the mystery of evil and the "profundity of sin" and know it will not necessarily all be wiped away. In this shift, we move beyond projections to wider and humbler perceptions of the divine.[12]

Again, tragedy cannot be avoided in a world marked by a riotous diversity of life in flux. As within the Whiteheadian understanding of freedom and multiplicity, in Jungian thought there is a similar level of importance placed upon decision and differentiation. In contrast to the classical Christian belief that evil entered the world through human disobedience, McGehee and Thomas note Jung's view that evil is an undifferentiated force that works in the world through human experience. They see humans as naturally dualistic until they can consciously integrate opposing forces in the psyche.[13] In fact, in a Jungian view, the process of becoming conscious is a dynamic one in which the tension between the opposites of good and evil force us to make the human decisions that are both life's "grace and [its] burden."[14]

In Jung's *Seven Sermons to the Dead*, the *pleroma* is described as the primordial state where all the opposites negate each other. This is the unconscious unity within which there is no tension and no conscious differentiation, so all qualities are balanced and devoid of energy. It is due to conscious differentiation that the opposing forces become distinct and efficacious. In this way, according to Singer, humans are "the victims of the pairs of opposites. The *pleroma* is rent in us." As a self-regulating system, the psyche, too, is inherently polar. Human distinctiveness—value—is achieved not by seeking only what is good or beautiful, leading us to "forget our own nature." Rather, Jung argued that when we work to achieve only one polar value we invariably attach to its opposite, but when we focus on our natural distinctiveness, we achieve distinguishing value. To do otherwise is to fall into "nothingness and dissolution";[15] or, as Keller might phrase it, to do otherwise is to fall into the *tehomic* abyss.

Yet it is not just decision and opposition that cause suffering and neuroses; early life trauma seems to be yet another influential factor. Young-Eisendrath and Hall discuss the "heavily defended person" who inevitably manifests a "pathological false self" that is split from one's shadow and therefore "inaccessible to ordinary awareness."[16] The need for such heavy defenses arises, according to Kalsched, because trauma experienced by children who cannot bear its weight consciously engenders internal division.[17] Though less than ideal, the self-divisions that result from early trauma have survival value. They are part of a *self-care system* that saves at least some of the child's "innocence and aliveness" through "sequestering" it in the unconscious where it can be retrieved later for "possible future growth." Kalsched argues that those who experience early childhood trauma or adverse experience are prematurely thrown into a *non-ordinary reality* wherein an *implicit narrative* comes alive. This alternate world is not created by the trauma, but is already there in an archetypal sense; it "surrounds the fractured soul with a dramatic *story* from the archetypal repertoire of the ancient psyche . . ." This narrative that surrounds the split off part of the self is made explicit in dreams and other nondirected thinking through what Kalsched calls *trans-egoic powers* or *personified presences* that exist in the "mytho-poetic matrix between reality and fantasy"[18]

Such fracturing and subsequent recruitment of unconscious powers allows life to continue and protects the psyche from being shattered, but at a price: what is sacrificed is "the animation and vitality that have always been associated with ensouled living."[19] Another unfortunate result of such traumatic experience is the internalization of distorted perceptions of self. These then become disintegrating and fragmenting "*anti-wholeness factors* in the psyche" that become habitual and perpetuate suffering through the adoption of chronically negative self-identifications.[20] Such negative views of the self that result from unbearable alienation and rejection may then lead to despair and violence, according to Edinger, and such violence can either be self- or other-inflicted.[21]

When McGehee and Thomas ask, "How did we ever get to be so un-whole, so broken in the first place?" they explain that it is all-too-human to be divided against ourselves because of the inherent psychological struggle between what is conscious and what is unconscious.[22] In a resonant way, Whitehead believed that philosophy must critique abstraction and make explicit those unconscious—and often conflicting—presuppositions upon which our statements and actions are based.[23] How, exactly, can we do that? If an individual is torn asunder inside, feels unworthy to exist, and is incapable of recognizing or responding to what spontaneously arises from the unconscious and the environment, surely, this must be—at least in part—what lies at the root of the correlation between adverse childhood experiences (ACEs) and adult disease and risky behavior. Yet the current biomedical model has no way in which to understand such possible linkages.

Epperly, drawing from George Engel, describes the biomedical model of health and illness as both reductionistic and dualistic, noting that although that model has successfully addressed a significant number of health problems, "its failure to address the spiritual and emotional lives of patients renders it ineffective in dealing with chronic and terminal illness, patient responsibility for self-care, and bioethical decision-making." While modern medicine has saved multitudes, its "purely somatic" approach leaves it incapable of addressing "the deeper issues of meaning and values that are raised by critical illness and mortality." Its siloed approach has separated patients from "spiritual, relational, and environmental resources" and its "adherence to a linear cause and effect understanding of reality has blinded it to the impact of economics, emotions, spirituality, and the environment on issues of health and illness."[24] The results of our alienation—and our adverse childhood experiences—are the myriad of symptoms elaborated in chapter 1 of this current work. Certainly wounding, dualistic worldviews have played a part, but as Bulkeley and Zimmerman argue, coming to an intellectual appreciation of a non-dual worldview cannot transform our behavior. Conscious awareness alone cannot move us out of reactive mode. Only deeply felt *experience* of a transformative nature has any hope of changing our lives.

Pargament, Hood, and Walter Houston Clark have all made compelling claims about the healing power of religious or mystical experience. In describing Hood's research, Pargament explains that mystical experiences—even though such experiences are incredibly varied—are "generally marked by powerful emotions, consisting of feelings of numinous consciousness and feelings of unity." The sacred object encountered is "perceived to be absolutely real—'a foundational reality' in the words of Hood" and such experiences "can have long-lasting, life-altering effects."[25] Clark's understanding of mystical experience is key to making spirituality and religion more relevant today. He argues that while mystical experience is the essential principle that makes religious consciousness religious, ecstatic experience does not seem to be limited to believers, and such experiences can be triggered through art, music, and other such imaginal elements. The experiences themselves are strongly similar, and Clark believes that it is primarily the interpretation or the theology that differentiates the religious mystical experience from the secular ecstatic experience.

Useful to this project, Clark's central conviction that only religious or mystical experience can produce the kind of profound changes to personality that such experiences engender is of utmost interest. It is only in such "shattering" experiences where one comes face-to-face with oneself that can effect long-lasting changes to values and behavior. Mystical experiences are often interpreted as a "union" with a divine presence. Some researchers theorize this to be a return to the blissful experience of unity with one's mother, but Clark's work shows mystical experience to be more like a "rebirth" than a regression, because those who have experienced such an encounter claim a new power to be loving and compassionate with others.[26] The facilitation of more mystical experiences of "rebirth" may be the only way the Church can have any real impact on the human condition. How might we interpret the outcome of such experiences?

Wholeness and Flourishing

As can be discerned in previous chapters, the ultimate point of this work is the facilitation of psycho-spiritual *wholeness and flourishing*. As has been taught *ad nauseum* in business or strategic planning retreats, one cannot point one's ship in the right direction if one has not determined the destination. We must describe what success looks like—what its indicators are—if we are going to prove a means of getting there. Such is the point of this section wherein we will examine both Whiteheadian and Jungian understandings of wholeness and what it means for humans to flourish.

As already noted, Whitehead and Jung agree that there is a certain inevitability of dualism at the heart of reality and of our psychic lives. For Whitehead, because the universe is both transient and eternal, and exhibits both unity and multiplicity, it is inherently dual. Sounding like a Jungian, he writes, "Through the universe there reigns the union of opposites which is the ground of dualism."[27] As has already been discussed at length, Jung described the psyche as having an inherent polarity, resulting in the tension of opposites that we cannot avoid but which we can transcend. It is this transcendence of the opposites—while holding the contrast of both and rejecting neither—that is at the heart of how wholeness is understood in both systems. Singer writes that wholeness includes a harmony "in which everything is included."[28] Whitehead, too, speaks of the Harmony that is yet possible within the contrasts and discordant elements. The discord in reality cannot be blocked out, as that would result in what Whitehead called "anaesthesia," but even when elements cannot be harmonized, if we are willing to hold them in tension, Cobb and Griffin insist that they may be contained within "a larger, more inclusive novel pattern" where the contrast actually contributes to the overall intensity. Embodying novelty in this way means that "the occasion is creatively transformed in relation to its predecessors" and the contrasts then contribute to beauty and enjoyment of the whole.[29]

For the individual, Cobb describes wholeness as "at-homeness." Such people are

> "at-home" in their bodies, in their conscious and unconscious feelings and senses, in their human relationships, and in their total natural environment. They are "at-home" with who they are, and therefore they are comfortable being just that. Because they are "at-home" in themselves, they are free from defensiveness toward others. Others experience their warmth—that is their openness, their concern, and their affection. One is not the object of good deeds or just treatment from the whole person. One is the recipient of acceptance and understanding.[30]

For many, the central aspect of the experience of wholeness may be the greatest challenge of all—the acceptance of oneself. Jung writes that to be forgiving of others, to act in a caring way in the world, and even to "love my enemy in the name of Christ" are all "great virtues." But if I consider myself deeply unworthy and am my own enemy, where will I find the capacity to love this enemy within? Rather than self-love, we may "condemn and rage against ourselves," denying ourselves any mercy whatsoever.[31]

As will be shown later through the results of a qualitative study of Christians who use Jungian-influenced dream work as a spiritual practice, such self-acceptance and transformation can result from the healing experiences that working with one's dreams and synchronicities may bring. Yet it is not only true that dream work can facilitate healing encounters with sacred reality, the argument herein is that within a relational-imaginal praxis, dream work can be a means of discerning God's initial aims and fostering *conscious transmutation*. As noted earlier, aligning with God's aims and *transmutation*—the blocking out of unwelcome detail—are two ways of enhancing one's mental pole and thereby allowing complex societies to remain stable while still incorporating novelty and intensity. These separate methods of enhancing the mental pole—transmutation and discerning God's initial aims—are the very heart of what we might consider to be a *relational-imaginal praxis* for psycho-spiritual wholeness.

In Whiteheadian terms, *transmutation* is a "method of simplification" that allows us to focus our attention on the aggregate occasions or enduring objects within our environment.[32] Irrelevant details are subsumed, differences are eliminated, and we then feel our actual world as a community. Whitehead considers transmuted feelings to be akin to "propositional prehensions" or "propositional feelings" and Hosinski argues that while they arise unconsciously, they may acquire consciousness in more complex occasions with intellectual feelings. Transmuted feelings allow us to grasp purposes and intentions at a more abstract level.[33] It is my contention that if transmutation is made more conscious, it is healthier for the individual, because unconscious emotional transmutation—caused by the entrenched behavioral patterns and psychological complexes that trigger emotional reactivity—leads to repetitive and unhealthy life operating patterns as well as bad decisions.

Yet recognizing our unconscious patterns and agendas is no easy task in contemporary America. Our modern world is heavily skewed toward concentrated attention and this imbalance risks dissociation from the unconscious. Such dissociation is problematic because when we dissociate from the unconscious, the more likely that disruptive unconscious counter positions will operate beneath the level of consciousness and wreak havoc upon our lives.[34] In such instances, reactive patterns we have developed that result in our blocking out the detail of the real experience in front of us in favor of the projected imprint of emotional wounding and self-defeating thoughts prevent us from engaging in the world *as it is in the present moment*. In such cases, we are no longer responding to the dynamic flow of life but reacting from the perspective of past experience. In Whiteheadian terms related to the material already explored on formalism and history, we are more likely to repeat the past unless we can perceive the propositions that join the past world with our novel aims, and raise these propositions from unconsciousness to the level of intellectual feelings so that they may be consciously evaluated.

Before our rationalistic side gleefully grabs the steering wheel, we must keep in mind that this is an emotion-heavy and value-soaked endeavor. Hosinski describes propositions as lures for feeling that result from the integration of an eternal object with the physical prehensions of actual entities.[35] Regardless of the truth or falsity of a proposition, its purpose is simply to influence the process of concrescence and persuade us to act through the attraction of value.[36] While entertaining propositions, an actual entity unconsciously *feels* the difference between the "fact" of past entities and the "theory" of the new possibilities prehended; this is known as a propositional feeling and is an unconscious valuation. As noted in chapter 3, if the integration phase of concrescence is prolonged even more, such a proposition may become an intellectual feeling, wherein the contrast between "what is" and "what might be" is both *felt* and *known* consciously.[37] The importance of consciousness to higher-level organisms and human society cannot be overstated—it is the consciousness achieved in intellectual feelings that allows the subject "to criticize [its] propositional lures."[38] Hosinski argues that intellectual feelings that reach consciousness expand the awareness of the concrescing subject to include more of its unconscious experience and therefore empower that subject to better judge its possibilities before committing to them.[39]

Such consciousness lays the foundation for reason and rational thought and increases intensity of experience and the capacity to aspire toward such lofty ideals as truth, value, and beauty.[40] Moreover, "high grade," conscious occasions bring novelty and originality to life. Symbols play a role in this process, as Whitehead's symbolic reference is an intellectual feeling that has connected what is perceived through our senses with what is perceived through causal efficacy.[41] The knowledge that arises through intellectual feelings produces the data "which initiates rational or reflective thought," and it is only "active thought" that can "save symbolically conditioned action from quickly relapsing into reflex action."[42]

As mentioned, Whitehead suggests that conforming with God's initial aims is yet another way to enhance the mental pole and increase intensity of experience and enjoyment, yet there has been little guidance within Whiteheadian thought or process theology on how that is accomplished. Earlier, I argued for functional connections between eternal objects and archetypes, and propositions, propositional feelings, and archetypal images. I also posited a *relational-imaginal God-Self* as the historic route of initial aims. Here it is useful to combine Cobb's claim that "The primary aim of piety . . . is to conform one's decisions to the possibilities offered by God"[43] with his understanding that the way we conform with our highest possibilities is not a conscious activity but through more subtle principles and lures of the future.[44] Armed with our *relational-imaginal theory of dreaming*, and aware of a *relational-imaginal God-Self* within, combined with the recognition that our tasks are to (1) improve our conscious transmutation, (2) raise unconscious propositions to intellectual feelings, and (3) discern—and better conform to—God's initial aims, I now propose a transformative *relational-imaginal praxis of dream work for psycho-spiritual wholeness and flourishing*.

Dream Work as Spiritual Praxis

A *relational-imaginal theory of dreaming* is a foundation upon which we can posit a praxis of dream work for harmonization of contrasts, discernment of aims, and conscious transmutation through raising unconscious propositions to intellectual and religious feelings resulting in more conscious decisions, less reactivity, better alignment with initial aims and more wholeness and flourishing. Let us now explore why this is considered a *spiritual* praxis.

Human spirituality has long been a topic of interest, although it has remained primarily a religious or theological matter until more recent decades when both the soft and hard sciences became interested in understanding this aspect of human life. From a psychological perspective, the core question about religion and spirituality has seemed to center on whether or not religiousness is a unique human behavior—one that requires a specific set of concepts and practices in approaching it systematically—or if religiousness can be reduced to some other more elemental human behavior. Related to that is whether religiousness should be looked at in this more reductive way or if it requires a more holistic approach wherein the data collected is understood within a wider field of scope. As well, researchers in brain science have been wiring experienced meditators to monitors to get a clearer picture of exactly what is happening on a physical level in the brain as people pursue such a practice.

There are also differences in the way spirituality has been defined. For example, Andrew Dreitcer focuses on spirituality as a "style of intimacy" one uses in approaching sacred reality.[45] Saint-Laurent describes spirituality as the "inner meaning of human experience" as people seek transformation under a particular sacred worldview,[46] and Pargament describes spirituality as the "search for the sacred."[47] Another way to look at these various definitions is to say that spirituality can be approached as *a way of being*, as *a system of meaning*, or as a *technique* or *set of practices*. Which is "correct"? It is possible they all are. For purposes of this project, spirituality is defined as incorporating: (1) a way of perceiving *ultimate Reality*, (2) a set of tools or techniques to approach that Reality, and (3) the hope of being in some kind of communion and transformative relationship with this Reality as a way of navigating the human experience.

Are dreams like a "sacred text" one can contemplate as in *lectio divina*? Or is a dream an imagistic icon one can "see through" to sacred Reality? In the work of George J. Tanabe, Jr. with Buddhists who practiced image-generating techniques, Bulkeley notes that the techniques were shared because the monks discovered their dream-visions to be highly valuable to their journey toward enlightenment.[48] In a 2005 article in the *Journal of Counseling & Development*, Timothy L. Davis and Clara E. Hill detailed the results of a study that compared spiritual and non-spiritual approaches to dream work and concluded that their results "suggest the benefits of incorporating spirituality into dream interpretations for spiritually oriented clients."[49] Clients in what they identified as the "spiritual condition" in the study "gained more spiritual insight into their dreams and gained more existential well-being than volunteer clients in the waking life condition."[50]

THE LIVED EXPERIENCE OF CHRISTIAN DREAM WORKERS: A QUALITATIVE STUDY

In some spiritual experiences, individuals may meet the hiddenness or dark side of God. Could meeting God in a way that deconstructs one's God images be a positive move for our communal wellbeing? Taylor points to the surging interest worldwide in dream sharing as symptomatic of our growing communal anxiety and evolving relationship with God. Myriad factors have historically contributed to a sense of "chaos, uncertainty and increasingly urgent spiritual need," including horrific or sadistic crimes, long-lasting wars, and social unrest and changing demographics. Add an unhealthy contemporary dose of natural disasters and unease about a changing climate, growing ideological tensions, and other "sociocultural markers" of "collective distress and uncertainty," and Taylor finds it unsurprising that interest in "all manner of techniques for 'spiritual renewal and discernment' in general, and in the spiritual implications of dreams and dreaming in particular" are on the rise, especially in a time when "traditional religious practices and institutional leadership" seem less and less relevant.[51] One of the regions witnessing a particular growth in dream-sharing groups is the southeastern part of the United States wherein it was estimated that over 400 dream groups were operating in Christian congregations in 2006.[52] This has been fostered, at least in part, by the writing of Joyce Rockwood Hudson and Bob Haden's establishment of the Haden Institute, both of which integrate Jungian psychology into Christian belief and practice.

In the Spring of 2014, I conducted an exploratory phenomenological study utilizing a methodology developed in the United Kingdom by Jonathan A. Smith, Paul Flowers, and Michael Larkin called Interpretative Phenomenological Analysis (IPA)[53] that sought to describe the nature of the shared experience of using Jungian dream work as a Christian spiritual practice. IPA is considered *doubly hermeneutical* because "the researcher is trying to make sense of the participant trying to make sense of what is happening to them."[54] Considered a pilot study, my research was not exhaustive and did not seek data saturation, but recruited a small number of Christian dream workers who had registered to attend the Haden Conference in 2014. Data was gathered to answer this primary question: *What is the essential nature and meaning of the practice of Jungian dream work in the spiritual lives of Christians who attend the Haden Conference?* The purpose of the study was to gather rich accounts from a small group of Christian dream workers to gain insight into their own interpretations of their experiences. Moreover, I sought to understand whether participants believed their dreams were a place for encountering God, or had any effect on their spirituality, their theological insights, and their experience of religious community.[55] To counter the potential bias in conducting research as a participant observer, I focused on the participants—on *their* accounts, *their* descriptions, and *their* interpretations—during data collection and engaged in deep reflection afterward. Five major themes emerged in data analysis regarding dream work in the lives of these five Christians. Of course, it is impossible to completely isolate the effects of their dream work practice from other aspects of their spiritual and psychological journeys, but what is reported is based on their accounts.[56]

First, all made experiential claims of a mystical nature that included feeling God's presence, experiencing an inner knowing, a heightened sense of the reality of a "spiritual realm," energy or *numinosity* in dream images, and sometimes particular physical sensations.

Susan: I had some negative experience with religious people. Struggled with that. Then in my mid-20s, I had a horrible, horrific family issue come up and thought I would lose my mind. And I had one of those—gosh, I would almost call it a Damascus road type experience. I was talking to my boss, who was also a good friend, about this young man who—well, actually, he had molested my daughter. And I said, "He needs to get in a church," and this stuff people say. And he looked at me and he said, "Do you think it would help you?" And it was like the weirdest thing. It was like this—it was like sitting out on a hot summer day and a cloud goes over the sun . . . And this cool comes over you. And it was really weird. The whole rest of that day, I went around thinking, even saying—"Everything's going to be okay." No reason for it.

Thomas (speaking about his dream group experience): . . . and I get a sense now, part of interpreting the language of wetness. Fluid of movement. When that happens the spirit is there and I often see in the dream group—water. Great spiritual sign. And I get that feeling sometimes. When somebody interprets something, I get a flowing feeling when it's right. You know, I'd say, "mmm." I get this flowing feeling inside.

June (speaking about her bi-polar son): So it felt like he was just dead and so that was another time where I was just brought to this place of sheer broken nothingness, but God came—God was there.

Second, all claimed, in one way or another, that dream work has played a significant role in their spiritual lives, and that dreams themselves hold important meaning and value. All of them have recorded their dreams in writing and analyzed them in some way.

John: I started off way back in the 80's just writing my dreams down. Sometimes I'd go back and look at them. Then when I hit the skids I started working with my dreams more analytically out of just a survival necessity . . . over time my dream work became more—I put more energy into it and thought more about it. Then when I hit midlife the dream work became the life preserver that I clung to when all hell broke loose.

Susan: What I would call my greatest gift from the dream work is basically the veil that separates . . . it's coming down. And I've read somewhere—and I don't know who wrote it—that there are many veils over our consciousness or whatever. Between us and the spiritual realm. And as they come off, you see more clearly and you become more conscious. But I perceive it as a tremendous gift to me. That there is little separation between the waking physical realm and the spiritual realm. And dreams, visions, waking dreams, whatever. They're more and more the same for me. They're carrying as much weight, one as the other. Because they complement one another, and they confirm one another. That's the greatest gift.

June: . . . it's both cognitive and affective. The "aha" moments are just incredible . . . I feel gratitude when I write a dream—a lot of times we just don't remember our dreams and then—but to write down a dream and to look at the richness of it and I think—praying without ceasing. I never would've understood that, but instead of having a prayer time now, my centering prayer time is [dream work].

Third, they interpret their dreams (and often synchronicities) as divine communication that provides insights, guidance, loving support, hope, and healing.

Elizabeth (speaking about how dream work has affected her spiritual life): You know, it's just—I'm conscious of it. I'm really aware that dreams are part of my spirituality. It's like God speaking to me and there's something significant happening in the dreams even, you know, ordinary dreams. And so I'm aware of that.

John (speaking about two dreams where Jesus came to him): It was very clear to me that God was speaking to me and teaching in dreams . . . . Toward the end of my pastoring I have to say that my morning dream work became my primary spiritual discipline. That was the way that I felt God was communicating with me most clearly.

Susan: And I used to—I'd work a dream to exhaustion. And I finally came to realize that if it's something I need, it's going to come. And I started seeing a pattern where [God] would use an entirely different dream to reflect on the same issue . . . . Very often dreams came to me as confirmation on things. And then too it's just become so much a part of my connection to the Divine. Just His presence, you know?

Fourth, they saw their dream work as an enriching and transformative practice in relation to their experience of self. It typically helped to increase their sense of self-acceptance, self-knowledge, and self-forgiveness; they described themselves as happier, healthier, more integrated and more whole as a result of this practice.

June: (speaking about dreaming and sleep) So you're letting go of control, conscious thought, and that's when the real person, good, bad [emerges] . . . so I think—I don't feel as guilty and I don't really feel shame anymore about who I am. For some reason, every time I messed up somehow or things didn't go the way society said they should, I felt a sense of shame, but I don't really much feel that anymore.

Elizabeth: (again speaking of how dream work has affected her spiritual life) I think it's broadened it; my life is more enriched because of it. I bring a lot more to it, you know, like I'm a lot more aware that my life is filled with all kinds of prayer practices and sometimes when I'm developing prayers, they don't look very Catholic anymore. They tend to look more pagan because I'm looking for symbols that speak, that are rich, kind of like, you know, as they would come to us in dreams . . .

Susan: (who credits dream work with helping her survive a battle with cancer over the previous year) I feel whole. And I know there's more. But yeah. People tell me how radiant—I hear it constantly . . . And at first I thought, well, they're just trying to make me feel better because I'm not looking as sick. Because I looked like death for many months. But it's like—it got to be so constant. I would see people in Wal-Mart—"You're so radiant." That word, constant, "radiant" Radiant, radiant, radiant. There must be something to it. And it's more than my shiny make-up. And I feel that.

Lastly, they saw their dream work as an enriching and transformative practice regarding their relationships with God and others. They feel it helped to broaden their spiritual perspectives, change their images of God, deepen their friendships, heal past hurts, and increase their appreciation of, or participation in, other religious traditions.

Thomas: (speaking about a dream he had) I had one particularly dark time where I remember myself falling down in blackness and then reaching a point where I felt a hand under my rib cage and that stopped the fall . . . I knew there was a bottom and that somebody was there observing and caring.

Thomas was then asked what had changed for him after that experience, and he said,

Thomas: Like, it wasn't so dark and I knew if I kept on putting one foot ahead of the other I would get through. That there was an invisible means of support . . . After that hand on the rib cage I saw [God] was not only real, but he was for me. And then with [the dreams of] my parents, I could see that this is bigger than anything I ever imaged. [God's] really there.

Elizabeth: . . . just more recently I've started noticing—like after a dream group session I might pick up on the same symbols as another person. That's just kind of a recent thing. Like, oh, that's interesting for my own dreams. And then whenever I promote dream work, I talk about it in terms of that it's not just a personal thing. But it's, you know, we help to heal society and to contribute to healing our shadow stuff so that we're not projecting so much and that, you know, the world is a better place if we participate in dream work and get to know our shadows better.

Susan: So, I don't know how much longer I have. I know this particular cancer, if it returns, it returns quickly and ferociously. And I believe that I'm well. I think that all is well. But what a glorious thing to have arrived where I am before it's all over. Because that was one thing with me. It was like, okay, life is painful. And I know it's a growth thing from start to finish. But shouldn't you be able to arrive somewhere, you know? And I would like to—right at this moment, I really like where I'm at. And I know there's more. But I'm just really grateful. *Grateful*. I feel like the Beloved. Finally.

Bulkeley acknowledges that dream interpretation "may seem more trouble than it is worth" for pastoral counselors because they can be dismissed as mere "wish fulfillment" or even as satanic, on the one hand, or, on the other, naively elevated to the status of "instant enlightenment."[57] Yet he offers a very helpful perspective when he notes the positive uses of dream work in pastoral counseling, especially in times of personal struggle. At such times, dreams may provide key insights that are spiritually transformative.[58] The participants interviewed in this project would most likely agree. At the end of June's interview, she was asked to summarize how dream work has impacted her spiritual life.

> The one word that comes to mind is connection. I feel *connected* to my inner self; most days, not all the time. I feel connected to who I really am and I feel connected to the life force . . . the poem "Desiderata" used to make me cry, you know, "you're a child of the universe." And I never knew why it made me cry—because it's really kind of corny, but now it's not corny to me at all and I just feel like dream work cuts across the entire universe. It feels to me as though it

opens us up or has opened me up to forces that I don't really have to understand, but that there is guidance—loving guidance—and that's what I think.

For those who resist the use of subjective accounts and interpretations of dreams for meaningful research, Bulkeley argues both that dream recall is reliable and that we need not be overly skeptical of introspective reports when we remember that "*all* the contents in our minds are subjective."[59] We might also keep in mind that a scientist cannot objectively *prove* that she loves her husband, nor can patients who fill out pain scales objectively *prove* the level of their pain, yet such subjective accounts are widely accepted. Though investigators cannot be sure that people may not misrepresent their experiences, Bulkeley argues that such concerns need not lead us to overreact by rejecting all personal, introspective data. We must accept that others' subjective experiences are real and valid.[60]

At this stage of our knowledge, it is certainly impossible to completely pin down the nature of the dream experience. Jung himself remained somewhat mystified about its nature. Yet he knew that despite our prejudices against dream interpretation as uncertain and arbitrary, intentionally working with dreams often leads to positive results.[61] Additional qualitative studies of this emerging movement in Christian spirituality are called for and can broaden the scholarship regarding transformative practice, new religious movements, and offer a rich area of interdisciplinary potential between the fields of theology, religious studies, contemplative spirituality, psychology, and spiritual formation. Moreover, if using a practice of dream work within a Christian context has a positive impact on people's lives, and if such a practice helps them to become aware of the transformative presence of God in the "small spaces" of their lives, then teaching and encouraging such a practice in congregations should be a vital ministry of the church—possibly even one of its core ministries. Such a ministry has the potential to be enlivening and revitalizing not only for currently active churchgoers but also for those who have become disengaged with congregational life, as well as for those with no religious affiliation who are seeking to deepen their spiritual lives.

SUMMARY

In chapters 4 and 5, we examined the role that dream work plays in Jung's analytical psychology as well as how it might be viewed from scientific, communal, and mystical viewpoints. Yet we saw each viewpoint is limited by obstacles to greater adoption mostly due to the lack of a metaphysical-theoretical framework within which dreams and dream work could be understood as revealing something crucial about the very nature of reality. In chapter

6, I showed how a synthesis of Whitehead and Jung lays the foundation for generative constructive work. In this chapter, I have shown how the constructed *relational-imaginal theory of dreaming* combined with awareness of a *relational-imaginal God-Self* within allows us to see spiritual dream work as a *transformative relational-imaginal praxis* in which we can engage to (1) improve our conscious transmutation, (2) raise unconscious propositions to intellectual feelings, and, (3) discern—and better conform to—God's initial aims. Moreover, I have described wholeness and flourishing as ultimately being marked by increased enjoyment and intensity of experience achieved through being able to respond consciously and creatively to life as it is in the present moment. I have therefore shown dream work to be a transformative *relational-imaginal praxis for psycho-spiritual wholeness and flourishing.*

CONCLUSION

I have spun here a relational-imaginal web of theory and practice: of Whitehead, Jung, and dream work. We have explored reasons for our divided and divisive culture. We have envisioned integrative theoretical, empirical, and practical resources to address our fragmentation. We have witnessed signposts for transpersonal reality, unconscious perception, vision, value, novelty, and change. We have imagined a cosmos and psyche where everything formed is formed in relation to everything else. We have sounded the depths of reality and found at its heart deep feeling, aesthetic value, imagination, and image. We come now to the proverbial "so what?" question. What is the ultimate value of a *relational-imaginal theory of dreaming*, or of a theory of a *relational-imaginal God-Self* in the human being, or of a *relational-imaginal praxis* in the greater scheme of things? After this long, interdisciplinary weaving project, I must return to my social location as one who claims a pluralistic, ecofeministic, and panentheistic Christian identity. Because of that identity, I first claim the value of such a relational-imaginal web of theory and practice as *Christian*—as reflecting the good news of Jesus the Christ, and therefore as robust and liberative for Christians. But then, like one who takes a step onto the spiral pathway back out from the center of the labyrinth, I also claim this relational-imaginal web to be *transreligious*—as offering value, belonging, and transformation for any who seek psycho-spiritual wholeness and flourishing.

In his *Lure of Divine Love*, W. Norman Pittenger called for a "radical reconception of the Christian tradition in which we stand and from which we look at things," asking us to "work through once more, the things that are both human and Christian."[62] Christians have for millennia described the human condition as one of both sin and grace—although it can be argued that the

Church has more often focused on the sin. Beldon Lane, in his beautiful and evocative writing on Calvinist spirituality and its core aspect of desire, notes Calvin's "extravagant" description of the "radical unity of nature and God" as counterbalanced by a pessimism regarding humans' capacity to choose what is most attractive because of disjointedness throughout creation.[63] Yet maybe Morton Kelsey is correct in his view that humans exist more as wanderers than as fearfully hovering "over the abyss of nothingness." As wanderers, we humans possess a "compass" that helps us "sense" the direction we must go if we "hearken to revelation." For him, each human is on a pilgrimage to the absolute that is not a thing to be owned but a missional journey.[64]

The mission of the Christian community, like all that are built around revelation and revelatory experience, is to communicate—*and live out*—its good news in a way that is meaningful. No matter how "startling" or "original" a revelatory vision is, Rosemary Radford Ruether insists that it still "must always be communicated and made meaningful through some transformation of ideas and symbols already current."[65] While Athanasius and Leo I claim to be true to tradition, Ruether insists they "are in fact engaged in a constant process of revision of the symbolic pattern in a way that reflects their experience." If Ruether is correct that the only way a "religious pattern" can remain "vital" is if the symbols used to communicate it are alive, evocative, and redemptive within a community,[66] then, based on the evident decline of participation in Christian churches, the symbols used to communicate the Christian revelation seem no longer vital or effective.

Hosinski is deeply correct when he notes that the Trinitarian and Christological doctrines of the Church that attempted to describe the presence of God in the human Jesus were written using fourth- and fifth-century substance-based metaphysics that no longer hold sway.[67] Such concepts cannot do the work required today. I have shown in this project through the synthesis of Whiteheadian and Jungian theory and empiricism with a practice of spiritual dream work and a relational-imaginal understanding of the presence of God in each entity, of our inherent relationality with God and the entire cosmos, of our thrust toward value and the purposiveness of human life, and of the accessibility of real, positive transformation through alignment with God's desires and possibilities is robust and liberative. This view is robust and liberative for Christians because the relational-imaginal practical theology expressed herein is "faithful to the heart of Christian revelation"[68]; it is as much so in this time and place as earlier articulations were in their own times and places. Yet the final proof of this claim lies in the pudding of experience. "Theology," Jung claims, "demands faith, and faith cannot be made; it is in the truest sense a gift of grace."[69] Faith arises from experience, from relationship with the living God. The life of the spirit, when experienced anew for ourselves, is, Jung writes, the only way to break free from the bondage of biological events.[70] Such faith in the constantly fluid life of the spirit is a commitment to align oneself with ultimate reality whether that reality conforms to one's previously held beliefs or not. Such faith is renewed by the healing and wholeness experienced when one's heart is opened to God's transformative power and presence. This is a Christian message, but it is also more expansive and inclusive than that.

Even while the relational-imaginal web of theory and practice advocated in this work can be distinctly Christian, I strongly believe that this is also a *transreligious* project. If to be human is to dream, then this is a universal and transpersonal truth, even if those dreams are not easily recalled for every individual. If the cosmos itself is, at its very core, relational, value-soaked, and transformative, then all humans—regardless of location—inherently have the capacity to participate in and experience those qualities. Drawing from Pittenger and Ogden, the relational-imaginal web woven herein better "re-presents" what "God is always and everywhere up to, what God is always and everywhere doing, and what God is always and everywhere seeking to achieve in the world—with which God is unfailingly related and with which God is in a relationship of mutual influence."[71] If this relational-imaginal web represents what God is doing everywhere and all the time, then it need not be limited to any one religious tradition or even to religion itself. It is what Hudson refers to as a *natural spirituality*[72] or what Roland Faber might call a *process spirituality*. In Faber's "spiritual vision" for the Center for Process Studies he describes process spirituality as being about "experience."

> A process spirituality is about "organic" life and (to live within) its experience. Whitehead's understanding of the universe allows for a spirituality of interconnection through empathy, through which we are enabled to "feel" everything, and to feel everything differently. We begin to "experience" flux, relatedness, transformation, and "permanence," or should we better say: the "persistence" of the creative Eros in all. We know of the tragic complexities of such feelings but we might become able to search for their meaning differently: we seek ecological, social, and religious peace.[73]

There are many who run for the hills any time the word "religion" comes up, yet is such a knee-jerk response more because of the prevailing concretized meaning of religion in institutional churches rather than the potential for religion to be an "imaginative and aesthetic response to the human situation and to whatever is supremely worshipful in the cosmos—that is, to what religion calls 'God'?"[74] Returning to Jung's view that a "religious outlook" is the sense that there is a wholeness to the world that then facilitates wholeness in each individual,[75] may we not embrace a relational-imaginal web of theory and practice as religious in this *transreligious* sense? I believe that we can and we must because the theological and psycho-spiritual perspective articulated herein is one pathway toward healing the alienation and fragmentation that currently plagues our culture and our culture *will no longer welcome* an exclusive Christian message.

Based on the only-surface-scratching symptoms and realities described in chapter 1, I agree with Bernard Loomer that, for all intents and purposes, American culture has failed,[76] especially regarding the overall wholeness and flourishing of both people and planet. As a conglomerate, the American people are not whole; we are not "at home" in our bodies or at peace in our minds and spirits; we do not, according to Kearney, "know our center to be a larger stream of life transcending the ego and going on beyond our death" that is somehow still "in union with" the individual soul.[77] Loomer's answer to the failure of an American ethos rooted in a flawed individualistic, dualistic, and mechanistic worldview was *aesthetic* and based on what he called "stature" or "size."

> By size I mean the stature of a person's soul, the range and depth of his love, his capacity for relationships. I mean the volume of life you can take into your being and still maintain your integrity and individuality, the intensity and variety of outlook you can entertain in the unity of your being without feeling defensive or insecure. I mean the strength of your spirit to encourage others to become freer in the development of their diversity and uniqueness.[78]

As with Loomer's emphasis on *size*, my emphasis on psycho-spiritual wholeness and flourishing leans more toward the "size-producing capacities" than the "justice-producing capacities of society" because I agree that the pursuit of justice in a "statureless society" will likely only offer the formerly oppressed their own "opportunity to be truly dehumanized, insensitive, and materialistic, the way the elites of today are."[79] Life is wounding, and wounded people wound: there is no avoiding that reality, no matter how religious one is or is not. But this wounding reality—where everything is in flux and everything perishes—is also healing; brimming with grace and with a fluid, transpersonal, and creative reality that we can call "God" and in whose wholeness we can be made more whole, more loving, and more beautiful. In this wounding *and* whole-making reality—no matter how many categories of adverse childhood experience you have survived, no matter how divisive your politics, no matter how lonely or addicted your life is, no matter how fragmented and alienated we all are—we *matter*, we *belong*, and we can be *transformed*.

NOTES

1. We might turn to the book of Job 33:14–15, "For God does speak—now one way, now another—though no one perceives it. In a dream, in a vision of the night, when deep sleep falls on people as they slumber in their beds . . ."

2. Anderson, *The Shape of Practical Theology*, 12.
3. Sarkar, *Whitehead's Four Principles from West-East Perspectives*, 67.
4. Hopper, "Once More," 109.
5. Sarkar, *Whitehead's Four Principles from West-East Perspectives*, 63.
6. Whitehead, *Religion in the Making*, 149.
7. Griffin, "A Metaphysical Psychology to Un-Locke Our Ailing World," 249.
8. Griffin, 248.
9. Faber, *God as Poet of the World*, 311.
10. Keller, *The Face of the Deep*, 220.
11. As I believe I did when I "broke up" with God (as described in the Introduction).
12. Ulanov and Ulanov, *Religion and the Unconscious*, 40.
13. McGehee and Thomas, *The Invisible Church*, 101.
14. McGehee and Thomas, 103.
15. Singer, *Boundaries of the Soul*, 384.
16. Young-Eisendrath and Hall, *Jung's Self Psychology*, 29.
17. Kalsched, *Trauma and the Soul*, 10.
18. Kalsched, 4.
19. Kalsched, 11, 23–24, 30.
20. Kalsched, 159.
21. Edinger, *Ego & Archetype*, 44.
22. McGehee and Thomas, *The Invisible Church*, 49.
23. Hosinski, *Stubborn Fact and Creative Advance*, 5.
24. Epperly, "Process Theology and the Healing Adventure," 95.
25. Pargament, *Spiritually Integrated Psychotherapy*, 70–71.
26. Walter Houston Clark, "The Psychology of Religious Experience," in *Current Perspectives in the Psychology of Religion*, ed. H. Newton Malony (Grand Rapids: William B. Eerdmans Publishing Company, 1977), 230.
27. Whitehead, *Adventures of Ideas*, 190.
28. Singer, *Boundaries of the Soul*, 350.
29. Cobb Jr. and Griffin, *Process Theology*, 99.
30. John B. Cobb Jr., "Wholeness Centered in Spirit," in *Spirit-Centered Wholeness: Beyond the Psychology of Self*, ed. H. Newton Malony, Michele Papen-Daniels, and Howard Clinebell (Lewiston, NY: Edwin Mellen Press, 1988), 230.
31. Jung, *Modern Man in Search of a Soul*, 235.
32. Hosinski, *Stubborn Fact and Creative Advance*, 144.
33. Hosinski, 145–48.
34. Jung, *The Portable Jung*, 276–77.
35. Hosinski, *Stubborn Fact and Creative Advance*, 105.
36. Hosinski, 100, 102.
37. Hosinski, 108–13.
38. Hosinski, 115.
39. Hosinski, 113.
40. Hosinski, 124.
41. Hosinski, 118.
42. Whitehead, *Symbolism*, 82.
43. Cobb Jr., "Spiritual Discernment in a Whiteheadian Perspective," 359.
44. Cobb Jr., 366.

45. Andrew Dreitcer, "Lecture Notes on 'Spirituality and Spirituality Studies'" (Claremont School of Theology, Fall 2012).
46. Dreitcer.
47. Pargament, *Spiritually Integrated Psychotherapy*, 32.
48. Bulkeley, *Big Dreams*, 129.
49. Timothy L. Davis and Clara E. Hill, "Spiritual and Nonspiritual Approaches to Dream Work: Effects on Clients' Well-Being," *Journal of Counseling & Development* 83 (Fall 2005): 492.
50. Davis and Hill, 499.
51. Taylor, "Ambiguities of Privilege," 236–37.
52. Taylor, 237.
53. Jonathan A. Smith, Paul Flowers, and Michael Larkin, *Interpretative Phenomenological Analysis: Theory, Method and Research* (London: SAGE Publications Ltd, 2009), 1.
54. Smith, Flowers, and Larkin, *Interpretative Phenomenological Analysis*, 3.
55. Five participants were interviewed for sixty to ninety minutes; they self-identify as Christian, are active in a congregation (with "active" defined as having the status of "member" in the congregation and attending worship at least twice per month), and have been regularly practicing spiritual dream work for at least one year, whether only individually or also within the context of a dream group. Most have attended the Haden conference multiple times.
56. To protect participants' privacy, pseudonyms have been used.
57. Kelly Bulkeley, "Dream Interpretation: Practical Methods for Pastoral Care and Counseling," *Pastoral Psychology* 49, no. 2 (2000): 95–96.
58. Bulkeley, "Dream Interpretation," 95.
59. Bulkeley, *Big Dreams*, 78.
60. Bulkeley, 86.
61. Jung, *Modern Man in Search of a Soul*, 62.
62. Pittenger, *The Lure of Divine Love*, 192.
63. Beldon C. Lane, "Spirituality as the Performance of Desire: Calvin on the World as a Theatre of God's Glory," *Spiritus* 1, no. 1 (Spring 2001): 7–11.
64. Kelsey, *Encounter with God*, 97.
65. Ruether, *Sexism and God Talk*, 14.
66. Ruether, 15–16.
67. Hosinski, *Stubborn Fact and Creative Advance*, 243.
68. Hosinski, 244.
69. Jung, *Modern Man in Search of a Soul*, 122.
70. Jung, 122.
71. Pittenger, *The Lure of Divine Love*, 65.
72. Hudson, *Natural Spirituality*, passim.
73. Roland Faber, "'. . . Adventure of the Spirit . . .': My Vision for the Center for Process Studies," *Process Perspectives*, no. Summer (2006): 11.
74. Pittenger, *The Lure of Divine Love*, 51.
75. Kalsched, *Trauma and the Soul*, 169.
76. Dean, "Introduction: From Size to Integrity," 9.

77. Kearney, "Healing the Soul in a Culture of Fear," 42.
78. Bernard M. Loomer, "S-I-Z-E Is the Measure," in *Religious Experience and Process Theology: The Pastoral Implications of a Major Modern Movement*, ed. Harry J. Cargas and Bernard Lee (New York: Paulist Press, 1976), 70.
79. Dean, "Introduction: From Size to Integrity," 9.

References

Adelson, Rachel. "Stimulating the Vagus Nerve: Memories Are Made of This." American Psychological Association, April 2004. http://www.apa.org/monitor/apr04/vagus.aspx.

Advokids: A Legal Resource for California Foster Children and Their Advocates. "Adverse Childhood Experience Study (ACES)." Accessed September 16, 2016. http://www.advokids.org/adverse-childhood-experience-study-aces/.

Aizenstat, Stephen. *Dream Tending: Awakening to the Healing Power of Dreams*. New Orleans: Spring Journal Books, 2011.

———. "Jungian Psychology and the World Unconscious." In *Ecopsychology: Restoring the Earth, Healing the Mind*, edited by Theodore Roszak, Mary E. Gomes, and Allen D. Kanner. San Francisco: Sierra Club Books, 1995.

Anderson, Ray S. *The Shape of Practical Theology: Empowering Ministry with Theological Praxis*. Downers Grove, IL: IVP Academic, 2001.

Argyle, Michael. *Psychology and Religion: An Introduction*. London, New York: Routledge, 2000.

Arlow, Jacob A. *Legacy of Sigmund Freud*. New York: International Universities Press, Inc., 1956.

Ballard, Edward G. "Kant and Whitehead, and the Philosophy of Mathematics." In *Studies in Whitehead's Philosophy*, 10:3–29. Tulane Studies in Philosophy. New Orleans: Tulane University, 1961.

Bergland, Christopher. "How Does the Vagus Nerve Convey Gut Instincts to the Brain?" *Psychology Today*, May 23, 2014. http://www.psychologytoday.com/blog/the-athletes-way/201405/how-does-the-vagus-nerve-convey-gut-instincts-the-brain.

Bosnak, Robert. "The Physician Inside." In *Imagination and Medicine*, edited by Stephen Aizenstat and Robert Bosnak, xv–xxiv. New Orleans: Spring Journal Books, 2009.

Bowman, Donna, and Jay McDaniel, eds. *Handbook of Process Theology*. Annotated edition. St. Louis, MO: Chalice Press, 2006.

Boyd-MacMillan, Eolene. "Loder and Mystical Spirituality: Particularity, Universality, and Intelligence." In *Redemptive Transformation in Practical Theology: Essays in Honor of James E. Loder Jr.*, edited by Dana R. Wright and John D. Kuentzel. Grand Rapids, MI: Wm. B. Eerdmans Publishing Company, 2004.

Bracken, Joseph A. *The Divine Matrix: Creativity as Link between East and West.* Maryknoll, NY: Orbis Books, 1995.

———. *The One in the Many: A Contemporary Reconstruction of the God-World Relationship*. Grand Rapids, MI: Wm. B. Eerdmans Publishing Company, 2001.

Brinkley, Alan, B. "Whitehead on Symbolic Reference." In *Studies in Whitehead's Philosophy*, 10:31–45. Tulane Studies in Philosophy. New Orleans: Tulane University, 1961.

Bulkeley, Kelly. *An Introduction to the Psychology of Dreaming*. Westport, CT: Praeger, 1997.

———. *Big Dreams: The Science of Dreaming and the Origins of Religion*. New York: Oxford University Press, 2016.

———. "Dream Interpretation: Practical Methods for Pastoral Care and Counseling." *Pastoral Psychology* 49, no. 2 (2000): 95–104.

———. "Dream-Sharing Groups, Spirituality, and Community." *Journal of Religion and Health* 35, no. 1 (Spring 1996): 59–66.

———. *Visions of the Night: Dreams, Religion and Psychology*. Albany, NY: State University of New York Press, 1999.

Burkhart, Ford. "Edward F. Edinger, 75, Analyst and Writer on Jung's Concepts." *The New York Times*, August 2, 1998. http://www.nytimes.com/1998/08/02/us/edward-f-edinger-75-analyst-and-writer-on-jung-s-concepts.html.

Card, Charles R. "The Archetypal View of C.G. Jung and Wolfgang Pauli." *Psychological Perspectives* 24, no. Spring–Summer 1991 (1991): 23–33.

Chalquist, Craig. "Who Was Carl Jung and Why Should We Study Him and His Work?" *Pacifica Post* (blog), October 17, 2016. http://www.pacificapost.com/who-was-carl-jung-and-why-should-we-study-him-and-his-work.

Christ, Carol P. *She Who Changes: Re-Imagining the Divine in the World.* New York: Palgrave Macmillan, 2004.

Christ, Carol P., and Judith Plaskow. *Goddess and God in the World: Conversations in Embodied Theology*. Minneapolis: Fortress Press, 2016.

Clark, Walter Houston. "The Psychology of Religious Experience." In *Current Perspectives in the Psychology of Religion*, edited by H. Newton Malony, 227–37. Grand Rapids: William B. Eerdmans Publishing Company, 1977.

Clayton, Philip. *Mind and Emergence: From Quantum to Consciousness*. Oxford: Oxford University Press, 2006.

Clayton, Philip, and Simpson Zachary. *Adventures in the Spirit: God, World, Divine Action*. Minneapolis: Fortress Press, 2008.

Cobb Jr., John B. "Eternal Objects and Archetypes: A Response to Stanley Hopper." In *The Archetypal Process: Self and Divine in Whitehead, Jung, and Hillman*, edited by David Ray Griffin, 1–76. Evanston, IL: Northwestern University Press, 1990.

———. *God and the World*. Philadelphia: Westminster Press, 1969.

———. "Spiritual Discernment in a Whiteheadian Perspective." In *Religious Experience and Process Theology: The Pastoral Implications of a Major Modern Movement*, edited by Harry J. Cargas and Bernard Lee. New York: Paulist Press, 1976.

———. "Wholeness Centered in Spirit." In *Spirit-Centered Wholeness: Beyond the Psychology of Self*, edited by H. Newton Malony, Michele Papen-Daniels, and Howard Clinebell. Lewiston, NY: Edwin Mellen Press, 1988.

Cobb Jr., John B., and David Ray Griffin. *Process Theology*. Louisville, KY: Westminster John Knox Press, 1976.

Coleman, Monica A. "An Exchange of Gifts: Process and Womanist Theologies." In *Handbook of Process Theology*, 160–76. St. Louis, MO: Chalice Press, 2006.

———. *Making a Way Out of No Way: A Womanist Theology*. Minneapolis, MN: Fortress Press, 2008.

Coward, Harold. "Taoism and Jung: Synchronicity and the Self." *Philosophy East and West* 46, no. 4 (1996): 477–95. https://doi.org/10.2307/1399493.

Crouse, Janice Shaw. "The Loneliness of American Society." *The American Spectator* (blog), May 18, 2014. http://spectator.org/59230_loneliness-american-society/.

Daugherty, Alane. *From Mindfulness to Heartfulness: A Journey of Transformation through the Science of Embodiment*. Bloomington, IN: Balboa Press, 2014.

Davis, Timothy L., and Clara E. Hill. "Spiritual and Nonspiritual Approaches to Dream Work: Effects on Clients' Well-Being." *Journal of Counseling & Development* 83, no. Fall 2005 (Fall 2005): 492–503.

Dean, William D. "Introduction: From Size to Integrity." In *The Size of God: The Theology of Bernard Loomer in Context*, edited by William D. Dean and Larry E. Axel. Macon, GA: Mercer University Press, 1987.

Dourley, John P. *The Psyche as Sacrament: A Comparative Study of C.G. Jung and Paul Tillich*. Toronto: Inner City Books, 1981.

Dowd, Michael. "Is Biblicist Christianity Bankrupt?" *Evolutionary Christianity* (blog), n.d. http://evolutionarychristianity.com/blog/general/is-biblicist-christianity-bankrupt/.

Dreitcer, Andrew. "Lecture Notes on 'Spirituality and Spirituality Studies.'" Claremont School of Theology, Fall 2012.

Edinger, Edward F. *Ego and Archetype: Individuation and the Religious Function of the Psyche*. Boston; London: Shambhala, 1992.

Epperly, Bruce G. "Process Theology and the Healing Adventure: Reflections on Spirituality and Medicine." In *Handbook of Process Theology*, edited by Donna Bowman and Jay McDaniel. St. Louis, MO: Chalice Press, 2006.

Faber, Roland. "'. . . Adventure of the Spirit . . .': My Vision for the Center for Process Studies." *Process Perspectives*, no. Summer (2006): 11–12.

———. *God as Poet of the World: Exploring Process Theologies*. Louisville, KY: Westminster John Knox Press, 2008.

Fang, Jiliang, Peijing Rong, Yang Hong, Yangyang Fan, Jun Liu, Honghong Wang, Guolei Zhang, et al. "Transcutaneous Vagus Nerve Stimulation Modulates Default Mode Network in Major Depressive Disorder." *Biological Psychiatry* 79, no. 4 (February 15, 2016): 266–73. https://doi.org/10.1016/j.biopsych.2015.03.025.

Felitti, Vincent J., and Robert F. Anda. "The Relationship of Adverse Childhood Experiences to Adult Medical Disease, Psychiatric Disorders and Sexual Behavior: Implications for Healthcare." In *The Impact of Early Life Trauma on Health and Disease: The Hidden Epidemic*, edited by Ruth A. Lanius, Eric Vermetten, and Clare Pain, 77–87. Cambridge, New York: Cambridge University Press, 2010.

"Findings from the Philadelphia Urban ACE Survey." Philadelphia: Institute for Safe Families, September 18, 2013.

Franz, Marie-Louise von. "Conclusion: Science and the Unconscious." In *Man and His Symbols*, edited by C. G. Jung. Garden City, NY: Doubleday, 1969.

Freud, Sigmund. *The Basic Writings of Sigmund Freud*. Translated by A. A. Brill. New York: Modern Library, 1995.

Frey-Rohn, Liliane. *From Freud to Jung: A Comparative Study of the Psychology of the Unconscious*. Boston: Shambhala, 2001.

Goehler, Lisa E. "Vagal Complexity: Substrate for Body-Mind Connections?" *Bratislavske Lekarske Listy* 107, no. 8 (2006): 275–76.

Goldenberg, Naomi R. "Archetypal Theory and the Separation of Mind and Body: Reason Enough to Turn to Freud?" *Journal of Feminist Studies in Religion* 1, no. 1 (Spring 1985): 55–72.

———. "Jung After Feminism." In *Beyond Androcentrism: New Essays on Women and Religion*, edited by Rita M Gross. American Academy of Religion Aids for the Study of Religion. Missoula, MT: Scholars Press for the American Academy of Religion, 1977.

Griffin, David Ray. "A Metaphysical Psychology to Un-Locke Our Ailing World." In *The Archetypal Process: Self and Divine in Whitehead, Jung, and Hillman*, edited by David Ray Griffin, 239–49. Evanston, IL: Northwestern University Press, 1990.

———. *A Process Christology*. Philadelphia: Westminster Press, 1973.

———. "Holy Spirit: Compassion and Reverence for Being." In *Religious Experience and Process Theology*, edited by Bernard Cargas and Harry J. Lee. New York: Paulist Press, 1976.

———. "Introduction, Archetypal Psychology and Process Philosophy: Complementary Postmodern Movements." In *The Archetypal Process: Self and Divine in Whitehead, Jung, and Hillman*, edited by David Ray Griffin, 1–76. Evanston, IL: Northwestern University Press, 1990.

———, ed. *The Archetypal Process: Self and Divine in Whitehead, Jung, and Hillman*. Evanston, IL: Northwestern University Press, 1990.

Halligan, Fredrica R. "Jungian Theory and Religious Experience." In *Handbook of Religious Experience*, edited by Ralph W. Hood. Birmingham, AL: Religious Education Press, 1995.

Hartmann, Ernest. *The Nature and Functions of Dreaming*. New York: Oxford University Press, 2010.

Haule, John. "Personal Secrets, Ethical Questions." In *Teaching Jung*, edited by Kelly Bulkeley and Clodagh Weldon, 151–68. AAR Teaching Religious Studies. New York: Oxford University Press, 2011.

Heisig, James W. "The Mystique of the Nonrational and a New Spirituality." In *The Archetypal Process: Self and Divine in Whitehead, Jung, and Hillman*, edited by David Ray Griffin, 167–202. Evanston, IL: Northwestern University Press, 1990.

Hillman, James. "Back to beyond: On Cosmology." In *The Archetypal Process: Self and Divine in Whitehead, Jung, and Hillman*, edited by David Ray Griffin, 129–32. Evanston, IL: Northwestern University Press, 1990.

———. "Forward." In *Ecopsychology: Restoring the Earth, Healing the Mind*, edited by Theodore Roszak, Mary E. Gomes, and Allen D. Kanner. San Francisco: Sierra Club Books, 1995.

Hood, Ralph W. "Mystical, Spiritual, and Religious Experiences." In *Handbook of the Psychology of Religion and Spirituality*, edited by Raymond F. Paloutzian and Crystal L. Park, 348–64. New York: The Guilford Press, 2005.

Hopper, Stanley R. "Language as Metaphorical: A Reply to John Cobb." In *The Archetypal Process: Self and Divine in Whitehead, Jung, and Hillman*, edited by David Ray Griffin, 129–32. Evanston, IL: Northwestern University Press, 1990.

———. "Once More: The Cavern beneath the Cave." In *The Archetypal Process: Self and Divine in Whitehead, Jung, and Hillman*, edited by David Ray Griffin, 107–24. Evanston, IL: Northwestern University Press, 1990.

Hosinski, Thomas E. *Stubborn Fact and Creative Advance*. Lanham, MD: Rowman & Littlefield Publishers, 1993.

Hoss, Robert J. "Evidence of a Cognitive Function within Dreams." www.dreamscience.org, July 2010. http://www.dreamscience.org/articles/Cognitive_Function_Dreaming-Hoss.pdf.

———. "Evidence of Wisdom in Dreams." Asheville, NC, 2010.

———. "Image Activation Dreamwork." Accessed December 16, 2016. http://www.dreamscience.org/articles/image_activation_dreamwork.htm.

———. "Recent Neurological Studies Supportive of Jung's Theories on Dreaming." Berkeley, CA, 2012.

Hudson, Joyce Rockwood. *Natural Spirituality: Recovering the Wisdom Tradition in Christianity*. 2nd ed. Danielsville, GA: JRH Publications, 2001.

Huffaker, Lucinda A. "Feminist Theology in Process Perspective." In *Handbook of Process Theology*, edited by Donna Bowman and Jay McDaniel, Annotated. St. Louis, MO: Chalice Press, 2006.

Johnson, A. H. *Whitehead's Theory of Reality*. New York: Dover Publications, 1962.

Johnson, Robert A. *Inner Work: Using Dreams and Active Imagination for Personal Growth*. San Francisco: HarperOne, 1989.

Jung, C. G. *Modern Man in Search of a Soul*. Orlando, FL: Harcourt Harvest, 1955.

———. *Psychology and Religion: West and East*. Translated by R.F.C. Hull. Corrected. Vol. 11. The Collected Works of C.G. Jung, Bollingen Series. New York: Pantheon Books, 1963.

———. *The Basic Writings of C. G. Jung*. Edited by Violet Staub De Laszlo. Reprint. New York: Modern Library, 1993.

———. *The Portable Jung*. Edited by Joseph Campbell. New York: Viking Press, 1971.

———. *The Structure and Dynamics of the Psyche*. Translated by R.F.C. Hull. Corrected. Vol. 8. The Collected Works of C.G. Jung, Bollingen Series. New York: Pantheon Books, 1969.

———. *Two Essays on Analytical Psychology*. Translated by R. F. C. Hull. Vol. 7. The Collected Works of C.G. Jung, Bollingen Series. New York: Pantheon Books, 1953.

Kalsched, Donald. *Trauma and the Soul: A Psycho-Spiritual Approach to Human Development and Its Interruption*. London, New York: Routledge, 2013.

Kearney, Michael. "Healing the Soul in a Culture of Fear." In *Imagination and Medicine*, edited by Stephen Aizenstat and Robert Bosnak, 35–44. New Orleans: Spring Journal Books, 2009.

Keller, Catherine E. "Psychocosmetics and the Underworld Connection." In *The Archetypal Process: Self and Divine in Whitehead, Jung, and Hillman*, edited by David Ray Griffin, 133–56. Evanston, IL: Northwestern University Press, 1990.

———. "Self and God: Separation, Sexism, and Self." In *Creating Women's Theology: A Movement Engaging Process Thought*, edited by Monica A. Coleman, Nancy R. Howell, and Helene Tallon Russell. Eugene, OR: Pickwick Publications, 2011.

———. *The Face of the Deep: A Theology of Becoming*. London, New York: Routledge, 2003.

Kelsey, Morton T. *Dreams: A Way to Listen to God*. New York: Paulist Press, 1978.

———. *Encounter with God: A Theology of Christian Experience*. New York: Paulist Press, 1988.

———. *God, Dreams, and Revelation: A Christian Interpretation of Dreams*. Revised and Expanded. Minneapolis: Augsburg Books, 1991.

Kim, Chae Young. "A Comparison of Alfred North Whitehead's and Carl Gustav Jung's Idea of Religion: Special Reference to Their Lectures on Religion." *Journal of Dharma* 27, no. 3 (July 1, 2002): 417–28.

Kirkpatrick, Lee A. "Evolutionary Psychology: An Emerging New Foundation for the Psychology of Religion." In *Handbook of the Psychology of Religion and Spirituality*, edited by Raymond F. Paloutzian and Crystal L. Park, 101–19. New York: The Guilford Press, 2005.

Klarer, Melanie, Myrtha Arnold, Lydia Günther, Christine Winter, Wolfgang Langhans, and Urs Meyer. "Gut Vagal Afferents Differentially Modulate Innate Anxiety and Learned Fear." *The Journal of Neuroscience: The Official Journal of the Society for Neuroscience* 34, no. 21 (May 21, 2014): 7067–76. https://doi.org/10.1523/JNEUROSCI.0252-14.2014.

Kling, Sheri D. "Avoiding a Fatal Error: Extending Whitehead's Symbolism beyond Language." In *Rethinking Whitehead's Symbolism: Thought, Language, Culture*, edited by Roland Faber, Jeffrey Bell, and Joseph Petek, 124–43. Edinburgh: Edinburgh University Press, 2017.

———. "Whitehead's Metaphysics as a Cosmological Framework for Transpersonal Psychology." *The Humanistic Psychologist* 47, no. 2 (2019): 181–200. https://doi.org/10.1037/hum0000124.

Kolk, Bessel van der. *The Body Keeps the Score: Brain, Mind, and Body in the Healing of Trauma*. Reprint edition. New York, NY: Penguin Books, 2015.

Kradin, Richard. "Reply to Bessel van Der Kolk." In *Imagination and Medicine*, edited by Stephen Aizenstat and Robert Bosnak, 189–95. New Orleans: Spring Journal Books, 2009.

Kraus, Elizabeth M. *The Metaphysics of Experience: A Companion to Whitehead's Process and Reality*. New York: Fordham University Press, 1979.

Kripal, Jeffrey J. "Visions of the Impossible." The Chronicle of Higher Education, March 31, 2014. http://www.chronicle.com/article/Embrace-the-Unexplained/145557/.

Lane, Beldon C. "Spirituality as the Performance of Desire: Calvin on the World as a Theatre of God's Glory." *Spiritus* 1, no. 1 (Spring 2001).

Lauter, Estella, and Carol Schreier Rupprecht. "Feminist Archetypal Theory: A Proposal." In *Feminist Archetypal Theory: Interdisciplinary Re-Visions of Jungian Thought*, edited by Estella Lauter and Carol Scheier Rupprecht. Knoxville: University of Tennessee Press, 1985.

Lee, Bernard J. *The Becoming of the Church: A Process Theology of the Structures of Christian Experience*. New York: Paulist Press, 1974.

Liu, Jun, Jiliang Fang, Zengjian Wang, Peijing Rong, Yang Hong, Yangyang Fan, Xiaoling Wang, et al. "Transcutaneous Vagus Nerve Stimulation Modulates Amygdala Functional Connectivity in Patients with Depression." *Journal of Affective Disorders* 205 (November 15, 2016): 319–26. https://doi.org/10.1016/j.jad.2016.08.003.

Loomer, Bernard M. "S-I-Z-E Is the Measure." In *Religious Experience and Process Theology: The Pastoral Implications of a Major Modern Movement*, edited by Harry J. Cargas and Bernard Lee, 69–76. New York: Paulist Press, 1976.

———. "The Size of God." In *The Size of God: The Theology of Bernard Loomer in Context*, edited by William D. Dean and Larry E. Axel. Macon, GA: Mercer University Press, 1987.

Mattingly, Susan Shotliff. "Whitehead's Theory of Eternal Objects." PhD, University of Texas at Austin, 1968.

Maxwell, Grant. "Archetype and Eternal Object: Jung, Whitehead, and the Return of Formal Causation." *Archai: The Journal of Archetypal Cosmology* 3 (Winter 2011): 51–71.

McGehee, J. Pittman, and Damon J. Thomas. *The Invisible Church: Finding Spirituality Where You Are*. Westport, CT: Praeger, 2008.

Mersbergen, Miriam van. "Viva La Vagus!" *Choral Journal* 55, no. 3 (October 2014): 67–73.

Mesle, C. Robert. *Process-Relational Philosophy: An Introduction to Alfred North Whitehead*. West Conshohocken, PA: Templeton Press, 2008.

Moltmann, Jürgen. *God in Creation: A New Theology of Creation and the Spirit of God*. Minneapolis, MN: Fortress Press, 1993.

Monbiot, George. "Neoliberalism Is Creating Loneliness. That's What's Wrenching Society Apart." *The Guardian*, October 12, 2016. https://www.theguardian.com/commentisfree/2016/oct/12/neoliberalism-creating-loneliness-wrenching-society-apart?CMP=share_btn_fb.

Moore, Robert L. "Psychocosmetics: A Jungian Response." In *The Archetypal Process: Self and Divine in Whitehead, Jung, and Hillman*, edited by David Ray Griffin, 133–56. Evanston, IL: Northwestern University Press, 1990.

Muray, Leslie A. *An Introduction to the Process Understanding of Science, Society and the Self: A Philosophy for Modern Humanity*. Vol. 26. Symposium Series. Lewiston, NY: Edwin Mellen Press, 1988.

Nelson, Geoff. *Dreaming in Church: Dream Work as a Spiritual Practice for Christians*. Eugene, OR: Wipf and Stock, 2016.

Nicolaus, Georg. *C.G. Jung and Nikolai Berdyaev: Individuation and the Person: A Critical Comparison*. London, New York: Routledge, 2010.

"'Nones' on the Rise." The Pew Forum on Religion & Public Life. Washington, DC: Pew Research Center, October 9, 2012. http://www.pewforum.org/2012/10/09/nones-on-the-rise/.

Odin, Steve. *Process Metaphysics and Hua-Yen Buddhism: A Critical Study of Cumulative Penetration vs. Interpenetration*. Albany, NY: State University of New York Press, 1982.

Pagels, Elaine. *The Gnostic Gospels*. Reissue. New York: Vintage, 1989.

Palmer, Parker J. "The Gift of Presence, the Perils of Advice." *On Being* (blog), April 27, 2016. http://www.onbeing.org/blog/parker-palmer-the-gift-of-presence-the-perils-of-advice/8628.

Pargament, Kenneth I. *Spiritually Integrated Psychotherapy: Understanding and Addressing the Sacred*. New York: The Guilford Press, 2011.

Perera, Sylvia Brinton. "The Descent of Inanna: Myth and Therapy." In *Feminist Archetypal Theory: Interdisciplinary Re-Visions of Jungian Thought*, edited by Estella Lauter and Carol Scheier Rupprecht. Knoxville: University of Tennessee Press, 1985.

Perrin, David B. *Studying Christian Spirituality*. New York: Routledge, 2007.

Petek, Joseph. "Introduction." In *Rethinking Whitehead's Symbolism: Thought, Language, Culture*, edited by Roland Faber, Jeffrey Bell, and Joseph Petek, 1–10. Edinburgh: Edinburgh University Press, 2017.

Pittenger, W. Norman. *The Lure of Divine Love: Human Experience and Christian Faith in a Process Perspective*. New York: Pilgrim Press, 1979.

"Political Polarization in the American Public." The Pew Research Center for the People and the Press. Washington, DC: Pew Research Center, June 12, 2014. http://www.people-press.org/2014/06/12/political-polarization-in-the-american-public/.

Poplin, Mary, and Dallas Willard. *Is Reality Secular? Testing the Assumptions of Four Global Worldviews*. Downers Grove, IL: IVP Books, 2014.

"Population Clock." Accessed January 3, 2020. https://www.census.gov/popclock/.

Porges, Stephen W. "Social Engagement and Attachment." *Annals of the New York Academy of Sciences* 1008, no. 1 (December 1, 2003): 31–47. https://doi.org/10.1196/annals.1301.004.

Potok, Mark. "The Year in Hate and Extremism." Southern Poverty Law Center, February 11, 2016. https://www.splcenter.org/fighting-hate/intelligence-report/2016/year-hate-and-extremism.

Robertson, Robin. *Jungian Archetypes: Jung, Gödel, and the History of Archetypes*. Revised. New York: iUniverse, 2009.

Rossi, Ernest Lawrence, and Kathryn Lane Rossi. "How the Mind and Brain Co-Create Each Other Daily." In *Imagination and Medicine*, edited by Stephen Aizenstat and Robert Bosnak, 135–68. New Orleans: Spring Journal Books, 2009.

Rowland, Susan. *Jung: A Feminist Revision*. Cambridge, UK; Malden, MA: Polity Press, 2002.

Ruether, Rosemary R. *Sexism and God Talk: Toward a Feminist Theology*. Boston: Beacon Press, 1993.

Sanford, John A. *Dreams: God's Forgotten Language*. San Francisco: HarperOne, 1989.

———. *Evil: The Shadow Side of Reality*. New York: The Crossroad Publishing Company, 1986.

Sarkar, Anil Kumar. *Whitehead's Four Principles from West-East Perspectives: Ways and Prospects of Process-Philosophy*. Patna: Bharati Bhawan, 1974.

Segal, Robert A. "Jung on Myth." In *Teaching Jung*, edited by Kelly Bulkeley and Clodagh Weldon, 75–92. AAR Teaching Religious Studies. New York: Oxford University Press, 2011.

Sellery, J'nan Morse. "The Necessity for Symbol and Myth: A Literary Amplification." In *Archetypal Process: Self and Divine in Whitehead, Jung, and Hillman*, edited by David Ray Griffin, 93–104. Evanston, IL: Northwestern University Press, 1990.

Shaviro, Steven. "Whitehead on Causality and Perception." In *Rethinking Whitehead's Symbolism: Thought, Language, Culture*, edited by Roland Faber, Jeffrey Bell, and Joseph Petek, 13–28. Edinburgh: Edinburgh University Press, 2017.

Shelburne, Walter. *Mythos and Logos in the Thought of Carl Jung: The Theory of the Collective Unconscious in Scientific Perspective*. Albany, NY: State University of New York Press, 1988.

Sherburne, Donald W., ed. *A Key to Whitehead's Process and Reality*. Chicago: University of Chicago Press, 1966.

Siivola, Markku. "Montague Ullman, Biographical Note." Accessed December 17, 2016. http://siivola.org/monte/biographical_note.htm.

Singer, June K. *Boundaries of the Soul: The Practice of Jung's Psychology*. Revised. New York: Anchor Books, 1994.

Slusser, Gerald H. "Jung and Whitehead on Self and Divine: The Necessity for Symbol and Myth." In *Archetypal Process: Self and Divine in Whitehead, Jung, and Hillman*, edited by David Ray Griffin, 77–92. Evanston, IL: Northwestern University Press, 1990.

Smith, Jonathan A., Paul Flowers, and Michael Larkin. *Interpretative Phenomenological Analysis: Theory, Method and Research*. London: SAGE Publications Ltd, 2009.

Stein, Murray. "Jung's Green Christ." In *Jung's Challenge to Contemporary Religion*, edited by Murray Stein and Robert L. Moore. Wilmette, IL: Chiron Publications, 1987.

Sternberg, Esther M. "Can Believing Make You Well? A Decade Later." In *Imagination and Medicine*, edited by Stephen Aizenstat and Robert Bosnak, 79–106. New Orleans: Spring Journal Books, 2009.

Tacey, David. "The Challenge of Teaching Jung in the University." In *Teaching Jung*, edited by Kelly Bulkeley and Clodagh Weldon, 13–28. AAR Teaching Religious Studies. New York: Oxford University Press, 2011.

Tarnas, Richard. *Cosmos and Psyche: Intimations of a New World View*. New York: Viking Adult, 2006.

Taylor, Jeremy. "Ambiguities of Privilege." In *Dreaming in Christianity and Islam: Culture, Conflict, and Creativity*, edited by Kelly Bulkeley, Kate Adams, and

Patricia M. Davis, 236–48. New Brunswick, NJ; London: Rutgers University Press, 2009.

Thayer, Julian F., and Richard D. Lane. "Claude Bernard and the Heart–Brain Connection: Further Elaboration of a Model of Neurovisceral Integration." *Neuroscience & Biobehavioral Reviews*, The Inevitable Link between Heart and Behavior: New Insights from Biomedical Research and Implications for Clinical Practice, 33, no. 2 (February 2009): 81–88. https://doi.org/10.1016/j.neubiorev.2008.08.004.

National Science Foundation. "The Profound Power of Loneliness: National Science Foundation," February 3, 2016. http://www.nsf.gov/discoveries/disc_summ.jsp?cntn_id=137534.

Tillich, Paul. *Systematic Theology, Volume I.* Chicago: University of Chicago Press, 1973.

Ulanov, Ann Belford. *The Functioning Transcendent.* Wilmette, IL: Chiron Publications, 1996.

Ulanov, Ann Belford, and Alvin Dueck. *The Living God and Our Living Psyche: What Christians Can Learn from Carl Jung*. Grand Rapids, MI: Wm. B. Eerdmans Publishing Co., 2008.

Ulanov, Ann Belford, and Barry Ulanov. *Religion and the Unconscious*. Philadelphia: Westminster John Knox Press, 1985.

Wagner, Suzanne. *Remembering Jung: Conversations about C. G. Jung and His Work*. DVD. Los Angeles: Bosustow Video Production, 1986.

Watts, Alan W. *The Tao of Philosophy*. Audiocassette. Electronic University Publishing, 1995.

Watts, Fraser N. *Theology and Psychology*. Hampshire, England: Ashgate Publishing, 2002.

Wehr, Demaris S. *Jung & Feminism: Liberating Archetypes*. Boston: Beacon Press, 1987.

Wehrwein, Peter. "Astounding Increase in Antidepressant Use by Americans." Harvard Health Blog, October 20, 2011. http://www.health.harvard.edu/blog/astounding-increase-in-antidepressant-use-by-americans-201110203624.

Weldon, Clodagh. "God on the Couch: Teaching Jung's Answer to Job." In *Teaching Jung*, edited by Kelly Bulkeley and Clodagh Weldon, 111–26. AAR Teaching Religious Studies. New York: Oxford University Press, 2011.

Whitehead, Alfred North. *Adventures of Ideas*. Paperback. New York: The Free Press, 1933.

———. *Modes of Thought*. New York: The Free Press, 1968.

———. *Process and Reality*. Edited by David Ray Griffin and Donald W. Sherburne. Corrected. New York, London: The Free Press, 1979.

———. *Religion in the Making*. Reissue. Cambridge: Cambridge University Press, 1927.

———. *Science and the Modern World*. New York: The Free Press, 1967.

———. *Symbolism: Its Meaning and Effect*. Revised. New York: Fordham University Press, 1985.

———. *The Function of Reason*. Boston: Beacon Press, 1958.

Woodman, Marion. "Coming to a Door." In *Imagination and Medicine*, edited by Stephen Aizenstat and Robert Bosnak, xi–xiv. New Orleans: Spring Journal Books, 2009.

Young-Eisendrath, Polly, and James Hall. *Jung's Self Psychology: A Constructivist Perspective*. New York: The Guilford Press, 1991.

Zimmerman, Michael E. "Quantum Theory, Intrinsic Value, and Panentheism." In *Postmodern Environmental Ethics*, edited by Max Oelschlaeger, 277–307. Albany, NY: State University of New York Press, 1995.

Index

Page references for tables are italicized

ACEs. *See* adverse childhood experience
actual entities, 61–66, 71, 218; as dipolar, 61; living *vs.* nonliving, 168; mental pole, 61, 62, 201, 218–19; physical pole, 61
actual occasions. *See* actual entities
Adelson, Rachel, 188
Adler, Gerhard, 41
adverse childhood experience (ACEs), 5, 74, 95, 98, 214; categories of, 8–9; score, 8–9; study, 7–9
aesthetics, 64–65, 69, 78, 164, 178, 182
agency. *See* freedom
aim(s), initial and subjective, xiii, 44, 61–62, 65, 66, 70, 77, 159, 162–64, 192–93, 201–2, 217; discernment of, 44, 75, 201, 218–21
Aizenstat, Stephen, 93, 99, 122–23, 145–46, 199
alienation, 4, 15, 56, 198, 212, 215, 229
analytical psychology. *See* psychology, analytical
Anda, Robert F., 7–9
Anderson, Ray S., 57, 211–12
anima–animus, 42, 94
appetition, 64
archetypal images, 39, 94, 103–4, 122, 158, 162, 166–68, 179–83
archetypal imagination, 67, 158–60
The Archetypal Process, xvii, 28, 165
archetypal Self, xvii, 13, 90–91, 96, 98–99, 159, 163, 193–95; Christ as, xviii; as God–image, 90–91, 100, 103, 163, 184, 193; as historic route of initial aims, 200–203, 219; images (symbols) of, 91, 103, 194; as ordering, unifying/unitive, 90–91, 99, 103, 164, 201; as pattern of wholeness, 100, 184; as processive, 194
archetypal theory, 39–41, 92–93
archetypes, 103, 159–69; as androgynous, 40–42 ; as bipolar/dipolar, 40, 103, 181; and collective unconscious, 103, 160–69; and determinism, 38, 166–69; as educating to the ego, 98; as embodied, 40, 92, 103; and emotion, 104; as historical, 162, 166; and human behavior, 39, 160; as inborn/inherited, 40, 101; and instinct, 160; as irrepresentable, 40, 162; and meaning, 104, 105;

not observable, 104; and numbers, 105, 160; ontological status of, 161–2; as organizing structures, 40, 103; as patterns, 120, 160, 180; as transcendent, 161–62; and valuation, 180; *vs.* eternal objects, 165–68; *vs.* Platonic ideas /forms, 38, 161
Argyle, Michael, 18, 178
Arlow, Jacob, 88

Bergland, Christopher, 188
Berry, Thomas, 18–19
bifurcation between humans and nature, 15, 72
Block, Robert W., 9
body and nature, 73, 92–93, 177–79, 191
The Body Keeps the Score, 9
Bosnak, Robert, 136
Bracken, Joseph A., 77
Bulkeley, Kelly, 13, 17, 98, 115–18, 130, 135, 137, 215, 220, 225–26

Cacciopo, John, 6
Card, Charles R., 41, 104
causal efficacy. *See* perception
causality, formal. *See* formalism
Center for Process Studies, 229
Chalquist, Craig, 26
choice. *See* freedom
Christ, xviii, 217
Christ, Carol P., ix, xiii, 26, 36, 60, 74, 198
Christianity, x, xii–xviii, 14–15, 106–7, 158, 200, 226, 228, 230. *See also* dream work, and Christianity
Christology, xviii
Clark, Walter Houston, 215–16
Clayton, Philip, xviii, 125
Cobb, John B., Jr., 10, 14, 28, 45, 73, 164–65, 217, 219
Coleman, Monica A., 37, 57
common flourishing, 27
comparative feeling, 65
complexes, 94–95, 97, 101, 135, 218. *See also* ego, as complex
concrescence, 32, 60–66, 201, 219; eternal objects. *See* eternal objects; initial (receptive) phase, 61–62, 70; as integration of relationships, 71; integrative and supplemental phases, 65–66, 181, 219; responsive phase, 62–63; satisfaction, 65; *superject*/objective datum, 65, 70
consciousness, 88–90, 125
constructivism. *See* social constructivism
contrasts. *See* opposites (contrasts)
cosmos: as matrix/web, 71, 74, 77
creative transformation, 192–93, 201–2, 217
creativity, 59, 63, 75, 77, 99, 165
Crouse, Janice Shaw, 6

Daugherty, Alane, 130, 135–36, 185, 189–90
Davis, Timothy L., 220–21
default mode network (DMN) of the brain, 100, 128, 176, 184
depression, 7, 56, 189
depth and past, 45, 176
Descartes, René. *See* worldviews, Cartesian
dipolar. *See* actual entities; God; psyche
dissociation, 8, 218
diversity, 55, 57
Dourley, John P., 106
Dowd, Michael, 15
dream images, 91, 94, 100, 101, 119–21, 181–91; Central Image Intensity, 129, 140; as picturing inner landscape, 119; as representing intrapsychic aspect of dreamer's life, 122
dreaming; and the brain, 124–36, 185–91; functions of, 118; sleep lab effect, 124; and stages of sleep, 124, 126–27, 131; and the vagus nerve. *See* relational–imaginal theory of

dreaming; waking–to–dreaming continuum, 130
dream interpretation, 119, 121–24, 182, 226; active imagination, 117, 122; amplification, 117, 121–23; animation, 117, 122–23; association, 117, 119, 120, 122; Dream Tending, 123; image activation, 123
dreams: big/divine, 118, 223–24; as carriers of significant content, 222–23; continuities with waking life, 118; and culture, 116, 122; and emotion, 119, 129–31, 185–86; examples of, xi–xii, 118, 131, 195; and healing, 136–38, 142, 216–21; and illness. *See* dreams, and healing; interpretation of. *See* dream interpretation ; *The Interpretation of Dreams* (Freud), 117; and learning, 128, 130, 187; and memory, 129–30, 187; and psychology, 116, 117, 138; recording, 121; and religion, 116, 117, 142; as religious experience, 117, 142–45, 185–91; and science, 116, 124–27; of snakes, xi–xii; transforming/healing power of, 17, 130, 143
dream sharing groups, 116, 138–41, 221; and Jung, 140. *See also*, dream work, group projective dream work
dream work, 115, 220–27; and Christianity, 144–45, 226; group projective dream work, 139–41; qualitative study of dream workers, 211, 217, 221–26; risks of, 145; as spiritual, 139, 220–27
Dreitcer, Andrew, 220
dualism. *See* worldviews
Dueck, Alvin., 100

ecofeminism, 17
ecological concerns, 16–19
ecstatic experience, 216. *See also* religious experience
Edinger, Edward F., 12, 13, 101, 194, 197–98, 214
ego, 88, 96, 177; as complex, 88; as historic route of images, 90, 177; not substantial, 88–89
ego inflation, 4, 13–14, 74, 197, 199
ego–self relationship, 90, 145, 197–98, 201
embodied experience of wholeness, 17, 190, 211–26
embodied theological method. *See* theology, embodied
enantiodromia, 41
entities. *See* actual entities
epistemology, 68, 176
Epperly, Bruce G., 73, 215
Eros, 33, 56, 202
eternal objects, 59, 63–64, 159–69, 218; as inexhaustible, 63; ingression of, 63–64; not causal, ideal/deterministic, 63; as novelty, 64; and numbers, 105; as patterns, 64, 160, 180; as transcendent, 63, 161–62; *vs.* archetypes, 165–68; *vs.* Plato's ideas/forms, 64, 161
events, 71
evil, 213–14
experience, importance of, 29, 32, 58, 59
extensive continuum, 72

Faber, Roland, 57, 212, 229
feelings. *See* comparative feeling; intellectual feelings; propositional feelings; religious feelings
Felitti, Vincent, 7–9
feminine principle, 42, 94
flux, 26, 77–78
formalism, 105, 144, 157–69
fragmentation, 25; interpersonal, 6; intrapersonal, 7–9; societal, 5–6
framework of the book, 25
freedom, 60, 70, 77, 164–69, 213. *See also* relational–imaginal reality of form and freedom

Freud, Sigmund, 18, 88, 100, 117, 119, 142, 177
Frey–Rohn, Liliane, 40, 163, 167
functional resonance(s) between Whitehead and Jung, xvii, 25, 28–32, 45, 155–57

gender identity, 93
God: consequent nature of, 75–76, 158, 166, 192; death of, theology, 15; definition, xviii, 76; as dipolar, 59, 158–59, 166; encountered within, 67, 90, 105, 143–45, 167, 202, 212–19; as entity, event, 75, 163–64, 192; envisagement of future, 63, 164, 166–68; image, xvii, 13–14, 100, 105, 221, 224; as immanent, 75, 105, 178, 182, 192, 212; as lure for feeling, 75; as necessary, 76–77, 163; as not coercive/deterministic, 64, 162–69, 192; as not supernatural, 12, 143, 183; as poet of the world, 76; and power, 78; primordial nature of, 67, 75, 158, 166, 192, 202; and suffering, 75; traditional doctrines of, 31, 158, 212; transcendence *vs.* immanence, xiii, 18; and world, 17, 28, 57–58, 67, 76, 163, 175–203, 212
Goldenberg, Naomi, 18, 38, 41, 92–93
Griffin, David Ray, xvii, xix, 10, 14, 26, 28, 31, 33, 36, 67, 73, 161, 212, 217
gut–brain axis, 188

Haden, Bob, 144, 221
Haden Institute, xi, 146, 211, 221
Hall, G. Stanley, 18
Hall, James, xvii, 95, 103, 180, 214
Halligan, Frederica R., 93, 121, 142
Hartmann, Earnest, 100, 118, 127–30, 140, 184, 189; contemporary theory of dreaming, 129–30
Hartshorne, Charles, 26, 60, 74
Haule, John, 91, 99, 105
Heisig, James W., 4, 17–19, 29, 31, 34, 95
hero's journey, 198–99
Hill, Clara E., 220–21
Hillman, James, 28–29, 45, 93, 121, 123, 161, 191
Hood, Ralph W., 215
Hopper, Stanley R., xiv, 33, 165, 168, 212
Hosinski, Thomas E., 57, 60, 61, 65–67, 73, 78, 160, 180, 218–19, 228
Hoss, Robert J., 103, 118, 120, 130–34, 194–95
Hudson, Joyce Rockwood, x, 144–45, 221, 229
Huffaker, Lucinda, 37
hybrid physical feelings, 164

imagination and healing, 137
Imago Dei, 99, 103
immortality, objective, 59, 65
individualism, 56
individuation, 96–99, 118, 195–200
initial aim(s). *See* aim(s), initial and subjective
inner marriage, 94
intellectual feelings, 65–66, 159, 183, 218–20
intensity of experience, 67, 158, 200–201, 218–19
internal relations. *See* relationality
International Association for the Study of Dreams (IASD), 118
Interpretative Phenomenological Analysis (IPS), 221

James, William, xviii, 18
Johnson, Robert A., 122, 184
Jones, William R., 37
Journey of the Universe, 16
Jung, C. G.: criticism of, 25, 35, 38–44, 94; critique of religion, 43; and exploration of his own unconscious, 119, 145, 185; and gender essentialism, 25, 41–43;

and God, 107, 143, 158, 167, 178; influence of, 26; and mass mindedness, 12; and morality, 97; and Nazism/anti–Semitism, 25, 39, 41; and a religious outlook, 11, 32, 229; *Seven Sermons to the Dead*, 214; and Sigmund Freud, 10, 88; as supporting the status quo, 43–44, 97; and Whitehead, A. N., functional resonances. *See* functional resonance(s) between Whitehead and Jung

Kalsched, Donald, 8, 90, 97–98, 122, 190, 214
Kearney, Michael, 199, 230
Keller, Catherine, xvii, 4, 28, 33, 35, 45, 165, 176–77, 198–99, 202, 213, 214
Kelsey, Morton T., 102, 103, 116, 119, 122, 144–45, 228
kenosis, xviii
Kim, Chae Young, 28, 30, 32
Kirkpatrick, Lee, 39
Kradin, Richard, 130
Kraus, Elizabeth M., 79, 180
Kripal, Jeffrey, 185–86

Lane, Beldon, 228
Lauter, Estella, 41
LeBarge, Stephen, 136
Lee, Bernard, 26, 163, 192
living immediacy, 62, 67, 70, 164
loneliness, 6, 56
Loomer, Bernard, 27, 36, 69, 191, 230
Lorenz, Konrad, 162

masculine principle, 42, 94
materialism. *See* worldviews
Mattingly, Susan Shotliff, 57, 63, 162, 168, 181
Maxwell, Grant, 28, 45, 105, 159–60
McDaniel, Jay, 192
McFague, Sallie, 16
McGehee, J. Pittman, ix, 90, 94, 107, 144, 200, 213, 215
meaning, 30
mental pole. *See* actual entities, mental pole
Mersbergen, Miriam van, 189
Mesle, C. Robert, 75
metaphysical proposition. *See* propositions
metaphysics, 29, 33–34, 45, 57, 58, 156, 177; processive, 57, 58; substance, 56, 78
methodologies used, xiv
mind: and body, 10, 43, 71–74, 92–93, 126, 135–38, 184–91; strong emergence theory, 125; theory of, 10, 116, 125, 184–86
modernism. *See* worldviews
Moltmann, Jürgen, 4
Monbiot, George, 56
monism, 68
Moore, Robert L., 4
multiplicity, 55, 77–78, 195, 213, 216
Muray, Les, 62, 202
mysterium fascinans, 143
mysterium tremendum, 143
mystical experience. *See* religious experience; primordial experience
myth and mythologems, 40, 101, 103, 158

National Center for Health Statistics, 7
National Science Foundation, 6
natural spirituality, x–xi, 229
Nelson, Geoff, 116, 121, 139–40, 143
neoliberalism. *See* worldviews
Neumann, Erich, 97
neuroplasticity, 135–36
neurosis, 93–96
nexus. *See* society of occasions
nondirected thinking, xv, 10, 100, 214
nonrational, dismissal of. *See* worldviews
novelty, xiii, 37, 65, 79, 101, 162–65, 201, 217–21
numinosum. *See* numinous

numinous, 11, 12, 31, 32, 101, 103, 104, 143–45, 166, 181, 215

objectification, 61
object relations, 213
occasions. *See* actual entities
occasions, route of. *See* personality, presiding (route of occasions)
Odin, Steve, 28, 64, 67, 158, 166, 180
ontological circle, 34, 35
ontological theory, 59, 77
opposites (contrasts), 67, 76, 164, 194–5, 198, 214, 216–17; union of, 216–17
order, 37
Otto, Rudolf, 32, 101, 143

panentheism. *See* worldviews, panentheism
panexperientialism, 74, 104, 125
pansomatism, 74, 125
paranormal experience, 30
Pargament, Kenneth, 18, 165–66, 215, 220
past, objective, 62
past and depth. *See* depth and past
patriarchy, 37, 56, 58
perception: in the mode of causal efficacy, 34, 66, 69–71, 176–91, 219; in the mode of presentational immediacy, 69–70, 176, 182; nonsensory, 30–31, 69, 176–91; of past world. *See* perception, in the mode of causal efficacy; sensory, 67–70, 73, 176–79; sensory, reliance on bodily organs, 69, 73, 177; sensory data, 68–70, 177
perpetual perishing, 77
Perrin, David B., 18
persona, 93–96
personality, presiding (route of occasions), 71, 202
Petek, Joseph, 67
Pew Research Center, 5, 14
physicalism, 30
physical pole. *See* actual entities, physical pole
Pittenger, W. Norman, xviii, 29, 37, 59, 66, 72, 76, 227, 229
placebo effect, 137
Plaskow, Judith, ix, xiii
polarization, 4, 95; political, 5
Poplin, Mary S., 57
Porges, Stephen W., 189
possibilities, 59, 60, 62, 74, 159–69, 219; real potential *vs.* pure potential, 63; as relevant for the occasion, 62
postmodernism. *See* worldviews
potentials. *See* possibilities
Potok, Mark, 5
prehend. *See* prehension
prehension, 60, 62, 64, 70, 166, 176–91, 218
presentational immediacy. *See* perception
primary–process thinking, 10, 100
primordial experience, xv, xvii, 12, 15, 74, 87, 100–101, 106, 143, 165, 178; as source of vitality, 100
Process and Reality, 36
propositional feelings, 65–66, 165–68, 181–91, 218
propositions, 65–66, 165–68, 218–19; as lures for feeling, 180–81, 218
projection, 13, 200; religious/transpersonal, 13, 15
psyche: archetypal. *See* unconscious, collective.; collective unconscious. *See* unconscious, collective; as compensatory/self–regulating, 42, 88–91, 118, 159, 163, 194; as embodied, 40; intrapsychic conflict, 88, 217; and matter, 92–93. *See also* psychoid; and nature, 40, 179, 191; objective, 39, 100–101, 143, 178; personal unconscious. *See* unconscious, personal; shadow, 11, 94, 96, 214; transcendent function of. *See* transcendent function; world psyche, 195

psychoanalysis, 18, 159
psychoid, 41
psychological circle, 34, 35
psychology: analytical, 28, 87–108, 142; evolutionary, 39; neuropsychology, 39; and spirituality, 18, 97, 165
psycho–spiritual. *See* psychology, and spirituality
purpose, 60, 124, 228

qualitative study. *See* dream work, qualitative study of dream workers
quantum physics, 17, 68, 105

rational thought, 66, 159
relational–imaginal God–Self, 47, 191–203
relational–imaginal praxis, 47, 211–21
relational–imaginal reality of form and freedom, 165–69
relational–imaginal theory of dreaming, 47, 176–91, 220
relationality: cosmic, 27, 31, 55, 58, 61–62, 69, 73, 177, 192, 200; psychic, 91, 202
religion: and human nature, 18; Jung *vs.* Freud, 11; Jung and Whitehead on, 32; and reformation, 43; and science, 15; as true container, 12, 16, 106
religious experience, xi, 67, 106, 107, 115, 143, 194, 211–16, 222; dreams as. *See* dreams, as religious experience
religious feelings, 220
religious outlook. *See* Jung, C. G., and a religious outlook
REM and NREM sleep. *See* dreaming, and stages of sleep
resonance, 29. *See also* functional resonance(s) between Whitehead and Jung
ritual, 13
Robertson, Robin, 4, 29, 34, 74, 88–90, 94, 96, 101, 162–63, 194
Rossi, Ernest Lawrence, 137
Rossi, Kathryn Lane, 137
Rowland, Susan, 27, 31, 40–41, 92, 100, 108, 121, 178
Ruether, Rosemary Radford, xiii, xv, 228
Rupprecht, Carol Schreier, 41

salvation, 19
Sanford, John A., 118, 122, 144
Sarkar, Anil Kumar, 36, 177, 212
secularization, 116
self: experience of, 224–25; modern self, 176, 195–97; unified. *See* personality, presiding (route of occasions). *See also* archetypal Self
Sellery, J'nan Morse, 29
shadow. *See* psyche, shadow
Shaviro, Steven, 68, 69
Shelburne, Walter, 88, 107, 162
Sherburne, Donald W., 68
Singer, June K., 89, 96, 98, 100, 101, 119, 161, 194, 214, 217
Slusser, Gerald H., 12, 29, 35, 158
social constructivism, 42
society of occasions, 71, 201
solitariness, 32
somatic awareness, 126
sphere of forms, 75
spiritual but not religious, 14, 147
spirituality, 18, 220–27; and human nature, 18, 25; and psychology. *See* psychology, and spirituality
spiritual practice/praxis, 25, 211–12. *See also* relational–imaginal praxis
status quo, 37, 43–44, 79
Stein, Murray, 10
Sternberg, Esther M., 137
subjective aim(s). *See* aim(s), initial and subjective
subjective form, 64, 178–80
subjective *vs.* objective world, 34, 60, 63, 178
subject *vs.* object, 4, 67, 68, 192, 195
Suchocki, Marjorie, xvii, 200
superject. *See* concrescence

suprapersonal categories. *See* transpersonal, categories
Swimme, Brian, 16
symbolic reference, 70, 183, 219
symbols, 11, 35, 40, 89, 94, 104, 119–21, 161, 163, 181–82, 219; Christian, 106; religious, 14, 43, 106
synchronicity, x, xi, 104–5, 217, 223; and Wolfgang Pauli, 105
synthesis, 55, 155–69

Tacey, David, 11, 30, 90
Tarnas, Richard, 4, 15, 105, 195
Taylor, Jeremy, 138–42
Teilhard de Chardin, Pierre, 73
teleology, 31, 97–98, 159–69
Terror Management Theory, 198–200
Thandeka, 37
theology: embodied, ix, xiii, xiv, 155; feminist, xiii, 197; liberation, xiii; practical, xii, 74, 228; process, xii, 79; relevance of, 57
Thomas, Damon J., ix, 90, 94, 200, 213, 215
Tillich, Paul, 4, 106, 212
transcendent function, 118, 163, 193–95, 201–2, 217
transformation, 17, 27, 57, 79, 136, 143, 200, 228. *See also* dreams, transforming/healing power of
transmutation, 201, 213, 217–18, 220; conscious, 217–18
transpersonal, 40, 55, 74–75, 89, 101, 116, 117, 119, 122, 135, 176, 192, 202, 229; categories, 12–13
transreligious, xvi, 142, 229
trauma, 8, 93–96, 214; changes to brain, 9. *See also* adverse childhood experience
Tucker, Mary Evelyn, 16
Turner, Victor, 13

Ulanov, Ann, 12, 98, 100, 140–41, 143, 159, 178, 181, 200, 213
Ulanov, Barry, 12, 98, 100, 143, 178, 213
Ullman, Montague, 138–41
unconscious, 55, 87, 88–90, 96, 101, 215; collective, 12, 31, 34, 67, 103, 119, 144, 158–69, 177–83; and God, 107, 158–59; healing power of, 108, 212–21; as memory, 158; personal, 88–90, 100, 103, 159; and symbolic thought, 119
universe. *See* cosmos
unus mundus, 105

vagus nerve, 125, 176, 187; polyvagal theory, 188. *See also* relational–imaginal theory of dreaming
value–free, 31
values, 15, 27, 31–32, 55, 58, 60, 64, 65, 66, 69, 78–79, 96–99, 124, 160, 180, 197, 214, 218, 228; inherent/intrinsic *vs.* instrumental, 70
van der Kolk, Bessel, 8
von Franz, Marie–Louise, 105

Watts, Alan, 74
Watts, Fraser N., 198
Wehr, Demaris, 38, 167, 194
Wehrwein, Peter, 7
Weldon, Clodagh, 104
Whitehead: and cosmos, 28, 55–80; and God, 59, 63, 75–77, 79, 158, 161, 178, 212; and indigenous religions, 37; influence of, 26; and Jung, functional resonances. *See* functional resonance(s) between Whitehead and Jung; ontological theory. *See* ontological theory
wholeness, 11, 12, 19, 30, 57–58, 90–91, 94, 98, 108, 190, 212, 214, 220
Woodman, Marion, 137, 187
worldviews, 9–10; Cartesian, 61, 67, 71, 116, 195; dismissal of the nonrational, 10, 146; dualism, 10, 56–58, 93, 116, 142, 195, 199, 215–17; Enlightenment, 71, 195;

humanism, 57; materialism, 12, 30, 56–58, 60, 67–68, 116, 195; mechanism, 10, 30, 56–58, 67–68, 142, 195; modernism, 30, 92; naturalism, 57; neoliberalism, 56, 58; nondualism, 17; panentheism, 17; pantheism, 57; postmodernism, 27, 31, 142; theism, 57; wounding and healing power of, 55, 78

Wright, Jerry R., 161

Young–Eisendrath, Polly, xvii, 95, 103, 180, 214

Zachary, Simpson, xviii
Zimmerman, Michael E., 17, 19, 115, 215

About the Author

In addition to being Associate Dean and Executive Director of the Beecken Center of the School of Theology at the University of the South in Sewanee, Tennessee, Sheri D. Kling is a theologian who works in the interdisciplinary space where worldviews, beliefs, and practices can create either disease and suffering or psycho-spiritual wholeness and common flourishing. Drawing from process philosophy/theology, Jungian psychology, and mystical spirituality, Sheri communicates theological ideas and practices that positively impact humans' relationships with God, self, and world, especially the use of dream work as a spiritual practice for divine encounter, personal integration, and widening our relationship to creation. She holds a Ph.D. from Claremont School of Theology and a master of theological studies from the Lutheran School of Theology at Chicago. She is a faculty member of the Haden Institute, a visiting lecturer with Palacky University (Czech Republic) in Social and Spiritual Determinants of Health, and a singer, songwriter, guitarist, retreat leader, and public speaker. Sheri has released three music CDs and a book of essays entitled *Finding Home: Rural Reflections on the Journey to Wholeness.*

www.ingramcontent.com/pod-product-compliance
Ingram Content Group UK Ltd.
Pitfield, Milton Keynes, MK11 3LW, UK
UKHW041841031026
15587UKWH00002B/937

9 781793 630421